Sacred Actions

Cover and interior design by Ashley Millhouse
Type set in Grand Duke/Bressay

ISBN: 978-0-7643-6153-1
Printed in India
6 5 4 3

Published by Red Feather Mind, Body, Spirit
An imprint of Schiffer Publishing, Ltd.
4880 Lower Valley Road
Atglen, PA 19310
Phone: (610) 593-1777; Fax: (610) 593-2002
E-mail: Info@schifferbooks.com
Web: www.redfeathermbs.com

For our complete selection of fine books on this and related subjects, please visit our website at www.schifferbooks.com. You may also write for a free catalog.

Schiffer Publishing's titles are available at special discounts for bulk purchases for sales promotions or premiums. Special editions, including personalized covers, corporate imprints, and excerpts, can be created in large quantities for special needs. For more information, contact the publisher.

We are always looking for people to write books on new and related subjects. If you have an idea for a book, please contact us at proposals@schifferbooks.com.

Sacred Actions

Living the Wheel of the Year through Earth-Centered Sustainable Practices

Dana O'Driscoll

REDFeather™

MIND | BODY | SPIRIT

4880 Lower Valley Road, Atglen, PA 19310

Contents

CHAPTER 3: SPRING EQUINOX
Spring Cleaning and Disposing of the Disposable Mindset 67

CHAPTER 4: BELTANE
Sacred Actions in Our Homes 99

CHAPTER 5: SUMMER SOLSTICE
Food and Nourishment 125

CHAPTER 6: LUGHNASADH
Landscapes, Gardens, and Lawn Liberations 156

CHAPTER 7: FALL EQUINOX
Earth Ambassadorship, Community, and
Broader Work in the World 190

CHAPTER 8: SAMHAIN
Sustainable Ritual Tools, Items, and Objects 208

CONCLUSION:
Growing Where We Are Planted 231

To Alfred

Eight Paths
through the Forest

It can be difficult to realize just how far the spiritual sensibility of the Western world has shifted over the last century or so. A hundred years ago, as it had been for most of the 2,000 years before that time, the world counted alongside the flesh and the devil as one of the three great enemies of the spiritually minded. Though a few voices, such as Francis of Assisi's, had always spoken out now and then for the holiness of living nature, the overwhelming consensus of the Western religious mainstream defined nature as humanity's enemy, fit only to be conquered and made subservient to the human will, and placed humanity's hope of salvation on an abstract otherworld on the far side of death.

There are still plenty of people in the Western world who cling to that way of thinking about the cosmos and humanity's place in it, to be sure, but each passing year seems to be bringing a radically different spiritual vision further to the fore. To this new sensibility, salvation is not a flight from nature but a return to it—or, more precisely, a recognition that we never really left it at all, that our place in living nature is essential to our being, and that nature and our many linkages with it deserve to be cherished and reverenced. In place of a quest for perfection that too often amounted to the amputation of whatever parts of human nature fail to measure up to some arbitrary theological standard, the keynotes of the new sensibility are wholeness, harmony, and healing: a quest for reintegration in which every aspect of ourselves, and likewise of the fragile and beautiful planet on which we live, can flourish in balance with all others.

The emergence of this new sensibility is timely in an obvious sense, as too long a pursuit of the shopworn fantasy of Man the Conqueror of Nature has already unleashed a rising spiral of ecological crises that bid fair to upend the arrangements that keep today's industrial societies from crashing into ruin. It's also timely in a less obvious sense, as the centuries the Western world has devoted to the pursuit of various arbitrary notions of human perfection have left very few of us with the inner resources we need to achieve wholeness of being. The erosion of the natural systems that sustain our outward lives is mirrored by the erosion of the values and meanings that sustain our inward lives: as without, so within.

Faced with the daunting challenges of the present age, many people feel lost, unsure of what can be done—if anything can—to move toward a way of life that's harmonious without and within and balances the requirements of life on a finite and fragile planet with the human needs for meaning, purpose, and relationship. It's for this reason that I was delighted to be asked to write a foreword to Dana O'Driscoll's *Sacred Actions: Living the Wheel of the Year through Earth-Centered Sustainable Practices*.

I have known Dana, first by correspondence and then in person, for many years now. During the time I spent presiding over the Ancient Order of Druids in America (AODA) as its Grand Archdruid, I watched her work her way through the grades of the order in an exemplary fashion, nominated her for the national office of Grand Pendragon, and welcomed her into the Grand Grove on her election as one of the order's four Archdruids. That she accomplished this while simultaneously completing a comparable course of study in another Druid order, the Order of Bards Ovates and Druids (OBOD), may be taken as a measure of the enthusiasm and commitment she brings to Earth-centered spirituality.

Her intention in *Sacred Actions* is as simple as it is profound. Many current Earth-centered spiritual paths work with a sacred calendar of eight festivals spaced equally around the cycle of the year. Whereas spiritual traditions attuned to the older spiritual sensibility used their holy days as opportunities to distance themselves from the world, *Sacred Actions* offers participants in the new sensibility a banquet of ways to use their holy days as opportunities to enter into closer relationship with the living Earth and the cycles of nature. Thoughtful discussions of the ways our current habits keep us apart from nature, suggestions for constructive change, exercises, rituals, and meditations—all these and more teach the reader how to plant the ideas and ideals of nature-centered spirituality in the fertile Earth of everyday life. Those who are looking for a profound and practical introduction to that essential task will find it here.

—John Michael Greer, Grand Archdruid Emeritus
of the Ancient Order of Druids in America (AODA), and author of *The Druidry Handbook and After Progress*

Acknowledgments

This book has been a six-year labor of love, and I am indebted to many individuals who have helped, in their own special way, bring this book into existence. To John Michael Greer and Sara Greer, who have nurtured and supported me as a writer, druid, and human being. To Anasazi, my beloved rooster, whose morning wake-up calls always encouraged me to move forward with my own learning and growth. To Michelle LaFrance, Jessica Tess, Adam Robersmith, and Robert Pacitti, giving me feedback on this work during the writing process. To Jim McDonald for his many sacred teachings of plants. To Deanne Bednar of Strawbale Studio for teaching and inspiration in natural building and sustainable living. To Kay Cafasso of Sowing Solutions, who taught an amazing permaculture design certificate course, and to Sirius Ecovillage for their work with the land. To members of the Oakland County Permaculture Meetup for sharing their knowledge and community. To Lisa DiPiano and Pandora Thomas for inspiring me to continue on the journey of teaching permaculture through my permaculture teacher training. To the Ancient Order of Druids in America's curriculum program, which gave me space and support to explore these topics. To Sandra Squires, Amanda Martin, Jess Tess, Tammie Heazlit, and Linda Jackson for their support and love. To my family for their long-term support and tasty mushrooms. And most of all, to the living Earth, from which all things flow.

Sacred Actions and the Wheel of the Year

Every human has an innate understanding of the sacred: it's that feeling of reverence that we get when we enter an old-growth forest, it's the wonder we feel when viewing a fresh snowfall, and it's the magic of the amazing Milky Way in the night sky. And those of us drawn to Earth-based and pagan paths are drawn to building and establishing that sacred connection. Our sense of the sacred emerges from the interaction between ourselves and our surroundings. It is through the combining of human reverence and thoughtful action with the outer energies of the land that the sacred is awakened. Another way we might think about the sacred is that it occurs when humans are living in harmony and balance with the living Earth, rather than living removed from it.

A sense of the sacred is part of our human heritage, and yet in today's mass consumer and industrial society, it seems rather hard to find. Part of the challenge we face in capitalist culture is that the reverence and respect for nature as sacred has been largely abandoned. Most of the spaces we live in, work in, and spend time in are not sacred and do not house sacred activities. One reason that one doesn't have a sense of the sacred in a shopping mall is that the shopping mall is not the product of a mutually beneficial relationship between nature and humanity. In the process of building the shopping mall, the land is stripped bare, the soil web of life is removed, the trees are cut, all without acknowledgment or respect— how can this space then be sacred? How can activities in this space be sacred? One might say that these modern buildings, and the activities that are within them, are working in opposition to nature or at least are working without any consideration of nature. This lack of sacredness that I describe is, unfortunately, the dominant one that many of us inhabit as we begin to walk our spiritual paths, and likely has encouraged us in pursuing an Earth-based spiritual path to begin with. But what if we could imagine our everyday living and work spaces differently? What if we could, instead, cultivate the sacred in everyday lives even in these kinds of spaces?

Many of us on a nature-centered spiritual path face additional challenges when it comes to these complex ecological and cultural realities: in my case, my spiritual beliefs and practices put me in a close, magical relationship with nature, and yet my behaviors and larger culture were exploiting and destroying that which I held most sacred. Because of my path, I could sense that damage in the land in ways that most typical Americans could not. We are drawn to Earth-based traditions because we know that what is happening in our world is unbalanced; we seek to regain that balance. And in walking these paths, the division between daily life and our inner beliefs is always present. While many Earth-centered spiritual traditions give us avenues of cultivating a sacred relationship with nature on a spiritual level, they often lack the tools that can help us weave that sacred relationship into the physical level and allow our spiritual practices to align with our daily living. To me, the simple things such as recycling and bringing reusable bags to the grocery store didn't seem to be enough to address my own lack of tools—and the thinking, principles, and practices that I learned over the years and that I share in this book helped me move forward.

I learned that my actions can't just be sacred when I walk into a forest and honor the spirits there by using ritual—my actions have to be sacred when I am going to work, paying my bills, spending time with my family, and buying food, or when I'm deciding how to spend my money. I started to realize that my offering, and my path, was how I lived my life and how I interacted with those around me.

Everything became a potential for sacred action. Sacred action is a journey and also a mindset. On the basis of those experiences, I've come to see the importance of weaving in magical traditions with more-practical action, of embracing sustainability and more Earth-centered living as a fundamental part of any Earth-based spiritual path.

Learning sustainable and ecologically sound skills and practicing them regularly as part of our spiritual practice gives us a meaningful response to the predicament we face in this current age. When we read about the rampant destruction, the pollution, the mass extinctions, peak oil, industrial decline, and so on, we feel powerless and wonder, "What can we possibly do?" This feeling of powerlessness stifled me for years; it prevented me from doing anything except thinking, "I hope they come up with a way to fix it," and living my life pretending it wasn't there. It wasn't that I didn't care. It was just that the problem seemed so big, so all-encompassing, so much larger than I was, that I didn't even know where to start. In fact, when I first began writing this book, my original introduction outlined all the issues we were facing in detail: from reaching our limits, overpopulation, pollution, mass extinctions, deforestations, ocean acidification, glacial melting, unsustainable resource extraction, and more. After nearly twenty-five pages and two months of writing, I could barely read what I wrote. Those dear druid friends who read this early chapter said the same thing: I had to find a different path into this predicament. Plenty of other books already detail the issues at hand that we face—and there is no need to rehash them here. And so, instead of rehashing the insurmountable problems before us, this book is about personal empowerment and sacred actions that help nurture ourselves and the Earth: it's about people care, Earth care, and fair share, as we'll explore in chapter 1.

Thus, this book is designed to help readers get past the stifling "What to do?" questions and integrate Earth-sustaining and regenerative living strategies with Earth-based spiritual practices—what I call "sacred action." This book is meant as a guide to aid those walking Earth-centered spiritual paths to further the sacred connections with the land through a weaving of spiritual practices and sustainable/regenerative living practices for all living situations. The book is part philosophy and part practical guide, weaving threads between the physical realities we inhabit, the spiritual and magical implications and connections, and the pragmatic "how-to" practices and tools to actually make those shifts. And in those tools, we seek the paths of wisdom and knowledge rooted in the work of our ancestors. We'll examine how spiritual practices can link up with regenerative practices, and I'll introduce many small—and large—modes of thinking and activities that you can do to live sustainably and regeneratively. We do this through exploring these practices as they connect to the Wheel of the Year (a cycle of eightfold celebrations at the solstices, equinoxes, and cross-quarter days celebrated by many Earth-based and neopagan spiritual traditions).

Challenges in Living an Earth-Centered Spiritual Path

If we want to build a sacred relationship with our landscape and engage in sacred action, we must find new ways of living, inhabiting, and being—with each moment and with each breath. The following is a triad, a kind of three-part verse used commonly within the Druid Revival tradition; it is wisdom in a triune form. Because of their usefulness, I'll use triads throughout this book. This triad describes the three challenges we face as we move from typical modern living into sacred action:

Three challenges we face:

1. Deprogramming our minds and opening our heart spaces
2. Reintegrating ourselves into the Earth's rhythms and cycles
3. Practicing sacred action as the wheel turns

First, we have the challenge of deprogramming ourselves. This includes shifting our mindsets and heart spaces to reawaken our human heritage of cultivating a sacred relationship with nature. Action starts with beliefs and mindsets, and it is our beliefs that drive our behaviors. As this reawakening takes place, we also have the second challenge, the physical work of reintegrating ourselves and our daily lives back into the land in a sacred manner. This work involves paying attention to our automatic activities that consume and produce waste, and instead living with intentionality and knowledge. The third challenge is external: as we make these shifts on the inner and outer levels, we also have the work of living differently in a disenchanted culture of conformity, and in sharing this new path with others.

Dana's Story

To show how the shift to embracing sustainable and regenerative practices can become sacred action, I'll use myself as a case study throughout this book. After growing up spending every free moment I had in the forest as a child, I fell into consumerism in my late teens and early twenties. During this period of my life, I didn't consider the impact of my actions on anything beyond me and lived to further my career goals and entertain myself. The painful loss of my best friend at the age of twenty-five woke me out of my slumber and had me reexamine everything; this loss also encouraged me to take my first steps on the druid path. I began working through the curriculum of two druid orders (the Ancient Order of Druids in America [AODA][1] and the Order of Bards, Ovates, and Druids [OBOD])[2] and had life-altering transformations along the way.

The AODA's first degree curriculum asked me to make three lifestyle changes: to minimize my impact on the living Earth, to spend time each week in direct observation and meditation in nature, and to celebrate the turning seasons. The OBOD's curriculum taught me about integration, balance, and cultivating relationships with the natural world. These simple, yet profound, practices began a growing process of awareness and awakening, kindling the spark of change. I made small but meaningful changes during the early part of my druid path.

I became a sponge, soaking up so many subjects and seeing how they could all be integrated into a deeper whole and be connected to my spiritual practices. That integration came more fully when I purchased my 3-acre homestead in southeastern Michigan, land that was deeply abused and in need of healing. With the inspiration of friends, teachers, and community, I continued to weave in more-sustainable practices and discovered permaculture design. With each shift, I felt my own awareness and oneness with the land deepen. This path into regenerative living allowed me to study and practice many skills: natural building and natural heating, compost toilets, compost systems, solar cooking, organic farming and gardening, animal husbandry, herbalism, wildcrafting, beekeeping, canning, fermenting, home brewing, wild foods and medicines, conservation, botany, bushcraft, and more. One thing I immediately noticed was that there was a lot of unarticulated overlap between my Earth-based spiritual community and the sustainable living and permaculture communities. The communities shared many values, but the groups weren't connected—and so I worked to integrate those two worldviews. Eventually, I completed a three-year self-designed project for my Druid Adept degree with the AODA, integrating permaculture, sustainable living, and druid practice. Years and revisions later, you are now reading one outcome of that project.

Because all the changes happened over a decade, I hadn't realized how far I had removed myself from the typical American lifestyle. Then, I ended up hosting a friend of a friend's family for a weekend. The children really illuminated differences for me, in ways that only children can do. "Why do you do everything the old way?" the eldest boy, nine years old, asked. "What do you mean?" I responded. He continued, "You don't have a TV here. You make popcorn on the stove from an ear of corn. The chickens lay eggs and we got to eat them. Everything here is done the old way." I didn't realize how different my life would seem to a typical nine-year-old who spent his time surrounded by convenience foods and various screens. I still saw myself as very much involved in typical America—I went to work, I lived in a more conventional house than I would have liked, I paid taxes, and I still drove a car (albeit as little as I could). However, these continual small shifts over time had led to more and more changes, until that twenty-something wouldn't recognize the woman I had become ten years later. It was this difference that the children picked up on. Through my own transformational process, I grew to have a profound understanding that encouraged me to write this book: every action, every choice, however small, can be done in a sacred, intentional manner, a manner that nurtures the Earth. Every action is important, and it is our daily actions that determine our relations with all living things. All of these can be interwoven into pagan, Earth-based spiritual practice.

Three Powerful Principles for Sacred Action

While we might not be able to change everything we'd like to change about our lives, the path of sacred action leads to deep spiritual connection and understanding. Most of us can't live 100% sustainably at this moment, but we can make consistent, manageable, and impactful shifts that do make a difference within and without. Given all this, this book rests on a few principles, again in the form of a triad:

Three principles of sacred action:

• Drawing together wisdom from the heart and mind
• Walking in harmony and care with the land
• Transforming our live, landscapes, and communities

First, in order to engage in sacred action, we need to draw together the necessary wisdom. For our purposes, this wisdom includes our mindsets, our ethics, and the knowledge and skills that we have or seek to gain. Our first chapter explores the ethics of sacred action and provides a framework for our actions, while chapter 2 explores the knowledge-and-skills part of this necessary wisdom. In a nutshell, if we want to engage in everyday sacred action and weave our spiritual principles into our physical realities, we need an ethical system that guides our paths, as well as a great deal of knowledge about the living Earth and what actions help nurture or harm our Earth. We need to understand and reclaim the human heritage that has been with us for millennia—the knowledge of root and seed, of stem and leaf, of feather and fur.

Second, in order to engage in sacred action we need to learn how to live in harmony with the land, despite the fact that most things in industrialized culture have encouraged us to do the opposite. Chapters 3 through 8 explore these sacred actions in depth. While it is certainly a meaningful practice to visit wild lands and old-growth groves as part of our spiritual practice—and one that I engage in regularly myself—it is our daily living that needs our attention, from both a spiritual and a physical viewpoint. In embracing sacred action, spiritual activity should not be disconnected from daily activity, something you do on the weekends or only during holidays, but rather something you live each day. To divorce our spiritual beliefs from our daily living is a tragedy: actions are what leave a lasting impact on the living fabric of our world. This is not to say that words don't have a power of their own, but words alone aren't going to produce less carbon, or save ecosystems, or regenerate landscapes. By the blending of Earth-based spiritual practices with principles of sustainability and regeneration, then, we can engage in sacred action.

Finally, when we engage in sacred action, we not only transform ourselves, we transform our communities and our world. Through focusing on our everyday lives and working to live in a sacred relationship at each moment—we can better not only our own relationship to the land but also our world for ourselves, our children, and the many other species that call this wondrous planet our home. I believe that Earth-centered spiritual practitioners, of any variety, can become invaluable resources and leaders to their communities and to the broader world concerning Earth-centered living.

On Making a Difference

I remember a conversation I had with one of my dear friends and mentors, John Michael Greer, while I was writing this book. At the time, I was struggling with articulating the focus of the book and said to him, "I'm not even sure if it will really make a difference." He looked at me intently and said, "It seems we need to interrogate the words 'make a difference' and ask, 'To whom? For whom? For what purpose?'" I smiled and realized exactly what he was getting at. We are programmed to think that making a difference must be done on a massive scale, rather than on a personal one.

So many of us get frustrated at what is happening nationally and internationally, but it's our own lives where the changes can start; that is, we can productively focus our energies and intensive efforts on those things that are closest to us. So as a permaculture designer and druid residing in western Pennsylvania, I have the most ability to change my own life, my immediate surroundings, and my immediate community. I'd have less control at the county or state level, and I'd have very little power over Wall Street executives or Congress, because they are so far away. Trying to change these things frequently ends in frustration rather than success. And so, when we think about meaningful change, it's not about waiting for someone else to change Wall Street or government—it's about starting with our immediate surroundings.

One way we might think about sacred action and our impact can be illustrated through permaculture design's[3] concept of the zone. When you are working with any space, whether it's in a town or community to a simple backyard garden, you want to think about what you are closest to, what you can most easily access, and how much it will take to maintain. I'll be using an example of a suburban yard and home (since so many live in that setting), but this can be applied to anything. A typical home has five zones, each zone getting a bit farther out and less visited or maintained. Zone 0 is usually the house itself—where you spend a majority of your time and what is easiest to access. (Even within your house, you can designate zones of use—think about the kitchen's or bathroom's daily usage compared to the basement or utility closet.) Moving to the yard: zone 1 is the area you access most frequently and is the easiest to get to and to tend—for a typical suburban home, this means the places we spend the most time or walk through every day. The path from the door to the mailbox, lined with herbs, and the back patio, where you enjoy dinner each night and spend time regularly, might all be considered zone 1. Zone 2 takes us just a little bit farther away; zone 2 is still visited and tended often, but perhaps not in the immediate pathways or energy flows. Zone 2 for our suburban house might be a kitchen garden, a compost pile, or the pathway to the chicken coop (even while a coop would be farther from the house, it would still be considered a lower zone because you must tend chickens at least two or three times a day). Zone 3 might be the chicken yard and some berry bushes and fruit trees that you cultivate on occasion. Zone 4 would be the wild edges of your yards, where you go even more infrequently. One can continue to build zones outward, eventually reaching zone 5, where don't actively cultivate but, perhaps, where you go to reflect and heal.

The principle of the zone is useful in thinking about our own sacred actions and where to begin, but it can also be applied to making change in our own lives and our communities—we have the most power and possibility for changing those

things that are closest to us geographically and physically. The third principle of sacred action, then, rests on the idea that we can make meaningful change, and change begins in our own lives, rippling outward like dropping a round stone into a still lake.

Meaningful change isn't just about the big events, the government's actions, or the UN climate talks. We are disempowered if we think that meaningful change occurs only if it's huge, massive, and global. This line of thinking stifles us from being those meaningful sources of change. It becomes easy to wait for someone else to fix it, and when "it" isn't fixed, it becomes easy to fall into despair.

But in this book, I argue that every action we take, each decision we make, and how we integrate sustainable practices into our daily lives give us the potential to be meaningful, powerful, and spiritually significant. Together, we stand united and strong, each of us individually weaving a better tomorrow. There is so much you can do that does matter. There is so much that you can do in your own life that does directly affect other lives. If you've been wondering, "What can I do?," the tools in this book provide a meaningful response. And so, given the landscape that is behind us, we move forward into a new year, a new day.

The Free-Range Fantasy

Another challenge that many of us trying to move into sacred action face is what I call the "free-range fantasy." In the same way that many people of previous generations were lured into the "white picket fence" narrative in the United States, those interested in sustainable living are often lured into the free-range fantasy today. The narrative goes something like this: You and your perfect partner decide to quit

your day jobs, purchase 30 acres in some remote area debt free, and build a fully off-grid homestead complete with solar panels, acres of abundant gardens, fields full of goats, happy free-range chickens, and two cute children covered in strawberry juice. Maybe you do have the opportunity to live off-grid in the circumstances I describe, and if so, you are certainly blessed! However, for most people, the free-range fantasy unfortunately sends the message that the only way to live sustainably is to live by this narrative. I was once trapped by this narrative, sorrowful and depressed that I didn't have two cute, strawberry-eating children, or a handsome partner, or the ability to go completely off-grid and retire to the land. This made me feel like I was never doing enough because I wasn't living this vision, rather than recognizing the good work I was doing in terms of sacred action and community building.

The truth is, this narrative can be as problematic as the white picket fence because it limits your vision, and it prevents you from doing something now that helps move into sacred action, rather than dreaming of some far-off thing. Further, if

PRODUCE NO WASTE

HERBS

LOCAL EATING

SOLAR COOKING

PEOPLE CARE

ANAGEMENT

RainGARDEN

ROCKET STOVE

IR SHARE

GROWING FOOD

COMMUNITY ACTION

every person wanted 30 acres, we wouldn't have enough land available for all. Part of sacred action is about living better in the circumstances that make up our current reality, not dreaming of a lifestyle that doesn't fit our current circumstances. We'll be exploring things that anyone, regardless of their living circumstances, can do; that is, we are focusing on "growing where you are planted." Everyone, whether living in an apartment, a suburban home, or rural land, will find much they can do to engage in sacred action.

Book Overview

This book has been a labor of love, written over a five-year period. While I was writing the first part of this book, I lived on the 3-acre homestead on the edge of the Detroit metro area in southeastern Michigan (USA) that I mentioned above. I wrote about the experience of recovering this land from the neglect and mishandling of previous owners at my blog, *The Druid's Garden*,[4] and the beginnings of this book were rooted in what I was sharing there. For the latter part of writing this book, after accepting a new job, I lived in a small rental house in a walkable town in western Pennsylvania. Given this, while writing I've experienced both "country living," owning abundant land, and "town living" while renting and having no land, no growing space, poor light, and little control over my physical environment. Prior to this, I also lived in an urban area in an apartment. These diverse living experiences have provided me with multiple perspectives and allow me to address issues of sacred action in many different living arrangements.

This book is arranged purposefully, to consider a set of spiraling actions that begin within ourselves and slowly transition us outward, finally moving into sacred action in our communities and then completing the cycle by moving back to ourselves. To use this arrangement, we use the triad of sacred action given above to guide our path. Further, this book is also purposefully arranged so that the eight chapters align with one of the eightfold holidays in the Wheel of the Year. Given this, one way to work with this book is to read each chapter on one of the eight holidays and work your way through the exercises contained therein; however, there are certainly many other ways to read and work with this book.

Drawing Together Wisdom from the Heart and Mind

In part I of the book, we lay the groundwork for sacred action through shifting our heart spaces and mindsets, and seeking a variety of new skills for regenerative ways of living.

Chapter 1: The Winter Solstice—the Ethics of Care. This chapter explores the root ethical principles that are woven throughout this book: the ethics of care. Through an exploration of people care, Earth care, and fair share, we can begin to see how shifts in living are a matter of mindset and practice. In this chapter we'll begin the inner work that manifests outward as sacred action in later chapters.

Chapter 2: Imbolc—Wisdom through Oak Knowledge and Reskilling. As many are deep in their studies in the dark winter months, so too should we begin the process of reskilling and knowledge building. This chapter encourages us to seek Oak knowledge and learn new skills for sacred actions.

Walking in Harmony and Care with the Land

In part II, we begin exploring specific practices to help us develop the practice of sacred action in our daily lives and through our daily choices.

Chapter 3: Spring Equinox—Spring Cleaning and Disposing of the Disposable Mindset. This chapter explores issues surrounding our culture of materialism and waste, showing how this is both an inner and outer challenge. We explore methods of reducing consumption and repurposing waste through a variety of techniques and consider the nonmaterial implications of these shifts.

Chapter 4: Beltane—Sacred Actions in Our Homes. This chapter explores everyday living and how we can walk a path of sacred action: from our homes as sacred spaces to heating, cooling, and lighting, and the many ways we can tread upon the Earth more lightly.

Chapter 5: Summer Solstice—Food and Nourishment. This chapter tackles the difficult issue of nourishment, and how the food that we eat can be linked to sacred action.

Transforming our Lives, Landscapes, and Communities

In part III, we consider actions in the broader world—in our landscapes and communities. We will also explore importance of sustainable practices when it comes to our spiritual tools.

Chapter 6: Lughnasadh—Landscapes, Gardens, and Lawn Liberations. This chapter explores the concept of sacred gardening and shares strategies for growing food, developing habitat, and cultivating sacred spaces that help regenerate our immediate landscapes.

Chapter 7: Fall Equinox—Earth Ambassadorship, Community, and Broader Work in the World. This chapter explores sacred actions in terms of our broader world—how we can be Earth ambassadors for our communities, and how we can integrate sacred action into our workplaces and transportation needs. It provides strategies to build and regenerate communities for broader action.

Chapter 8: Samhain—Sustainable Ritual Tools, Items, and Offerings. We conclude the book by looking deeply at the tools and items that we use every day as part of neopagan and Earth-based spiritual practices and how to make these more sustainable.

As the chapter listing indicates—this is a different kind of book. It's not just a book on how to live more sustainably, or a book on Earth-based spiritual practices. It is a book that attempts to synthesize, integrate, and expand those perspectives for people who are living in spiritual awareness of the living Earth. It provides the justification, the philosophy, the practical activities, and the spiritual actions to live in wholeness with the living Earth, through every action. In addition to the "outer" actions, the book also provides the necessary inner work: rituals, meditations, and other spiritual practices to help fully explore the path of sacred actions. Come, let us begin our journey!

CHAPTER 1

The Winter Solstice

The Ethics of Care

We begin our journey at the darkest point of the Wheel of the Year, when night seems to consume all, and when the blackness in the skies matches the sorrow in our hearts over what is happening to the Earth we love. Behind us are yesterday's problems, but at this moment, at the point when the light returns into the world, we are hoping, working, praying, believing, and enacting a better tomorrow. This is the energy of the winter solstice; the time when at the moment of utmost darkness, the light glimmers with the promise to return. The light of our sacred action is rooted in what I call the ethics of care.

Many of today's problems are rooted in a lack of care, compassion, and connection for ourselves, for others, and for the living Earth and all of her inhabitants. Throughout this book, we'll come to see that the philosophy and practice of sacred action is ultimately rooted in an ethics of care. It is from care and connection to things that are not ourselves that all else stems. Many ancient and modern spiritual movements have a set of ethics or morals attached to them, and these ethics served guides for behavior and living. However, due to the newness of modern Earth-based spiritual traditions, and the fragmentary nature in which they were developed and evolved, not all of our current traditions have an explicit ethical system, although ethical systems are certainly implicit. The ethics of care presented in this book helps fill those gaps and gives us an ethical system that moves us into sacred action. It also presents a set of ethics that can be effectively woven into any Earth-based spiritual path and can serve as a guiding light for our practices in the world.

Care is an essential quality in all that we do as human beings in service and in connection with the land. It is care that allows us to work to better our communities and world. Care is ultimately not just an ethic but a spiritual activity that we can use to center our practices in the world.

The Ethics of Care and Opening Heart Spaces

Industrialized cultures seem to have lost the ability, on an individual, community, and societal level, to care and be compassionate toward other people, the land, the animals, and the plants. When we look at the kinds of movements driving much political change and laws being enacted in the early twenty-first century, care is an essential quality that is missing. In part, it is the lack of care and compassion that can drive ordinary citizens to oppose feeding hungry children in the name of tax cuts; it is the lack of care and compassion that can allow public lands to be sold off to the highest bidder and fracked for natural gas; it is the lack of care and compassion that make people keep buying products even though they know those products are being made at the extreme expense of others. I have witnessed all of these things living in western Pennsylvania—the economics are the only metric through which success is measured or decisions are made. And so, our lands are fracked, the waterways are poisoned with acid mine runoff, and the people drink poisoned water—and the economics of it all are the only thing that have voice.

The triad of sacred action I shared in the introduction includes "opening a heart space," which is an essential part of cultivating an ethics of care. The herbalist Stephen Harrod Buhner is one of many recent authors to point out the disconnection in our modern culture between the mind and the heart. In his *Sacred Plant Medicine*,[5] he discusses the challenges with modern industrialized society in that we always "live in our heads" and allow decisions to be made without feeling out their consequences (since it is different to understand a situation rationally than to experience a situation emotionally firsthand). Our education systems encourage this rational thought at the expense of all feeling, so by the time we make our way out of formal education, there isn't always a lot left of the heart. The traditional symbolism in the Tarot associated with "heady" actions and the mind is helpful here: the heady actions are situated in the suit of swords. These swords are masters of logic, of the mind, but also bring about much of the carnage that is present in our lives. So much of our cultural value systems place emphasis on economics, on personal gain, on possessiveness, and on profit—all of which reside in the head. As Buhner describes, Native American indigenous cultures believed that one's consciousness resided in the heart and that care and compassion, especially toward the living Earth and one's community, were critical values.

Joanna Macy in *Coming Back to Life*[6] suggests that the greatest difficulty in our "turning" toward a life-sustaining society is in the deadening of the mind and the heart. We have to learn to recognize and avoid apathy (literally, nonfeeling) or refusal to feel. It is this deadness that we find at the root of so many problems of industrial culture that we hope to solve—and it's in the reawakening of heart spaces as how to begin to shift.

Even for those who do care deeply, compassion fatigue is a common problem. Those living in industrialized cultures are constantly bombarded with demands for time or resources; people grow numb to the amount of need and end up shutting down. I believe part of this has to do with the fact we aren't in an environment that encourages or facilitates care (care for others or self), and, because of this lack, the current environment burns us out. Self-care is an important aspect currently missing from so many of our lives—and that's where all care begins, from within. Care of all kinds is one of the necessary areas for sacred action.

Exploitation and Nurturing as Mindsets for Care

Another way to consider "care" is through exploring mindsets that underlie humanity's relationship with nature. In *The Unsettling of America: Culture and Agriculture*,[7] Wendell Berry describes two mindsets surrounding care and that can be tied directly to sacred action—exploiting and nurturing.

The nurturer, who embraces the ethics of care, is one whose livelihood, goals, and interactions focus on healing, regenerating, and maintaining as core values of the work they do in the world. Idealized by Berry as a small-scale organic farmer, but applicable to anyone following a path of sacred action, the nurturer is concerned with the long-term health of the land and its people, and they make decisions accordingly. Berry suggests that the nurturer isn't as concerned with efficiency or profit as they are with working "as well as possible" with an emphasis on care, health, and quality. That is, we can produce food, clothing, shelter— whatever we need—in ways that support and even enrich our lands through the ethics of care. For example, a farmer can raise chickens for egg production by allowing them to free-range. This practice is good for the chickens, but also good for the land, since their manure enriches the soil. (In fact, many regenerative agriculture systems are based on working with animals to quickly improve degraded ecosystems; see Mark Shepard's *Restoration Agriculture*[8] for one such method.) Nurturing can be applied to everything that we do, purchase, or support.

The exploiter, epitomized by Berry in the image of the strip miner, abuses the land for short-term profits made with as little work or investment as possible. Unfortunately, this is the model that capitalism has given us, and the model that is dominant in industrialized cultures throughout the world. Exploiters are concerned only with how much and how quickly the land can be made to produce profits—the land is viewed, and used, like a machine. Exploitative policies aren't limited to the land; rather, exploitation works throughout all levels of a system: workers in minimum-wage and factory jobs producing and selling goods, the procurement of raw materials, the disposal of waste streams, the treatment of animals. Where I live in Pennsylvania, exploitation fuels every major economic boom: strip logging that took place over the last part of the nineteenth and early twentieth centuries, the coal mining that leaves our rivers and streams toxic and lifeless, the policies that exterminated or forced native peoples to relocate, and the current fracking industry. These systems and practices are concerned with only one thing: profit. Exploitation is now so ingrained in our lifestyles, in society, that it is completely normal. For example, in looking for new land in Pennsylvania, the ads say things like "18 acres, timber sold and to be cut, no mineral rights." Here we see it as the previous owner making as much money as he or she could get before selling the scrap of soil that remains—stripped and bare. This is a practice that is common and considered perfectly acceptable.

Exploitation comes in many forms: those who are directly making decisions that exploit, and those who passively or unconsciously support exploitation through a trickle-down effect. Passive exploitation is hidden, covert, and, yet, still a driving force. In modern industrialized society, even if we aren't making active exploitative decisions, we are still often participating in passive exploitation of someone or something, very frequently without knowing it. This is where the lines get a bit grayer, but make no mistake—when you purchase a product, you purchase everything that goes along with that product. A simple example here is clothing. Exploitation can happen all along the production line of your clothing: the farmers who grew the cotton, the land that suffered through pesticides and deforestation, the rivers where pollution ran off the fields, the people who were exposed to poison as part of processing and dyeing it, the factory workers who turned raw cotton into fabric, the people who stitched that shirt at a cramped machine for fourteen hours a day for poor wages, the people who packaged that shirt and prepared it for shipment (I worked in such a factory once), and the minimum-wage workers at the store selling you the garment.

Active exploitation is a problem, but it's usually a fairly obvious one that any discerning person can spot, especially if you are attuned to and aware of these concepts. Passive exploitation is an entirely different matter—it's designed to be hidden. Part of the work of sacred action is uncovering this hidden truth and using this knowledge to make decisions about purchasing and supporting materials that are more in line with the ethics of care. Purchasing, ultimately, is an ethical choice. We'll be covering many of these issues—and how to get around them—in this book.

Spiritually, exploitation of either variety creates a particular kind of energy: when we purchase a product or support a practice that is exploitative in nature, that energy enters our lives. And yet, we have to live, we have to eat, we have to work, and thinking about all the exploitation that's happening for profit, and on our behalf, can be overwhelming. The energy of the winter solstice is a powerful metaphor for understanding nurturing and exploitation: the darkness seems to be all powerful, but the light of nurturing comes into the world once again. Just as day and night find balance, so too can we find balance in our own ability to nurture while living in an exploitative society.

Nurturing and exploitation are not mutually exclusive; Berry argues that each of us has the capacity for both kinds of action and that they are often conflict with one another, especially when we are living in industrialized societies. Each of us can be exploitative, in that we are causing demand that removes resources and causes pollution and damage; however, each us also has the opportunity to be nurturing, where we are regenerating and cycling resources and working to sustain and heal.

The Ethics of Sacred Action

Earth Care, People Care, and Fair Share

The following three ethical principles that we will use throughout this book are Earth care, people care, and fair share. These ethics provide us a profound ethical system that helps address the nature of care and allows us to avoid exploitation. These ethical principles are drawn from permaculture design, a set of powerful principles rooted in nature's patterns that help us design and enact more-conscious and Earth-centered communities, systems, and cultivated spaces. Our triad is as follows:

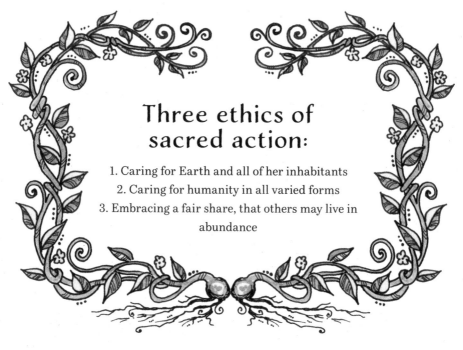

Three ethics of sacred action:

1. Caring for Earth and all of her inhabitants
2. Caring for humanity in all varied forms
3. Embracing a fair share, that others may live in abundance

These ethics provide us a way forward with understanding sacred actions through three focuses: an emphasis on caring for the Earth and all of its inhabitants, balanced with an emphasis on caring for people, and taking only our fair share and practicing restraint so that all may live in abundance.

Earth Care

Earth care is critical and central to sacred action and can take place on a number of levels: the mental, the physical, the spiritual, and the emotional. Earth care begins, always, with a mindset and orientation toward the Earth. With each breath, with each step, with each thought, caring for the Earth asks us to consider the impact of our actions: Will this action help and heal the Earth, or will it cause harm? This leads directly to our understanding of physical Earth care and what it actually looks like.

The problem with Earth care today is that consumerist framing has clouded cultural understandings of Earth care. For example, many things that are labeled as "caring for the Earth" are simply "less bad" options, rather than good options that actually constitute care. The consumer industry is driven by this principle. New products promote themselves as being "more sustainable" or "Earth-friendly," but what does that actually mean? If we want to care for the Earth, it has to move beyond just product choices. We cannot care for the Earth fully and meaningfully if it is only a consumer identity to us. It can go much deeper.

The terminology of Earth care is important here. Like many permaculture practitioners, I prefer the term "regenerate" to the term "sustain" for the simple reason that "sustainability" implies that we can, or should, sustain what is currently happening. "Regenerate" implies that to help heal our lands better, we can and should work to bring them back to healthy abundance for all life. To me, Earth care is not about doing less harm but, rather, active good. Given this, sacred action is about doing more than minimizing harm or choosing less bad options. Rather, we can actively be a force of good that transforms and heals our lands through our everyday life actions.

Stemming from this, Earth care includes how we use the land we are given and how we use and manage our resources. Exploitation of the Earth is easy to spot—but what does Earth care, Earth nurturing, look like? A simple example, explored further in chapter 3, may illustrate a principle here. When we cook and eat, we have parts of vegetables that we cannot use as well as food that sometimes spoils. These represent nutrients taken from the Earth. A regenerative perspective would suggest that we want to cycle these nutrients back into the ecosystem rather than disposing of them as waste. Composting is something that any person, regardless of their living situation, can do in some form or another. A vermicomposting (worm composting) bin in an apartment can help convert these vegetable scraps into nutrient-rich worm castings, which can then be used on a garden or even distributed back into a natural setting. These are nutrients cycling back into the ecosystem by using Earth care, rather than being thrown away to rot in a landfill. We will cover this, and many other aspects of Earth care, throughout this book.

Earth care is as much a spiritual practice as it is a physical one, and I would argue that they are one and the same. When we care for the Earth, that which we hold sacred, it is spiritual work. I think when we find nature-based spiritual paths, sometimes the immediate emphasis is on practices such as meditation, ritual, magic—but Earth care is as much a part of that spiritual practice as is a ritual, and learning how to integrate these is a key for sacred action.

People Care

A critical link exists between Earth care and people care. The United Nations has long recognized that ecological destruction and poverty are closely linked. People are more likely to take care for their lands if they are not destitute. United Nations data,[9] along with many other studies, clearly demonstrates that if people don't have their basic needs met, they will often strip their lands bare in desperation—or allow it to be stripped in pursuit of economic opportunity. Poverty leads to disempowerment and lack of agency over one's lands, livelihoods, and more. A good example of this can be seen from photographs on the border of Haiti and the Dominican Republic—the Haiti side is brown and bare, while the Dominican Republic side is lush and forested. A massive difference in the standard of living and the poverty rate of these two nations explains why those in Haiti stripped their forests bare for cooking fuel and food, and why those from the Dominican Republic did not.

While the UN discusses the link between people care and environmental protection primarily in terms of protection for people living in "developing" nations, industrialized nations such as the US and those in Europe also have a lot of work to do when it comes to people care. Even in industrialized nations, the poorest communities are often targeted for power plants, toxic factories, oil pipelines, and more. Poverty and related social justice issues seem more hidden here in "First World nations"—and when people are poor or suffering racial, religious, or any other form of injustice, they are often blamed, rather than recognizing poverty or racism as a systematic issue of exploitation. When I lived in Michigan, I taught classes in an extremely poor, urban, mostly minority suburb of Detroit. The auto industry had closed down the factories there in the mid-1990s, and poverty had skyrocketed in the years following. My students and I were there to help disadvantaged children build their literacy skills—and we realized that we couldn't help them read and write if they were hungry. When I watched laws being made and conversations taking place about (rather than within) this community, I couldn't believe how uncaring these conversations were: referring to the poor as lazy, leeches, unwilling to work—none of which was true. A community organization wanted to address the "food desert" problem and began urban farming and teaching children how to grow their own food—and this made tremendous inroads into bringing empowerment back into the community. Many poor communities are turning to food justice, urban permaculture, community gardens, and more for ways to empower and sustain livelihoods and lands. Sustainability and Earth care are thus inherently tied together with people care.

One of the ways to consider people care is how it aligns with Maslow's hierarchy of needs. The bottommost level of the hierarchy deals with the physiological needs: clean air, food, water, good sleep, and sanitation. The children I worked with

didn't have all of these extremely basic needs met, so attending to anything higher up on the hierarchy wasn't possible. The second tier in Maslow's hierarchy of needs is also as critical as the first: shelter, employment, base resources, family and community, and health. So, when we think about people care, a whole list of considerations takes place: access to healthful and nutritious food, clean water, meaningful and well-paying work, happiness, stable relationships, good education, safety, adequate housing, adequate transportation, and general fulfillment. We'll be talking about many of the needs on these two basic levels throughout this book.

Many of the practices much higher on Maslow's hierarchy—those surrounding Earth-based spiritual practices—are also about people care. In *Permaculture: Pathways beyond Sustainability*,[10] David Holmgren suggests that people care includes a sense of well-being that extends beyond material needs. The principle of nonmaterial well-being is part of many Earth-based spiritual traditions—we value the intangibles, the bardic arts,[11] the things that have little to no material value in our current culture, and also learn to better value ourselves and our gifts to the world. Our sense of community and belongingness, the ability to share our creations, supportive structures for empowerment—these all are important parts of people care.

A subset of the people care principle is self-care, or caring for ourselves in order to engage in the care of people and Earth. Ethical self-care realizes that we can't engage in any other kind of care if we, ourselves, are not taken care of first. Nature spirituality is a path that allows us much in the way of self-care, as do the practices of sacred action in this book.

Some readers may feel a strong draw toward the work of people care or may already be in "helping" professions. I would encourage those with this gift to consider how people care connects with Earth care and the next topic, fair share.

Fair Share

Fair share is the third ethical principle used in this book, the idea that we should take only our fair share so that others can also live comfortably and fulfilled (and by "others," I mean all other life, not just other humans). I was reminded of the principle of fair share each year in the fall, when the hickory trees on my Michigan homestead produced an abundant harvest of hundreds of pounds of amazing nuts. I could go and pick every last nut, but if I did so, there would be no nuts for the squirrels and chipmunks that depend on hickory as a major food source. I set a limit of gathering nuts to once every third day and would limit myself to never taking more than 20%. This allowed us all to have our share, and I still had plenty of nuts. This simple practice demonstrates aspects of fair share and its importance.

Fair share is not a value understood and enacted in our current industrialized culture, but it is a principle that is at the core of regenerative and sustainable societies. In American culture, a limit is consistently negatively framed: we hear of a credit card limit, a limit to your patience, a physical limit, being over the limit, being pushed to your limit—in each of these expressions, a limit is a challenge to be overcome. This idea of "limitless" possibilities and infinite growth focuses us on economic growth and "more" as the only productive way to be. If the economy isn't growing, if businesses aren't making more money each year, then there is a serious problem. (The entirety of the Western industrialized culture and nearly all systems within that culture function under this premise; their economic models assume infinite growth.) Limitless thinking is particularly problematic and destructive long term, given that we live on a finite planet.[12] Given this, we can reevaluate the concept of a limit—it's not something to overcome, but something that we willfully choose to enact because that limit encourages fair share and creates space for others to live. We can limit our consumption, because the less we use, the less demand there is and the more resources stay in the land. We can limit other things as well, such as our miles driven using fossil fuels, the purchases we make, the processed food we buy, the television we consume: all of these limits have real and lasting benefits to ourselves and our land. In nearly all cases, a limit we set in our lives means less demand on stressed ecosystems worldwide. Embracing the limit is a sound ecological and spiritual practice.

Fair share also is about resource distribution. A forest is a perfect example of a closed system—nothing at all is wasted in a forest. The trees fall and are host to fungi, bacteria, and lichens; these break down the remains of the tree into fertile soil; nutrients in that soil are taken up by plants, which are eaten by animals, who die and are returned to the soil, and so forth. There is no pollution, no waste, and nothing out of place. Engaging in sacred action encourages us to see everything in our lives—every object, scrap of food waste, and so forth—as something that we can redistribute, rather than throw away. Nothing truly goes "away," since the Earth itself is also a closed system, just like that forest. The spiritual principles of the cycle and circle are particularly useful here.

David Holmgren[13] suggests that fair share was actually one of the reasons that so many indigenous traditions (including our many spiritual ancestors) gave offerings. It was a sign of giving back, of recognizing the harvest and honoring the land, spirits, and gods who allowed that harvest to happen. One of the offerings we can give is living a regenerative life—this is a powerful way of enacting the principle of fair share. Another way of thinking about fair share is that of balance—a lesson that Earth-based spiritual practitioners are reminded of during the winter solstice.

Care as a Lifestyle and Spiritual Ethic

The ethical triad of care can help us understand and enact more sacred action in the world around us. The ethical triad has profound spiritual implications as well. For one, the ethical triad can form the cornerstone of an ethical system that provides us a guiding light in difficult times, an Earth-centered ethical system of sacred action in the world. When I'm encountering a situation and making a decision, I draw upon the ethical triad and carefully consider each aspect as part of that decision-making process—this has helped me even with mundane activities, such as ordering food for an event as well as more long-term ones. In my own teaching of herbalism or wild-food foraging, I teach the three principles prior to any other lesson. But even professionally, I use the ethical triad in my decisions and daily work life.

Spiritually, the ethical triad offers many possibilities (see the "Exercises and Rituals" section for a few possibilities). The ethical triad is a useful as theme for meditation or as mantras. I have found them of considerable use for themes for meditation, where I spend one or more weeks meditating on them (and repeat these meditations over a period of years to deepen my understanding). I found them so useful, I even created little colorful signs and placed them all over my house to remember them as I go about my daily living. They are simple to remember and yet profound on many levels.

The ethical triad also encourages another kind of thinking that links us to past indigenous understandings of a sacred partnership with the Earth. The "Great Law of the Iroquois"[14] asked tribal elders making decisions to make the decision so that it would benefit the next seven generations. The seven-generations principle has been adapted more broadly to provide a new way of thinking about our actions—what can we do now to benefit those who are yet unborn, seven generations after us?

Even if you aren't at a point to make many physical changes to your life, I do advocate for putting yourself in a nurturing and caring mindset and beginning to see this as part of your spiritual ethic. The mind is an extremely powerful tool—it is a tool of magic. Magic, in traditional terms, is about the process of focusing the will for outward change. Seeing ourselves as nurturers helps us be nurturers and practice these three ethics of care, even if those changes are slow. It allows us to be in the right mindset to take advantage of opportunities and make slow shifts. I'm not saying we can, or should, only think and not act, but shifting the mind is a powerful start that will lead to a shift in actions over time.

Exercises and Rituals

With each chapter in this book, I'll present a series of exercises, rituals, and activities to help you work with the concepts and practices of sacred action further.

Your Ecological Footprint

People in industrialized nations are often living lifestyles that this planet cannot support. One of the ways to measure your overall lifestyle impact is to use a carbon footprint calculation. While carbon is only one measure among many, it's a good place to get some general sense of how your actions affect our larger world.[15]

Your ecological footprint will give you a baseline assessment of how much of our natural world your current lifestyle requires; ecological-footprint calculators also will give you suggestions for change. These are generalized models, but I do find that they are useful for a baseline measurement tool.

I measured my ecological footprint by using the Center for Sustainable Economy's Ecological Footprint Calculator (www.footprintcalculator.org/) when I started this work many years ago, and I was shocked when I was at 6.62 Earths. This meant that if everyone on the planet lived like I was living, we would need 6.62 Earths to sustain that lifestyle. This was a wake-up call for me: I realized that simple changes in my life, such as bringing my own bags to the grocery store or recycling, were not really getting to the heart of shifting my practice. After a decade of dedicated shifts to sustainability, I took the calculation again and discovered I was at 1.5 Earths; this showed that I had made substantial progress, but that I was still very much on the journey. The two great challenges that remained were housing and transportation (especially work-related transportation). Airline travel three to four times a year for work continued to be my greatest waste area.

A Ritual of Change and Blessing upon Your New Journey

This ritual can help you begin your journey through the wheel of the seasons and set your intentions and actions for sacred actions that are to come.

Timing: This ritual is best completed at night, close to or on the winter solstice (the longest night of the year) or a new moon. Note: this book uses the solar Wheel of the Year beginning in the winter solstice, but if you decide you want to start this work at a different time and begin your sacred actions sooner, you can use the lunar wheel instead. The lunar phase repeats every twenty-eight days, while the solar repeats every 365. The correspondences are as follows:

Winter solstice (dark moon / new moon)

Imbolc (waxing crescent)

Spring equinox (first quarter)

Beltane (waxing gibbous)

Summer solstice (full moon)

Lughnasadh (waning gibbous)

Fall equinox (third quarter)

Samhain (waning crescent)

Performing this ritual on a dark/new moon will draw in similar lunar energy.

Preparation and Materials

Nine candles: Place one at a central altar location, and place the other eight at stations around the room in a circle. These should be unlit at the start of the ceremony, except for the central candle. In line with sacred action, consider candles purchased secondhand (thrift store, yard sale, etc.) or beeswax candles produced locally (see chapter 4).

A hooded lantern or other light-obscuring device. For the beginning of the ceremony, you will need something that obscures nearly all the light in the room. A hooded lantern or a coffee can with holes works well for this.

Journal: A journal that will help you document your journey and a writing utensil are needed for this ritual. This can be the same journal you use for discursive meditations and other aspects of your spiritual work and reflection.

Representations of the four elements: Place representations of Earth, air, fire, and water on your central altar in positions appropriate for each element. The central candle represents fire (placed in the south). You'll need a representation of air (incense, a bell, or a feather; placed in the east), water (bowl of water, shells; placed in the west), and Earth (bowl of Earth, stone; placed in the north).

Decorations: You may also include altar decorations appropriate to the season. For the winter solstice in the Northern Hemisphere, this would include a white altar cloth, evergreen sprigs, holly berries, dried grasses or flowers, winter root vegetables, or anything else you can gather from outdoors at this time of the year.

Ritual Overview

Sacred journaling: This ritual introduces the practice of sacred journaling. Journaling is a way to help you set a baseline, gauge your progress, and keep track of your successes. This particular exercise will ask you to write creatively, telling the story of your future self—the story of you, a year from now, and the sacred actions that you do each day. Describe this story in detail.

Continuing the energy forward: Like any magical act, it is equally important to carry the energy forward into manifestation in the physical world. After you conclude the ritual, in the next twenty-four to forty-eight hours, do something, even something small, to help you move forward on your path to sustainable, sacred living.

The Ritual Opening

This simple opening is inspired by the Druid Revival tradition. Instructions are in plain text; spoken words are in *italics*. Alternatively, feel free to use an opening and closing from your own tradition or experience.

Stand in front of the altar in the north, facing south.

Begin by taking three deep breaths. With each breath, allow the concerns and worries of everyday living to fade.

Raise your hands. *With the blessing of the land within and without, let it be known that I now open a sacred space.*

Move to the eastern side of the altar and pick up the incense in both hands. Move to the eastern part of the space, facing outward. Raise the incense into the air. *I call upon the east! The powers of the quickness of the mind, and the hawk in the spring skies! May the rising sun illuminate my path forward into sacred action.*

Move around the circle, carrying the incense, saying, *I cleanse and bless this space with the power of air.*

Move to the southern side of the altar and pick up the candle in both hands. Move to the southern part of the space, facing outward. Raise the candle into the air. *I call upon the south! The powers of the creative flow, and the stag in the summer forests! May the noonday sun bless my journey into sacred action.*

Move around the circle, carrying the candle, saying, *I cleanse and bless this space with the power of fire.*

Move to the western side of the altar and pick up the bowl of water in both hands. Move to the western part of the space, facing outward. Raise the bowl into the air. *I call upon the west! The powers of the passion of the heart, and the salmon in the sacred pool! May the setting sun illuminate my heart in enacting in sacred action.*

Move around the circle, sprinkling water, saying, *I cleanse and bless this space with the power of water.*

Move to the northern side of the altar and pick up the bowl of Earth in both hands. Move to the northern part of the space, facing outward. Raise the bowl into the air. *I call upon the north! The powers of the home and hearth, and the great bear and land around me! May the moon and stars guide my path in sacred action.*

Move around the circle with the bowl of Earth, saying, *I cleanse and bless this space with the power of Earth.*

Return to the center of the space and focus your mind on each of the four elements you have called. Then, draw a circle with your index and middle fingers around the space, beginning in the east. As you draw, envision a circle of white light protecting the space.

This circle is sealed. The wheel forever turns, but for this moment, time is still. In this hallowed place, all things are possible and hope springs eternal.

The Rite

Place the central candle in the hooded lantern or coffee can to obscure nearly all of the light. Then read or say something near to the following:

Today, I stand at the darkest day of the year. The sun hangs low in the sky, the land is bare, and all is obscured by the night. Our great mother Earth and her children seem to be in this same place of darkness. Many of us feel lost, confused, and hopeless, as though this dark night will never end. We fear the passage of time. We fear for the lives of so many of Earth's inhabitants. We fear for the future.

Spend a few moments sitting in this darkness, experiencing what it is like to be here, in this time, and in this place. Just be with any emotions you currently have[16]—sense them, experience them, for a short time. Then, remove the coffee can or open the lantern.

A light shines in the darkness, the light of hope! The ethics of caring once again for this land and her peoples! A light shines, and a path is revealed. I am this light, moving into the broader world.

Pick up the central candle and move to the first of the eight candles, in the eastern part of the circle. Light the candle.

The path of Oak knowledge brings light and hope to our Earth.

If you wish to speak about your journey toward sacred action through reskilling (learning new skills), it is appropriate here.

Move to the next candle, in the southeast, and light it.

The path of fair share brings respite and relief to our Earth.

If you wish to speak about your journey toward sacred action through reducing consumption and waste, it is appropriate here.

Move to the next candle, in the south, and light it.

The path of sacred action in the home brings peace and health to our Earth.

If you wish to speak about your journey toward sacred action in your home and daily living, it is appropriate here.

Move to the next candle, in the southwest, and light it.

The path of sacred action through nourishment brings abundance and regeneration to our Earth.

If you wish to speak about your journey toward sacred action through eating a more Earth-friendly diet, it is appropriate here.

Move to the next candle, in the west, and light it.

The path of sacred action in my immediate landscape brings blessings and joy to our Earth.

If you wish to speak about your journey toward sacred action through growing plants or gardens, it is appropriate here.

Move to the next candle, in the northwest, and light it.

The path of sacred action in my community and broader society brings vision and reconnection.

If you wish to speak about your journey toward sacred action through community or workplace actions, it is appropriate here.

Move to the next candle, in the north, and light it.

The path of sacred action in my own life brings nourishment and wisdom.
Return to the central altar and pause for a moment.

All these things are accomplished by caring for the Earth and her inhabitants, caring for those of my own human tribe, and taking only my fair share so that others may live. I (begin/continue) this path of sacred action in the world!

At this time, make yourself comfortable in the circle and meditate, for a time, on the journey that is to come. Envision yourself living a life of sacred action—what does that life look like?

After a time of meditation, pick up your journal and write creatively, telling the story of your future self and the life that your future self lives, the sacred activity that your future self engages in regularly. Write that story in your journal in as much detail and description as possible.

Closing

Stand in the north, facing the altar.

With the blessings of the elements, I unwind this circle and close this space. Although the ritual is ended, the journey has just begun. As these candles are extinguished in the apparent world, a fire is lit within me. To carry the flame forward on the path of sacred action!

Move to each of the quarters and cross-quarters, placing your hands together in thanks at each quarter. After giving silent thanks, blow out each of the candles. As you blow the candle out, envision a flame within you burning brighter and brighter—the light of hope. Say:

This flame burns within, the light of hope. The Wheel of the Year continues to turn, and my path before is clear.

Envision now the circle you cast at the beginning of the ceremony, and, using your two fingers, "unwind" it counterclockwise, beginning in the east and envisioning the circle being taken down.

May I carry the inspiration of this ceremony with me, this day and always.

Discursive Meditation on the Triads

The introduction and this chapter each introduced a triad of triads—one for the challenges we face, one for the work of sacred action, and one for the ethics that guide our path. These triads can be used in a variety of ways, and we can explore them here further through meditation. It is in meditation that a deeper understanding of the triads can be revealed.

Meditation, a practice of focused and directed thought, is an extraordinarily powerful tool not only for the development of a rich inner spiritual life, but also in the development of our sacred actions in the world. Meditation on concepts and experiences can help us, directly and powerfully, to come to a deeper understanding of those concepts and experiences and can lead to profound change. I would suggest that you spend time meditating on many concepts in this book, especially those presented in the introduction and first chapter. This isn't flashy work, but it allows these concepts to resonate at many levels, consciously and subconsciously, and work their way deeply into your understanding.

An extremely useful and simple meditative practice for this work is called discursive meditation; this technique is used by the Ancient Order of Druids in America,[17] among many other traditions. I'll briefly outline one approach to discursive meditation here, for use in meditating on the triads.

Preparation: Prior to beginning meditative practice, select a "theme" for meditation. Good ones to start with for the purposes of the exercises and philosophies in this book are any aspect of the ethical triad—the whole triad or a piece of it. The ethics of people care, Earth care, or fair share, or the principle of sacred action. These principles alone can result in powerful understandings.

Meditation: Begin by sitting in a straight-backed chair, or sitting on the floor, or lying comfortably flat on the floor. The important thing here is that you are comfortable and at rest, and that you aren't cutting off any major energy flows of the body.

Begin by taking three deep "clearing" breaths and then return to a slower pattern of breathing where you take a breath for the count of three, hold it for a count of three, and release it for a count of three. Once you have the pattern of the "threefold breath,"[18] you can do it naturally without counting as you find your rhythm. Spend a few moments in the threefold breath, just focusing and centering on your breathing.

Discursive meditation: The core part of the meditative practice can begin. I like to describe this practice as walking on a path in the forest, where the path is your consideration of the topic at hand. On your walk, you see many different junctures, and each time you can choose one and see how far it leads. At some point, you might backtrack and choose another one, and that's fine too. In this way, you begin to work your way through the theme you've chosen, exploring your insights, intuitions, associations, and experiences with the theme. This can be fairly free association, or it might be a logically progressed thought—the important thing is that you work with the idea intensively. If you find yourself veering radically off course—into a briar patch of personal issues—note whether there are any relationships between the topic at hand and where you mind has wandered. If not, just like walking in the forest, retrace your steps and follow your thought path back to where you veered off course.

A good discursive meditation session lasts at least ten or fifteen minutes. More-frequent short sessions are better than longer ones. I would also strongly suggest keeping a notebook where you can record your insights after you finish a meditation on the topic. Record your insights in your journal just after closing your meditation, since you will be in the best headspace to remember your insights. Trying to record them later, after the mind is full of other things, leads to incomplete recall.

Enacting the Ethics of Care

As you meditate on the principles in this first chapter and complete the energetic and ritual work to help your path, also work to enact them in your life over the next few weeks. Take three weeks and devote one week each to living your life with that principle in the forefront of your mind and meditating on that principle.

- Week 1—Exercises 1, 2, and 3: ecological footprint, meditation, and ritual
- Week 2—Earth care: living in a way that cares for the Earth, even in small ways
- Week 3—People care: putting people care at the forefront of your actions this week
- Week 4—Fair share: examining needs vs. wants, taking only what you need

Record your experiences with each of the four weeks in your journal and see how many of these practices you can turn into a regular part of the framework through which you observe and interact with the world.

CHAPTER 2

Imbolc

Wisdom through Oak Knowledge
and Reskilling

When I was a child, my grandma sang me a song called "A Froggy Would a Wooin' Go," a song that, to my young ears, had the strangest words. The froggy went "a wooin'" the mouse "sat to spin"; I had no real idea what this song was about. As an adult, I was interested in the history of this song and traced it back to its first appearance in the historical record in 1558.[19] For that song to make it to me, for 500+ years grandmothers passed it down to their grandchildren in a line that spanned back countless generations. One day, when I was still young, Grandmother sat with tears in her eyes on the stoop where she buried shiny new pennies. She said to me, "Things were different when I was a child, Dana. Even during the Depression, things were different. People needed each other then. We got on with very little. There is so much I could teach you that you just don't need anymore." Then we went inside and ate her homemade mushroom soup with herbs from her garden. Many of the older generations, like my grandmother, didn't pass on their skills because either we didn't want to learn them or they felt that what they knew no longer applied to our modern lifestyles. But I often wonder what my ancestors who first sang "A Froggy Would a Wooin' Go" knew and how they lived, how much of the knowledge I sought to embrace died with them. It is in many of these more traditional ways of life that we can rediscover, and learn, the ways of sacred action.

With the dawning of industrialization and consumerism, we've lost many skills and much knowledge; this is the loss of our human heritage of interacting and living with the land: the knowledge of root and stem, seed and growth, balance and restoration. That loss, at least in the Americas, included systematic genocide of the Native Americans who held such knowledge. But even among those who later settled the Americas, prior to the twentieth century, the knowledge that people had, and passed down, of how to live more-traditional lives, with closeness to the land, was often still plentiful. The knowledge may have changed on the basis of the part of the world in which you lived and your family's station in life, but knowledge of sustaining the land to sustain yourself was a considerable amount of what was passed on—from parent to child, from grandparent to grandchild. The lost ancestral knowledge isn't just about growing one's own food or making one's own medicine; it's also about how to work with each other, about how to build communities, how to raise barns, how to learn and grow. We live in those fragments.

Looking back on the memory of my grandmother long after she had died, I remember feeling that I had no heritage. I felt, for a long time, that the traditions and knowledge of my ancestors (primarily Irish and German) were completely lost to me. Much of my family line had come to the United States at least four or five generations prior to my birth; those who were native had long since been forced to lose much of their own history or had taken it with them to their graves. I had no traditional knowledge or skills associated with that heritage. This "lack of heritage" situation was compounded by the fact that I had rejected the religion of my parents and, therefore, had rejected most of their celebrations, holidays, and values.

I'm sure that many who read this book, those living in various parts of the world, understand what I speak of here. The last few generations have been swept up—in all parts of the industrialized world—in this frenzy of fast-paced, consumerist living, where knowledge and craft are replaced with efficiency and product.

For many, finding a nature-based spiritual path gives us the opportunity to reclaim and rebuild traditions and to give us more-meaningful interaction with the world around us. Over a period of years, I realized that through walking the path of sacred action, which encouraged me to continue to build my own knowledge, I was building something anew where I had perceived this empty wasteland of family tradition. I became obsessed with reading old books full of old knowledge (the 1970s has much to offer, as do those from earlier decades and centuries). I attended workshops and classes, learned by doing, sat at the feet of elders, and absorbed everything I could. So come with me now, back on a journey to understand our ancestors, the skills they had, and how we might begin to learn them again for the goal of engaging in Earth-based sacred action. This is sacred knowledge, the knowledge of our ancestors, and the knowledge that will help us sustain our world and save our future.

The Light at Imbolc

Imbolc is a time of new beginnings, an ancient holiday that marked the first signs of spring in the Northern Hemisphere. Although traditions varied, and vary widely in the Earth-centered and neopagan spiritual communities today, we can draw upon its energy for the purposes of sacred action. Using a traditional agricultural calendar, which still survives in many places, we see that winter is the time for study, reading, and reflection. The brightness of summer is the time for action, movement, and activity. In early February, children from agricultural areas still attended school so that when summer returned, they could work once again in the fields. We might mirror this tradition and draw up on the energy of this time of year for reading and study of our own, of the dedicated practice of learning a craft. Imbolc is a wonderful time to plant the seeds of inspiration for projects and activities for the coming light half of the year.

This chapter is the second of our "foundational" chapters for sacred action; it provides us with a road map of the skills and knowledge that we need in order to move forward. In this chapter, we explore the importance of knowledge and the kinds of places we might seek it, things worth learning that can help us engage in sacred action. Sacred action is firmly rooted in knowledge, dedicated practice, and an application of that knowledge to our actual living, as the triad suggests:

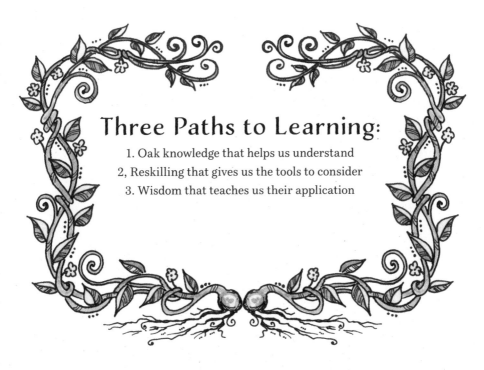

Three Paths to Learning:
1. Oak knowledge that helps us understand
2. Reskilling that gives us the tools to consider
3. Wisdom that teaches us their application

We need the wisdom to understand what is happening around us and to identify places that we can change. But we also need the actual tools to enact change—to go from saying, "This is a problem," to saying, "I have a solution." It is in wisdom that we find that application. So it is in this spirit that we explore knowledge, history, and reskilling as key principles that inform and lead to sacred action.

Oak Knowledge

In the ancient Celtic world, the word "druid" meant "Oak knowledge" or, more broadly, "deep knowledge."[20] This referred to the wide variety of activities that ancient druids participated in and the knowledge they held: the knowledge of the law, of nature, of astronomy, of mathematics, of the bardic (creative) arts, of divination, of healing plants, and of the spirit realm. This knowledge and set of associated skills is what made someone a holder of Oak knowledge. I suggest that we embrace this idea of "Oak knowledge" as part of sacred action. But what does "knowledge of the oaks" mean for us today?

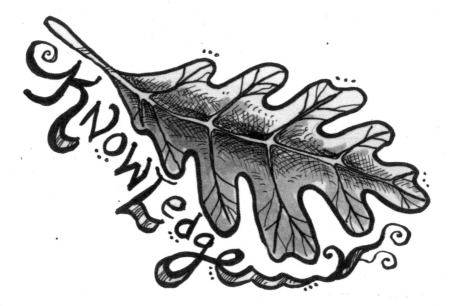

In the most literal sense of the words, "Oak knowledge" refers to knowledge of the oak: its growing habits and range, the ecosystems the oak creates, uses of acorns and the medicine of its bark, and so on. This is not only the knowledge of scientific fields, such as ecology or botany, but the folk knowledge of living close to the land each day and through the powers of careful observation. Knowledge of the oaks is knowledge of a range of aspects of the natural world.

To expand, we might consider "Oak knowledge" as knowledge directly tied to better understanding, healing, and consciously inhabiting our incredible Earth. In a modern sense, it can include having a deep understanding of the natural world and the medicine and teachings of the plants, an understanding of humanity's ecological impacts and how to mitigate them, a knowledge of how to nurture and regenerate our landscapes and communities and how to grow and preserve food, a knowledge of basic botany and ecology, and of water and energy systems, and knowing how to best reach others for larger-scale change.

What I have found is that a little bit of knowledge can go a long way, and immediately when you have it, people begin to gather and seek your expertise. Of course, in order to do this in our own lives and in those of our communities, we have to build the knowledge and the skills to begin with! I have found that this Oak knowledge is invaluable—I always have an opportunity to share something I know and to teach others about the natural world, which can lead to more-positive relationships for everyone involved. For example, I was recently camping at a spiritual gathering, and we didn't have quite enough to eat for our final meal. Since I was in the mood for salad, I produced a nice salad from wild greens out of a nearby field. At that same gathering, a friend's hand got cut fairly badly, and I stopped the bleeding with yarrow and healed it with plantain. These are small examples, but these small examples turned into a full-on plant walk for about ten people who were interested in learning more about the woods we were staying in. These kinds of opportunities occur all the time if we have the knowledge and are willing to share.

Reskilling

Everyone, to some extent, is a product of their culture and what skills and knowledge it values: our grandmothers were products of their time, just as we are products of ours. Certain sets of skills are privileged, and others are simply not taught, and in many cases, skill sets that are deemed no longer relevant are lost from the collective knowledge of many communities and families. Our culture's formal education system currently teaches a set of skills that are claimed to be beneficial and practical for functioning in modern society (although that is itself debatable); unfortunately, many of these skills teach us to be good consumers and participate in exploitation rather than nurturing. If we are hoping to engage in sacred actions in our lives, our current skill sets aren't enough to do this, and that's where reskilling comes in.

As this chapter's triad suggests, Oak knowledge gives us the practical knowledge of the living Earth and her systems, while reskilling provides us with the direct tools for change. Reskilling as a movement covers many of the traditional skills and crafts: home brewing, herb gardening, herbalism, fermentation, knitting, spinning, woodcarving, sewing, natural building, seed saving, foraging—all of these and many more represent some skills covered under the reskilling umbrella.

Reskilling entails learning broad sets of skills—skills often from times past, but also rooted in present needs, that are useful for sustainable living. Reskilling is about gaining the skills to live more regeneratively, which means being able to provide at least a few of the basic needs for ourselves, our families, and our communities. The broader reskilling movement is concerned with skills that help feed ourselves, clothe ourselves, provide daily functional items for ourselves from local materials, entertain ourselves, deal with our waste, keep ourselves healthy, create sustainable living spaces, keep ourselves sheltered and warm, and create our own useful arts and crafts. So, we can think about reskilling as the process of gaining a set of skills needed for meeting basic human needs—and for taking our power back from those who would seek to keep us consuming and passively exploiting.

A lot of reasons exist to encourage reskilling, and I'll share a few of mine. First, I found that each time I learn a new skill—from how to properly start seeds, forage for wild mushrooms, deal with an egg-bound chicken, or make my own medicines—I was taking one small step further away from modern industrial and consumerist society. This meant less dependence and financial support for the practices, companies, and lifestyles that I spiritually disagreed with and found destructive. Second, reskilling, while hard work, is fun and exciting—it has created a really fulfilling life full of activities, new interests, and new friends. Also, reskilling allows people like me, who were heavily trained in a specialty, to adopt a more generalist mentality and see a broader picture, and there is great benefit in such an approach. It allows me to realize that there is more than just one thing that I was good at, and become a more functional, independent person. Reskilling is extremely empowering—gaining new knowledge and doing something to make a difference. Finally, since my spiritual path is rooted in the living Earth, I see reskilling not only as a regenerative practice, but as a sacred spiritual practice— the Earth and the ancestors are honored, my needs are taken care of, and I live much closer to the land's rhythms and seasons.

In the process of building toward more-regenerative lifestyles, I have found that it is important to learn one or a few things comfortably at a time—when you start trying to do too much at once or trying to learn everything at once, you risk frustrating or overwhelming yourself. Start slow, read, talk to people, take classes, and find out what you are inspired to try. Consider also whether you want to specialize in one kind of skill extensively and master that skill or learn a bit of everything. To give you some reference, a typical community of 150 years ago had certain activities that everyone did (e.g., the home cottage industry, such as growing and preserving food, spinning, brewing, making cheeses, churning butter, raising some chickens), but then there were specialized skills that were marketable, such as a blacksmith, woodcarver, or herbalist. You want to think about your interests and see where they develop. I am much more of a dabbler myself, having decided to learn a lot of different skills and integrate them into my life, with a focus in a few key skills I work really hard at (such as herbalism and wild-food foraging). Others focus exclusively and get really good at that one skill.

When reskilling, one of the critical principles to remember is to move slowly and purposefully, integrating slowly over time. What can happen—and I speak from experience—is that in our enthusiasm for living more aligned with our principles, we make too many shifts too quickly, and those shifts are hard to maintain without burning us out, especially when juggling the other twenty-first-century responsibilities of taxes, bills, full-time jobs, family life, and so on. An example here from my own life is helpful: in my eagerness to provide for all of my own food and eliminate my lawn (the better part of 2 acres), in less than three years I put in a huge, 2,000-square-foot vegetable garden in addition to herb beds, perennial beds, fruit orchards, butterfly gardens, and much more. Not only was this garden a tremendous amount of work in a short period of time, the maintenance of the garden simply became more than I could manage—or eat! As a single woman in a full-time career, I simply did not have the time to tend all the huge gardens I had put in. I ended up growing more interested in permaculture design and converting much of the vegetable garden to perennials (such as golden raspberry, grape, strawberry, blueberry, and currant), and that made the space more manageable. But, regardless, my lesson here is an important one: manage the lifestyle shifts carefully and make lasting changes that are sustainable in the long run.

A Sample List of Skills and Knowledge

What kinds of skills and knowledge lead to sacred action? They are quite varied, but I want to encourage you in a few key areas that I have found really make a difference; other chapters will focus on covering some of the skills on these lists.

Knowledge of the natural world: This includes botany, ecology, plant identification, and knowledge of ecosystems. Knowledge of how humans can interact with the natural world is also quite powerful: how to build a safe and simple fire and shelter, gather medicine without damaging ecosystems, or walk carefully through the woods. You'll find classes like these under the heading of "bushcraft" or "wilderness skills." Knowledge of plants, ecosystems, and how they work is also very helpful. Probably the most-valuable knowledge I've gained, however, is of the plants themselves: learning what they are, their names, how to identify them in different seasons, and the role they play in our ecosystems. It is this kind of knowledge that can be usefully and readily shared with others, and there is a lot of interest in this broadly. In my own community, I have taught many herbalism and foraging courses, and people are very excited to learn. These skills often focus on the "Earth care" and "fair share" ethics we explored in the last chapter.

Sustainable living skills: These skills include a wide, wide range of skills and practices—many of which are covered in chapters 3–6. Key skills here include anything under the umbrella of "homesteading" (or, in the UK, "smallholding"), which refers to living on a patch of land closely and working to provide one's own needs: animal husbandry, organic farming, beekeeping, water catchment and movement systems, perennial agriculture and tree crops, irrigation strategies, integrated pest management, soil building, designing food systems, crop rotations, and more. Food preservation is a skill that anyone, regardless of living circumstances, can learn: fermentation, canning, drying, home brewing, drying, fruit leathers, and more. Waste management is also important: how do we handle repurposed waste (composting, humanure, vermicomposting) or repurpose / creatively use other waste streams. This list also includes how to manage home energy needs: solar power, wind power, and low-power living. In this list I would also include natural building: cob, straw bale, earth plasters, thatching, and more. These skills often connect the "people care" with "Earth care" and "fair share" ethics from the last chapter.

Crafts and bardic arts: Additionally, arts and crafts (including what we druids call the "bardic arts") are an important part of the reskilling movement. These are wide ranging and include a range of traditional crafts such as whittling, spoon carving, basket weaving, and soapmaking. It also includes what can be gathered from nature: foraging, wildcrafting, medicine making, natural arts, natural dyes, and more. Weaving, dyeing, making clothing, shoemaking/cobbling, leather tanning, leather working, blacksmithing, throwing pots and firing them naturally—so many more skills can show up under this list! We also have the skills that help us provide our own entertainment: dancing, singing, learning instruments, telling stories, and more. These skills often focus on the "people care" and "self-care" aspects of the ethics from chapter 1.

Community building: A final important set of skills (that we will cover in chapter 7) include community-building skills—consensus building, nonviolent communication, developing leadership skills, and the like—and can be useful here. Learning how to direct people to action, learning how to resolve conflict, and learning how to excite and motivate people are important skills for bringing our communities back together. These skills are rooted in all three ethics from chapter 1, but most directly in the "people care" ethic.

Although many of the kinds of skills I'm discussing are not part of "mainstream" industrialized living, a good deal of them can be found in certain niche communities and places all throughout the world. Beyond the skills covered in the remainder of this book, I would recommend expanding your horizons to learn new skills and knowledge for sacred action. Some of those places are as follows.

Learning Firsthand from Others

There is little substitute for learning firsthand, either one on one or in a group setting. Following are a few ways to learn.

Classes: These are a great way to learn many skills, and one of my preferred methods of reskilling training. Since I started reskilling many years ago, I have taken all sorts of classes—natural building (round-pole framing, thatching, plasters, straw bale construction), compost water heaters, rocket stoves, organic farming, winter organic farming / hoop house management, herbalism, foraging / wild foods, candle making, fermentation, mushroom foraging, mushroom cultivation, beekeeping, permaculture design certificate courses, livestock, wilderness survival, and so many more. Many of these classes were local, but others required me to do a bit of travel—and since sacred living is a lifestyle for me, I was happy to use my vacation time to, say, spend a few days in the woods learning how to build simple shelters and take care of my basic needs, rather than lie by the beach! I found these classes by reaching out to friends with similar interests and searching online.

Apprenticeships: These are great if you know someone experienced who knows how to do something you really want to learn. The basic idea is that you, as a novice, learn from a master of something and in exchange provide them assistance with that craft or skill. Learning under someone who has a skill allows you to have a mentor, to aid them in their work, and to learn firsthand. I was lucky enough to serve as an organic farmer's apprentice for a season, and there was no substitute for learning from her—she knew tips and tricks I had never read in any organic-farm book or learned from any class! Often, if you are a good apprentice, people who know things are glad to teach. You can also arrange more-formalized apprenticeships in certain areas (for example, herbalism is one area where such formal apprenticeships are more common).

Friends: Your friends may know all sorts of interesting things, and you won't know what they could teach you until you ask. For example, I learned how to make soap from two friends, and now already I've taught soapmaking to two more friends. Other friends taught me about woodcarving, knot tying, charcoal making, home brewing, composting, drying herbs, canning, beekeeping, starting fires with flint and steel, and so much more. Strike up conversations with people, see what they do in their spare time, and if it sounds interesting, ask them to teach you. Friends and family are also wonderful to learn skills with!

Community and professional organizations: These can be nonexistent or quite abundant, depending on where you are located. In the various places I've lived, I've had both abundance and famine as far as reskilling organizations and groups. I should also say that if a community organization or group doesn't exist, consider starting one. That's what a group of friends and I did to start a permaculture group in our local area in Michigan. That group ended up drawing groups of forty to fifty people each month and used a model of "members teaching members" that worked exceedingly well (see chapter 7 for more on building community). On the more professional side, if you are really interested in gardening, for example, you might find a sustainable agriculture organization that offers regional or local events. Campuses often have groups, some of which are open to outsiders in the community. There are also a range of nonprofit institutes and schools that offer lessons (the permaculture and reskilling movements have a number of these).

Reskilling festivals and fairs: These are another great way to learn. Some areas may have local reskilling fairs (for example, I attended one that took place in Ann Arbor, Michigan) or offer regional meetings. Perhaps the most well known currently in the US is the Mother Earth News Fair—there are now multiple fairs all over the country that are very well attended and quite educational! Keep an eye out— these kinds of events may not call themselves "reskilling" fairs, but if you take a look at the program and see what there is to learn, you will often be surprised by the offerings. Look for fiber festivals, farm festivals, home-brewing festivals, and any others offering traditional skills.

Learning from History and Historical Events

History in its various forms has so much to teach us in terms of reskilling, primarily because much Oak knowledge was held by our ancestors.

Living-history events/festivals: These offer a glimpse into the past, including the food, clothing, activities, and everyday living of various groups and time periods. These groups are a fantastic place to go to learn some traditional skills that help lessen our burden on the planet. In the US, these are put on by the Society for Creative Anachronism (SCA) and other groups. One year, some friends invited me to their reenactment camp, and I was really excited to see how many skills the reenactors were preserving. From that experience, I learned about camp cooking and iron cookware, simple blacksmithing, weaving, spinning, flint knapping, and tanning leather. While these camps provided me with "glimpses," I was able to be inspired, gain some basic instruction by talking to people at camp, and connect with others preserving these various skills. The camp cooking turned out to be the most useful, and it is a skill I now use quite regularly! A local SCA group in my community in Michigan also put on monthly activities surrounding skills including spinning/weaving, bread baking, cheese making, brewing traditional beers, and more. You could join them once a month to learn many different traditional skills.

Historical villages: These offer a more permanent form of "living history" is the historical village. In the US, you can find various kinds of historical villages peppered around the country, and visiting one can give you many insights into traditional skills. One of my favorites of these is called "Old Bedford Village" in Bedford, Pennsylvania, where all sorts of old traditions are preserved. They have a traditional print shop, an apothecary, a candle maker, various woodworkers, a blacksmith, a potter, a tinsmith, a spinner, a weaver, and more. It's an inspirational place, and while there are limited opportunities for hands-on experiences, you can learn a lot just studying the old tools and talking with the people who are demonstrating various skills. Even seeing a typical house in the colonial era (such as where the hearth was placed, the cooking instruments, etc.) gives lots of ideas.

Historical study: Looking through old books reveals a wealth of often-quite-useful knowledge. I found particular use in studying old local histories of various kinds. These include family history (if documents are present) and local and regional histories. Read family historical documents and journals, study old maps, and study what your town or city used to look like; these also give some hints as to life in centuries past and the skills that people had. Looking at maps and place-names tells important tidbits: "spring" indicates a source of water, while "mills" indicates some kind of mill (for grain, lumber, etc.), along with the river or stream that would likely power the mill.

More broadly, however, historical books give us a great sense of how people lived. One of my favorite series for this is a set of oral histories collected by Elliot Wigginton and his students, called Foxfire. These provide quite detailed accounts of all sorts of traditional skills—from building one's own log cabin to tanning hides to creating one's own musical instruments—all these books have much to teach. Another thing you might find useful in this manner are various public historical records—a bound copy of Pennsylvania's 1890 forestry report was particularly helpful for me to understand what the forests were like here in my home state before logging, for example, and what trees were abundant at that time. Other historical books showed simple recipes and glimpses of everyday life. Even historical children's books are useful: Laura Ingalls Wilder's *Little House*[21] books offer details on many traditional living experiences.

Historical shows: These offer more sustainable living ideas. You might check out a series of "living history" shows produced by the BBC, such as *Victorian Farm*. These programs share the story of historians who live a year on the farm and practice all sorts of interesting skills as the seasons go by—and while they aren't a substitute for a class, they can certainly provide insight.

Learning on Your Own

Sometimes it's best to learn just by doing or trying things out on your own. Following are some ways to do just that.

Books and magazines: These are the classic way to learn and often contain some of the best information available. I am especially drawn to books from the 1970s, since they have a wealth of good information, great graphics, humor, and wit. From building my own solar cooker to solar greenhouses to organic farming, there are wonderful books out there on literally any reskilling subject. Books with naked-hippie drawings in them often contain the absolute best information, such as the classic *Living on the Earth* from Alicia Bay Laurel.[22] Another good resource is the Foxfire[23] series of books. I like to collect these kinds of books throughout the year and then, in the dark winter months—at Imbolc—hole up in my home near the fireplace with a few good books and get ideas for the coming season. Throughout this book, I've included book recommendations for more information on a variety of topics.

Videos, blogs, websites and forums: All these provide such amazing knowledge. I've learned so much just by watching online videos, visiting websites, reading forums, and reading other people's blogs. Not all information is good information on the web, but much of it when it comes to "how-to" sets of skills is really quite good. I always suggest reviewing a number of tutorials or videos before trying anything—there are also a lot of bad sets of instructions out there that can steer you in a less-than-helpful direction.

Learning with Others

Given the right nurturing and cultivation, one blessing of reskilling is how it can bring a family together. For example, a few years ago I taught my parents about mushroom hunting, and they have become serious hunters and now are teaching me about new mushrooms. My sister and I are on parallel paths learning the ancient ways of herbalism and medicine making, and now we have much to share with each other. My family now gets together and goes foraging, makes medicine, and eats delicious dinners of wild mushrooms and food from the garden! I have seen this same thing occurring in the lives of many other friends' families—it is if we are all waking up to rediscover our relationship to the land and working, as families, to build that knowledge once again. We have, collectively, worked to rediscover the knowledge of our ancestors and have worked to build a new heritage and tradition for ourselves that allows us to once again live closer to the land and all of her inhabitants.

Oak Knowledge and Reskilling as a Spiritual Practice

Due to dominant religious and cultural influences, we often have a limited sense of what "religious" or "spiritual" practice looks like. Within Earth-based spirituality, spiritual activities are commonly viewed as things such as meditation, ritual, reflection, magic, prayer, or going into the woods. Part of this is that these larger cultural influences create a mental dividing line between "spiritual" practices and "mundane" ones.

What I've been suggesting in this book is that sacred action offers us a way of living in a sacred manner in each moment, with each breath, and with each day. It allows us to break down the barriers among mind, heart, body, and spirit and, instead, integrate those fully and fruitfully into our spiritual and everyday lives.

The practice of building Oak knowledge and reskilling, then, can be seen not just as "hobbies" that you engage in or learn about, but actual spiritual practices that bring you closer to the Earth. Oak knowledge teaches us deep knowledge about root, stem, seed, feather, and fur—this is the kind of knowledge that has not only practical sustainable outcomes but also deep inner truths.

As we learn about the land and her incredible inhabitants, new spiritual insights are revealed. For example, as part of my practice of herbalism and wild-food foraging, I have been deeply and closely observing plants—and as part of that observation, I have started noting that the pentacle and pentagram are repeated everywhere in nature. It is the pentagram we see in each chickweed, hawthorn, or apple flower; the pentagram also appears in a cross section of the blackberry cane. It is the same pattern, observed over 5,000 years ago, that led to the magical symbol and use of the symbol up through the present time. So much of the knowledge we have in our own spiritual practices and traditions can be cycled directly back to the living Earth—and we "rediscover" this as we learn Oak knowledge. Each time I learn something new about the living Earth, I am able to connect it with my own spiritual insights—this knowledge facilitates an awakening process within!

Reskilling, too, teaches valuable lessons. These lessons range from a deeper understanding of the Wheel of the Year and seasons over time to a deeper connection to our relationship to the living Earth. For example, after a long year of growing vegetables, planting fruit trees, and more, I can understand why the Celts celebrated so much during the fall seasons, and why the hunger months were so difficult. The cycle of the sun and the moon become more than representations on a calendar with associated holidays—they become living, breathing, realities that I live and experience through these reskilling activities. Composting and planting teaches many lessons, and those lessons replicate in my own rituals and celebrations, but also in other aspects of my daily life.

Oak knowledge and reskilling make the Wheel of the Year and the many other practices and teachings of pagan and Earth-based traditions come alive. They help us understand their deep and profound significance, a lesson that unfolds as our knowledge grows. I have found that these kinds of lessons have deeply affected every aspect of my druid path. Now that I understand and have interacted fully in the outer landscape, I see what happens to plants as Samhain approaches and why it has such power. I joyously await the return of the spring equinox. This allows me to understand that when I see these same cycles in my own life, and I celebrate them in ritual, I understand they are only a cycle—and that spring will return, that the darkness will give way to life and be born anew.

A common response to some of what has been presented in this chapter might be "But I don't have time for any of this!" Our time is one of the most precious resources that we have. Anything that we want to do requires—at the most basic level—energy and time. Other issues, such as physical resources, finances, lack of skill/ability, etc., may also be at play. But if we lack the time and energy to do something, nothing else is going to get that thing done. Linguistically, this is now how time is framed in our culture. Typically, we "spend" our time (like spending down a bank account) or we "save" our time (like a savings account; note the efficiency metaphor again). But we don't necessarily "protect" or "cherish" our time with the same positive qualities. This is part of why I'm talking about "time honoring" here—honoring this precious resource and all that it offers to us. By seeing learning some of these skills as a spiritual practice, perhaps we can feel more justified in "making time" for them.

A spiritual practice in our traditions can be thought of as anything that has spiritual significance and is an individual matter. Learning a new skill that can be used to heal the living Earth or her people is different than ritual or meditation, but no less significant. In fact, bringing the spiritual into your learning can be a moving and powerful experience. Part of this lies in our mindset—how does, say, learning to carve spoons connect with our inner worlds or with the energy of the trees? How does the act of sowing seeds or turning the soil also function as a meditative practice? How can learning and growth be an expression of a spiritual path? It is up to each of us to develop and explore those connections.

Exercises and Rituals

Building Relationships for Reskilling

You would be surprised where knowledge about reskilling can come from—sometimes from the oddest places! Seek out skills from those in your community. There are a number of ways to do this. Spend some time talking with friends and family about what they know, especially older ones and the young, strange ones. You might discover an avid canner, a home brewer, a mushroom hunter, a beekeeper, a wild-food forager, an avid gardener, or any other assortment of skills. Ask them about who else they might know who has a skill you'd like to learn.

When you find someone doing something you are interested in, ask them if they are willing to teach you in exchange for some help. I've learned—and taught—so many things by using this approach. For example, if someone wants to learn canning, I invite them over when I have lots of food to can, and then they can help me can the food, get a jar to take home, and learn a lot in the process. This has worked really well for my beekeeping and organic farming as well!

Your Future Self and a New Skill

Go back to last month's ritual and read the narrative you wrote of your future self. From that narrative, break down the different knowledge and skills that you might need. And then, take an afternoon or weekend to learn a new skill that will help you begin to achieve this goal—something that will help you become more sustainable. You might look for "Reskilling" fairs or events, which will help you learn from others. You'll be glad that you did!

History of Your Immediate Landscape

Studying the history of your landscape—as immediately as possible—is a useful activity as part of learning Oak knowledge. This helps you understand what your landscape was once like, what grew here, how people lived, and more.

A good historical society or library in your municipality would be a good place to start. For example, studying the history and former industries in my own home of western Pennsylvania provided me with a clearer sense of why we had no old-growth forests left, why the rivers were acidic and sulfurous, and also why people welcomed fracking to this region. This helped me get a clearer sense of what kinds of skills I needed and what kinds of knowledge would be most useful in my own sacred action. In the US, the following resources might be helpful (I encourage readers from other locations to seek out their own local resources).

• The National Archives (US), www.archives.gov/research/land/
• Geocommunicator, which allows you to see public lands as well as gas lines, oil wells, etc., www.geocommunicator.gov/GeoComm/
• United States Geological Survey, which includes watershed information, historical topographical maps of different decades, and much more: www.usgs.gov/core-science-systems/ngp/tnm-delivery/

A Good Library
I have found that part of reskilling is about having the resources, particularly books, on hand to refer to, learn, and grow. I would encourage you to start building such a library by visiting some used bookstores while you are working though this chapter. Some of my favorite books on a variety of topics are listed in the appendix.

Physical-Spiritual Connections
Part of the work of sacred action is integrating our inner spiritual life with our outer physical reality. One of the ways we can accomplish this is by making those connections conscious and using the spiritual tools we have available to us. Toward this goal, I would suggest trying to connect one of the skills you are learning explicitly to your spiritual practice, and seeing this as a sacred skill. Here are a few suggestions for how you might do this:

Timing and skill building: Pay attention to the timing of the practice and time your most important learning/work with that of the sun (Wheel of the Year), moon (phase), or stars (astrology). For example, I like to do a lot of my canning and herb gathering aligned with the summer solstice or fall equinox, and I start seeds and harvest using astrology (any farmer's almanac will give you information on this). This approach help you build a sense of sacredness in your own work and draw upon the subtle yet profound energies of the celestial heavens.

Ritual skill building and crafting: Before engaging in what others might observe to be a "mundane" skill, open up a sacred space and spend the duration of your practice while in a ritual space. You can use the sample opening and closing from the ritual offered in the exercise section of chapter 1 to create your sacred space. For example, when I make tinctures or teas for medicine by using my herbalism skills, I not only pay attention to the timing (moons, sun, and stars) but also open up a sacred grove when physically making the medicine. I then bless the medicine before closing the space. You could also build in a practice of a particular skill with other daily or regular spiritual work.

Meditation and reflection: After engaging in a skill, use discursive meditation (see chapter 1) to reflect upon the connection between the skill and what you've learned. Work to connect the skill with your own understanding of your spiritual path: the connection of the seasons, the patterns in nature, and your own relationship to spirit.[24] Returning to this activity multiple times as you are learning your new skill can be incredibly beneficial. After meditation, write about your insights in your journal. Record your thoughts often and note how your insights change and deepen over time.

CHAPTER 3

Spring Equinox

Spring Cleaning and Disposing of the Disposable Mindset

In my hometown in western Pennsylvania, a yearly spring ritual takes place—and not the kind of spring ritual you are probably thinking about! The ritual is known as "spring cleanup" week. This is the one week a year where the garbage company allows people to throw away anything and everything, with no limits. People end up with heaps of stuff on the side of the road: old TVs, appliances, furniture, boxes of junk, couches, boxes and bags, dishes, towels, bikes, wood, carpeting, anything imaginable. Some families have so much stuff that it covers 20 or 30 feet of their front yard in a line along the road. This "spring cleanup" ritual really helps illustrate one of the most pressing problems from a sustainability perspective: consumption and waste. This spring cleanup ritual is the end result of a system designed to encourage people to quickly consume and dispose of resources, but this consumption is quickly depleting the Earth of natural resources and polluting it with waste.

To demonstrate why consumption, waste, and materialism are at the heart of sustainability and why attending to them can be part of each person's sacred action, let's look at a few facts and statistics. Paul Hawken, Amory Lovins, and Hunter Lovins offer the following in their *Natural Capitalism*:[25] of the materials that are created, only 1% are still in circulation six months after they are produced. That is, 99% of what is produced from the living Earth (bottles, paper, plastic bags, coffee makers, clothing—you name it) is disposed of within a six-month period of manufacture and purchase. After World War II, US economist Victor Lebrow[26] articulated a vision for the US economy that could ensure consistent growth: "Our enormously productive economy demands that we make consumption our way of life, that we convert the buying and use of goods into rituals, that we seek our spiritual satisfactions, our ego satisfactions, in consumption.... We need things consumed, burned up, worn out, replaced, and discarded at an ever increasing pace." That is, consumption became not only a lifestyle for the last fifty years, but a spirituality, an identity, and a way of connecting with one's self. In the twenty-first century, we are seeing the incredible challenges that this unsustainable system creates: the disappearance of half the animals in the world since 1970 due to pollution and habitat loss, pollution now being the number one cause of disease and death worldwide for people, and the enormous amount of waste and garbage polluting our Earth.[27]

And so, we begin our journey into sacred action with examining waste and consumption and encouraging a bit of "spring cleaning" in each of our lives. Spring cleaning has its roots in pagan practices, even if the modern version I described in the opening is less ecologically sensible. Many traditions used spring as a time to clear out the home and hearth, dust out the house, and move into a new season with a fresh perspective. For example, where I live, many traditional spring-cleaning rituals in the Pennsylvania Dutch culture (brought over from the Old World and adapted for new soil) still remain: the hearth is cleaned, the home is tidied, and we move into the light half of the year. Waste and materialism is also a fitting topic for the spring equinox because the energy of the equinox is a time of new beginnings and new activities and thus encourages us to action.

Part of what I will do in this chapter is to frame our discussion of waste and consumption by using the hermetic magical adage "As above, so below, as within, so without," or, more directly from Hermes Trismegistus,[28] "That which is Below corresponds to that which is Above, and that which is Above corresponds to that which is Below, to accomplish the miracle of the One Thing." This saying helps us understand how our outer relationship with waste and consumerism can have inner ramifications, and by helping us "clean up" our waste and excess, we can build a more spiritually rich inner life in addition to supporting a more ecologically healthy world.

As in the other chapters of this book, I also offer a framing triad. The triad is a three-part saying used as a teaching tool in the druid tradition. This triad offers us insight into the material in this chapter and can be used as a mantra for action or meditation:

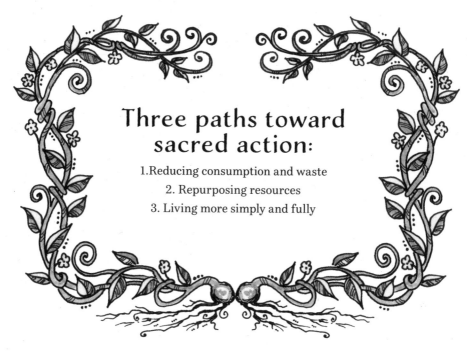

Three paths toward sacred action:

1. Reducing consumption and waste
2. Repurposing resources
3. Living more simply and fully

It is through this triad that we can deeply understand the effects of waste and consumerism in our lives and recognize some solutions. As we will explore in this chapter, we will see that the interplay between our inner worlds and our outer worlds is critical, particularly when it comes to waste and materialism. Thus, this chapter offers a broad variety of different sustainable-living techniques centered on materialism and waste. This choice of breadth over depth in this chapter specifically was made due to the wide variety of living circumstances that readers may find themselves in: the sacred actions done by someone living in a shared apartment in the city may not be appropriate for someone living in a big, empty house in the country. Thus, as a general suggestion for this chapter, I suggest that you first read through the many options presented. Then, make a choice of a few key things that you'd like to try over the next six weeks. The goal, overall, for this chapter is helping you consider more-sustainable options for how to reduce our demand for new goods and for the waste we produce. The material in this chapter has tremendous sustainable power: making a lifestyle change in this key area has potentially global implications.

Inner and Outer Problems of Consumerism and Waste

Materialism, in the simplest terms, is an obsession with "stuff," particularly the acquisition of stuff as a way to promote and maintain self-image, as the quote in the last section indicates. This stuff includes consumer goods, such as perfume, watches, televisions, vehicles, the latest fashionable clothing, gadgets, and technology, as well as services we consume, packaging of said products, and much more. Materialism is the end result of a culture designed to be voracious consumers. Materialism is a cultural philosophy that dominates modern industrialized cultures, where the products we purchase, the way we look, the things we consume, and the things we want to have in our possession define our reality and sense of selves. I think we can see it embedded in identity; the identities that people take on often refer to what stuff they buy, what products they align with, how they dress, and what hobbies they have.

The Story of Stuff,[29] a web documentary and book by Annie Leonard, describes two "automatic" behaviors that drive the consumerist system: acquisition and disposal. When I say "automatic" here, it refers to behaviors that are ingrained, require no thought, and may be subconscious or semiconscious. Purchasing, accumulating, and disposing of stuff is all about automatic conditioning. Consumerism is the ingrained solution to almost any problem or need: you buy something when you need to demonstrate affection, you purchase something when you need to solve a problem, you buy entertainment to "cure" boredom, and so on. When we don't want something, it is extremely easy to dispose of it. We don't even give this whole process a second thought—we just engage in it, over and over again. You can observe this for yourself by simply sitting by a public garbage can in a place with a lot of people: pay attention to how people throw things away without conscious effort.

The Outer Problem of Waste

Waste streams, completely nonexistent in nature, are ever present in modern industrialized and consumerist living. Yes, waste today is intentional; it is a matter of design. Today, as *The Story of Stuff* describes, goods are designed with two concepts: planned obsolescence (the idea that products are designed to fail after a certain period of time) or perceived obsolescence (the idea that something is out of date or no longer useful, such as computers, smartphones, and other technology). Beyond consumer goods, we also have other kinds of waste that simply are generated as part of doing business or living. This could include the millions of plastic cups that are waste generated by the airline industry daily, for example, or businesses that serve food in disposable containers, or the amount of food that is thrown away (see chapter 5). And since waste collection and processing itself is a now a profit-driven industry, there is resistance to change.

From the Great Pacific Garbage Patch, which is estimated to span 15,000,000 miles of ocean surface,[30] and its sister patches located in the other oceans, to food waste on the order of millions of pounds per year—up to 40% of the total food produced in the US[31]—to waste water from fracking, there seems to be no end to the waste that modern industrial societies produce. Waste accumulates in the ocean, including microbeads[32] from face scrubbers that end up in fish and then back in your own body, and our waterways are full of toxins and pesticides. Waste in the form of agricultural runoff ends up creating algae blooms and dead zones thousands of miles across. Waste and debris are even in orbit surrounding our planet—this is how bad our waste problem has become. Further, we have many waste streams that are invisible to us—the waste in manufacturing processes are unknown because they are considered proprietary—but when you buy that product, you buy the waste stream of that product.

Further, outer waste goes well beyond just physical objects. We have wasted energy—everything from heat leaking from our houses in winter to wasted clean water running down our drains and into our municipal sewage systems. We have wasted time in front of the various screens of our lives and wasted potential and creativity. We have so much waste in our lives that it's difficult to wrap our heads around it. We might say that more than anything else, industrialized culture produces waste.

We can turn to any system in nature for an example that produces no waste. Consider a forest, one of our greatest teachers. Every nutrient in the forest is cycled effectively through various systems, every drop of water stored, every ounce of sunlight used—all to the growth and benefit of specific plants, animals, fungi, and the larger habitat. When a tree falls and dies, its body is colonized by mycelium, ants, and other bugs, and quickly it is growing with new life. The decomposing body of the tree eventually turns into rich soil, taken up by other plants, and those plants are taken up by animals, in a great web of being. Each aspect of that forest is a nutrient, water, and energy cycle that wastes nothing. Nature's powerful lesson should not be wasted on us.

The Inner Problem of Waste

If we return to the hermetic principle framing this chapter, "As above, so below, as within, so without," magically, we can see a very serious problem in the waste generated by current industrialized culture. Not only are we destroying our planet, but we are destroying our inner worlds as well. Since what is reflected on one level of reality (the physical) happens on other levels (the mental, the emotional, the spiritual), the garbage piling up in our lives, our seas, and our lands is not just staying there. It is, and has, worked its way into our inner landscapes.

For a simple example, let's consider the difference in trying to cook dinner in a messy kitchen with a greasy stove, half-clean pans, cluttered-up counters, and stinky dishes piled up in the sink vs. cooking in a clean kitchen where everything is in order. Which leads to a healthy state of mind? Which leads to the better meal? Which leads to inner peace? This example illustrates that what is in our environment becomes part of what is reflected within us. What, then, is reflected in our inner realities, our magical selves, when we living in a world piling up with garbage, pollution, and waste? What happens when we want to relax and heal in nature, and we find it has become the next garbage dump?

One inner issue with waste is how it is framed in our minds through our language. Numerous linguists and philosophers have argued that language helps shape our realities and provides us with a particular lens or way of seeing the world. My town, like every other town in the US, asks me to label my "yard waste" and leave it on the corner like any other trash. This frames dead leaves, plants, and other nutrient-rich materials as "waste." What they are actually referring to are the dead plants that break down to create a rich layer of humus for more life to grow. That isn't waste; it's part of nature's perfect system. I call it a resource and eagerly seek it out each fall for my garden. The problem with terms such as "garbage," "waste," "dispose," and "throwaway" is that in our minds we hold these words to be true—we believe the meanings that have been constructed around them. When something is labeled with these words, it's easy to engage in the associated behavior of throwing away. Would the same behaviors occur if we labeled dead plant and leaf matter as "resources" instead?

On the mental plane, the implications of waste, piling up around us and infusing our natural world, are severe. Solastalgia is a concept within psychology that first was proposed by Glenn Albrecht and colleagues in 2007.[33] Solastalgia (tied to the word "nostalgia") describes the stress and mental health issues that people face when experiencing firsthand destruction and ecosystem loss of the places they consider "home." These researchers found that people who live in degraded and polluted ecosystems experience a range of negative emotions, a disconnection to their sense of place and belonging, extreme duress, and a strong sense of powerlessness. What they called "environmentally induced stress" was particularly difficult to manage because it happened in one's home environment, every day, and there was no escaping it. They described these chronic stressors as "generally not seen" by mental health professionals or researchers. These emotional impacts have profound psychological implications for all of us living in an increasingly shattered world. I am reminded of this fact living in western Pennsylvania, when I can't enter a local park or ecosystem without coming up on the many gas wells or deep injection wells that are now such a part of our landscape, the stumps or recently logged parts of our state forests, or the piles of trash along our roadways and even found deep within our state parks.

Just as our outer world impacts our inner world, what is within us also reflects outward. Many minds are drowning in detritus, not all of it avoidable. Estimates now suggest that most Americans see anywhere from 4,000 to 10,000 ads in one day.[34] Our attention is pulled in literally hundreds of different directions, and our minds are on overload. If our inner world is full of a kind of mental waste, it becomes so much easier, I believe, to accept waste in our outer world. Our inner and outer worlds are always informing and influencing each other; the relationship goes both ways. It is in our inner world where unconscious behaviors of waste are generated. And it is within that we can raise our awareness, be mindful of our actions, and begin to shift toward producing less or no waste. See exercise #2 at the end of this chapter for suggestions for mental decluttering.

Thus, understanding the waste streams in our lives and taking direct action to minimize them is a profound spiritual act: not only for cultivating our own relationship with ourselves and developing a richer inner life, but for connecting with nature on a deep level. So now, let's explore some opportunities to turn waste streams into resources or eliminate waste streams in our lives.

Shifting Away from the Waste Mindset and into Sacred Action

The problem of waste is a problem within and without—in our minds, in our language, and in the design of the systems in which we live. Because everything is designed as disposable, what we must begin with doing is to dispose of the disposable mindset. This section focuses on key strategies that we can do to engage in a new kind of spring cleaning and bring forth the energies of the balance at the spring equinox.

Recognizing and Attending to Behavior and Waste Monitoring

As I briefly mentioned in the opening to this chapter, throwing "away" is a mindset and a set of parallel behaviors so ingrained that they are at first quite difficult to even recognize. I had to travel by plane for my work while I was writing this chapter, and I carefully observed the endless waste streams on the airplane and airport: plastic cups come out, drinks are consumed, plastic cups and paper and various other "waste" are collected and whisked off so quickly. I inquired about whether or not the cups were recycled, and I was told by the steward, "On certain flights." I asked if this was one of those flights, and he could not tell me, but I watched him throw everything into one garbage bag. These actions of disposal are so embedded, so thoughtless, that they happen automatically for most of us. Most people hardly realized they were throwing things away—it did not register on their conscious reality.

Automatic behaviors are behaviors that repeat and that are extremely difficult to recondition. This is because we devote very little to no mental resources to engage in these behaviors. Social conditioning for waste in a throwaway society is so pervasive because it is culturally conditioned. On the extreme end, we simply buy and throw things away without thinking about it. How is this automatic behavior triggered with regard to waste? Because there is so much waste being generated all around us at every given moment with these consumptive behaviors, to think about it requires a great deal of mental energy that most people simply don't have. The second part of attending to behavior is being aware of, and avoiding, the social conditioning of what Sigmund Freud calls the "herd instinct." People will often "follow the herd" rather than be ostracized (from it) by deviating in their behavior, which means that even if we are conscious of it and want to change, the herd instinct may prevent us.

To begin working on the outer world, I would suggest some waste-monitoring activities. A good activity to start with is one I assigned my students when I was teaching an interdisciplinary/sustainability class. For one week, track all of your waste. Track every time you get a disposable cup, a takeout box, or unrecyclable packaging. What are you putting on the curb? Look at every item you throw away in the trash. Look at any waste produced by your family or workplace (the leftover food that gets thrown away, the waste paper, boxes, pens and pencils, packaging from shipped items, plastic in the trash bins, etc.). You will likely be surprised. Write every bit of it down (one of the things we know from behavioral research is that the act of writing something down helps shift behavior because it makes us more conscious). I've seen and experienced firsthand the transformative aspects of this practice: knowledge itself can be incredibly powerful. After you've done this work, mediate on how this activity has changed your relationship with waste, and develop a few strategies for making change.

Ecobricks

Think of all the plastic films, plastic bags, wrappings, and other plastics that you wish you could recycle but you can't! Ecobricks are a great solution to this, turning waste into a resource. Ecobricks are plastic bottles, usually 1- or 2-liter bottles, that are densely packed with plastic waste that cannot be recycled. The finished ecobricks are used as a sustainable and very hardy building material that can be used to build furniture, structures, or even whole buildings. Rather than throwing plastic away as you encounter it, you can carry a bottle with you along with a dowel rod or stick. As you encounter waste that cannot be recycled, you simply push the plastic into the bottle, compacting it with the dowel rod. The only thing that should go in the bricks is plastic: Styrofoam, cellophane, plastic bags, etc. When you start a new ecobrick, use something softer, such as a plastic bag, so you can get it into the crevices at the bottle bottom. A suggestion I have for this is to put an ecobrick station next to your recycling area in your home. Thus, you and any visitors you have are given several options: recycling, ecobricks for nonrecyclable plastics, and garbage. You'd be surprised how quickly you can produce ecobricks! Over time, once you've produced a number of bricks, you can build with them or contribute them to a community ecobrick project.[35] For example, I am producing ecobricks currently to use in an outdoor kitchen, where I will use the ecobricks combined with other natural building materials to create the counter spaces and benches for the project.

These Come from Trees: A Mindset Shift

A few years ago, I came across a great campaign called "These come from trees."[36] By putting a simple sticker that reads "These come from trees" near paper towels, toilet paper, office printers, and other paper-based sites of consumption, awareness alone is enough to reduce consumption. On the basis of some of the organization's data, one sticker could reduce up to 100 pounds of waste per year. I obtained some of the stickers and placed them around my campus and my home and in a few places in my community. I was surprised by how own mindset changed with the presence of the sticker—that simple reminder put it always in the forefront of my mind.

I believe that this same model can be applied to more than just paper products (although they are a wonderful start). When we look around, literally everything that we see is rooted somewhere in physical goods from our landscape—metal from mines, plastics from fossil fuels, glass from silica, wood from forests, and so on. In addition to the physical materials, there are the environmental costs of extraction and production of those goods. This makes each of them, in their own way, extensions of our living, breathing Earth. Given this, I have had good luck with signage, placed around my home and beyond, that reminds me of this fact and encourages me to be mindful in managing waste streams. By shifting to see all the things that surround us as intimately connected with the sacred Earth rather than as junk consumer goods, we change our relationship with our waste. As a simple activity, you might take one thing that you've purchased recently in your life (electronics are a particularly good choice for this) and trace its origins: what raw materials go into making it? Where do they come from? How much energy is needed? Where was it produced?

Trash into Treasures

On the positive side to the "spring cleanup" yearly ritual I discussed in the opening of this chapter, a whole counterculture is also present. People, often in old pickup trucks and rusty vans, go out "trash picking" through the piles. I, too, always go out. In the last few years alone, I have salvaged rakes, pots and pans, spades and shovels, canning jars, beads, paintbrushes, tools, solid-wood end tables, fabric, wooden boxes, yard furniture, cardboard boxes for sheet mulching, lamps, rugs, grills, windows for cold frames, a small boat, wood for the stove, and a working refrigerator—all from the side of the road. At first, I was nervous to dig in other people's garbage, but once I started doing so, I realized how important this work was. It was sacred action. If your own community has such "spring cleanup" rituals, consider gathering a few friends together and going "treasure hunting."

Another issue we need to directly confront here in "trash picking" is that of the relationship between certain kinds of activities (trash picking, dumpster diving, intentional downsizing, lawn alternatives, repurposing) and poverty. In the US, at least, one of the great social gaffes embedded into our cultural consciousness is the appearance of being poor. Trash picking certainly falls on the spectrum of activities that many people typically wouldn't engage in, and trash picking "marks" you as being poor. Part of this is addressing these feelings directly and changing how you see this activity in your own mind—as part of your own sacred action and spiritual practice. But part of it is also acknowledging—and working against—these larger systems that have gotten us into this mess. This is a process and can take time. For example, you might not feel comfortable trash picking in your own neighborhood, but going to a nearby neighborhood where nobody knows you might be a good first step. You might bring along some bold friends or family members and drive the car during your first few outings. If you are good at community organizing, getting a group together to raise awareness can also really be helpful (see "The Trash-to-Treasure Fairy"). Eventually, once you work through the feelings of embarrassment, you will find that this activity can be a wonderful treasure hunt and can be a great deal of fun!

The Trash-to-Treasure Fairy

Another strategy that takes the "trash to treasure" idea even further is something a friend of mine taught me during a recent "spring cleanup" ritual. He goes out with his car and doesn't just pick up stuff that he needs. Rather, he picks up everything that anyone can use that can be donated. He takes carloads of the donations to the local thrift store and works to keep as much out of the dump as possible. On a larger scale, the cleanup ritual is particularly bad in college towns; some universities are now organizing and mobilizing communities in order to move the stuff college students typically abandon into the hands of those who need it. This is a great activity for some community organization work (and a set of T-shirts with a group out in force describing the goals for the work can help address any embarrassment individuals may have over trash-picking activities).

Creative Repurposing

Creative repurposing is another fun way to turn trash into treasures. The most basic definition of creative repurposing is to use old, unwanted stuff in new ways. For example, the "upcycling" movement focuses on taking old clothing, books, and other items and using artistic processes to give them new uses and purposes. For example, I saved my old jeans that were worn out and cut them into strips, braided them, and stitched the braids together to make a braided rag rug. I gave that as a gift to a friend who had cold floors and liked handmade things. A friend of mine gathered up hundreds of 2-liter soda bottles, cut the tops off, stacked them together, sealed them, and made a small insulated greenhouse for starting seeds.

There are a lot of unique ways that people are turning trash into treasures. This creative repurposing is simply about seeing things not as "trash" but as something with possibility. Part of this is thinking creatively about how items can be reused. Here are a few examples:

- Used paper and plastic cups for plant seedlings (see chapter 6)
- Plastic bags knitted or woven into rugs, handbags, and more
- Old, abused clothing cut into strips, sewn together, and turned into braided rugs, recycled bags, or crazy quilts
- Newspapers and cardboard used for sheet mulching in a garden (see chapter 6)
- Plastic bottles turned into a greenhouse, cold frame, or roofing material
- Bottle caps as jewelry or artwork pieces
- Old, cracked plastic buckets or tubs turned into worm composters (see later this chapter)
- Altar cloth or robes cut out of an old sheet, cloth napkins out of an old sheet
- Candleholders made from tin cans, cat food cans, or small jars
- Aluminum cans used for growing small pots of herbs
- Wood pallets used for construction (make sure they are untreated)

I could fill a whole book with a list here, so I hope you get the idea—this is all about using your own creativity in giving something new life. Before throwing away, or even recycling, see what you can do to give your old waste new life or how you can solve a "need" with a waste material.

Shifting to Reusable Containers and Bulk Buying

Packaging waste accounts for a tremendous amount of what we throw away: shipping boxes, plastic that can't be recycled, food packaging, takeout containers, straws, and other "one use" plastics. Most of this ends up in the landfill. One way to address this packaging waste is to purchase food in bulk (or from bulk bins) and to use your own containers to do so. Mason jars are particularly useful for this; they have a multitude of purposes, and storing dry food goods is certainly one of them. Another common source of waste is storage intended for one-time use, such as plastic bags, plastic wrap, and aluminum foil. Again, shifting to glass containers, beeswax wraps, or other sustainable options can help mitigate these storage issues and allow you to reduce your waste.

The other thing is to pay attention to the packaging of things you buy regularly. You can evaluate similar brands to see which ones use less packaging (or compostable packaging) if bulk foods aren't available. Finally, there's a lot of power in writing to companies and asking them to reduce the plastic packaging in products.

Bringing your own takeout containers or take-home containers to restaurants can help substantially reduce waste. Foam containers can't be recycled and are really wasteful, but a nice set of glass or stainless-steel containers allow you to easily get things home. While all of these suggestions seem like little steps—remember that water dripping onto a stone will eventually create a hole right through that stone, and tackling small bits of waste in any area can create lasting change.

Bringing Your Own Cups/Plates/Straws/Silverware

Disposable plates, cups, chopsticks, and silverware contribute to substantial portions of waste and can add up very quickly. These plastics are also almost never recyclable. Avoiding these one-use items as much as possible can help reduce waste. One thing you can do is bring your own. Lots of options exist here: foldable cups, stainless-steel straws, carrying a water bottle, bringing your own bowl/silverware. So as an example, if you go to get takeout once a week, and each time they give you plastic silverware, using reusable keeps fifty-two sets of plastic silverware out of the landfill. If you give two sets of reusable chopsticks and silverware away to friends who will use them, you've now kept out 156 sets. I'll also mention that when I pull out my stainless-steel chopsticks or silverware and put them together, people are often excited and want to know more—so these also represent ways of engaging others in good conversations about waste.

Transforming Waste through Composting

Many of the above suggestions refer to waste in terms of plastic and one-use products, but the other major area of waste we have throughout the industrialized world is food waste. Just as the ancient alchemists worked to transform dross into gold, so too can we engage in an alchemical, sacred act of our own: transforming waste into a valuable resource, powerful for our own lives and useful to the natural world. Thus, the following section offers a discussion of various kinds of composting you can do to begin to "transform" waste into nutrient-rich soil.

Composting

If you aren't already doing so, composting is a great way to begin to address the high amount of food waste present in many households (as mentioned above, almost 40% of food is currently wasted in the US alone). Composting basics are really easy—you simply set it up and nature does the work. Different kinds of composting can be adapted to your local circumstances: vermicompost (*see below*) is excellent for small-space and apartment living, while compost piles or animal-supported compost may be more appropriate for those with land.

The basics of compost are fairly straightforward. Compost typically contains two kinds of materials, both of which are needed in balance:

1. **High-carbon materials (browns)** include leaves, shredded paper, shredded cardboard, pine needles, dead/dried plants, or wood shavings (only untreated ones, of course). Animal bedding, such as from ferrets, chickens, or rabbits, works well for this, as does old newspaper, cardboard, or fall leaves.
2. **High-nitrogen materials (greens)** include kitchen fruit and vegetable scraps (anything nondairy and nonmeat), recently cut grass, fresh animal manures (livestock), seaweed, and fresh plant matter of any kind.

The ratio of these two materials is important to achieve quick decomposition in a typical compost pile: 25–30 parts carbon (brown) to 1 part nitrogen (green). Your materials should be in smaller pieces if possible: large pieces take a long time to break down, although anything will break down if given time. In addition to the materials, compost systems typically need four other things to be successful:

1. **Decomposers:** Worms, bacteria, protozoa, nematodes, and mycelium (fungus) all help break down material and turn it into soil. Specific compost systems

may rely on one or more of these kinds of decomposers, as we'll explore.

2. **Oxygen.** Oxygen must be present in any compost system. For compost piles, regular turning of your compost pile helps speed up the process and prevents the pile from getting compacted and going anaerobic (which makes it smell). Turning can be done with either a simple pitchfork (readily available at yard sales or secondhand stores) or with a compost tumbler.

3. **Heat.** Heat is generated by bacterial action, which is useful for a compost pile since it helps speed up the process. Good placement of a pile in a sunny spot can substantially help speed things up. Heat is also useful for other methods of composting, since mushrooms or worms need certain optimal temperatures.

4. **Water.** A slightly moist pile will break down faster than one that is dry. Food scraps and other green materials often add a lot of moisture, but you might need more moisture (like a sprinkling of water).

While creating an efficient compost pile is an art form on its own, if you just pile up everything and leave it, you'll still have compost. All materials will eventually break down, but the difference between a quick three-month turnaround and a long one-year turnaround is determined by the ratio of green to brown as well as the airflow, heat, water, and bacterial action in the pile.

The next step of composting is creating the right kind of "pile" for your compost. There are a lot of options, and some may be better suited to your living circumstances than others. You don't have to buy anything to set up a compost pile—a simple barrel or two will do, or a few pallets nailed together to make an open box in the middle. Following are some options.

Open compost piles work best for places that are far from neighbors or that can be contained in some way. They also work best for material from outdoors, such as fall leaves, not necessarily food waste unless they are somehow enclosed or fenced (otherwise, various critters and your neighbor's pesky dog will be at the pile). You can turn the piles to encourage faster decomposition, but letting a pile sit for one to two years is a fine way of letting nature do the work.

Closed compost tumblers and bins work best for smaller spaces, such as in-town living. I purchased a wonderful metal spinning composter with two chambers—as one chamber fills and needs time to decompose, you switch to the second. While I was in a rental house, it sat on the patio, taking up only a few feet of space. The closed tumbler prevents odor or critters from getting in. You can also easily make your own compost tumbler with a large 50-gallon plastic barrel that can be added to and rolled around (you can also find these used or recycled). A garbage can with a lid (bungee-corded shut) and some holes drilled into it also works great.

Semiclosed compost bins also work great for suburban or rural living. When I was in Michigan, the previous property owners left rolls of wire fencing that had rusted. I uncoiled one and used it as a wonderful compost pile. I added compost to the top; the wire kept out animals, and critters offered plenty of aeration. As the material composted down, I dug out finished compost of the bottom from a cutout area in the wire near the ground. I moved it every few years, and the spot where it previously sat was nutrient rich, so I planted squash on that spot. (Squash love growing near and out of compost piles!)

Vermicomposting is an indoor composting method using a worm bin, perfect for those in apartments, cities, or other small living spaces. My students in a recent sustainability class created gallon-size worm bucket composters and kept them quite successfully in their dorm rooms! While you can purchase commercial worm composters, you can also easily make your own. I have several bins—one with three cracked 5-gallon buckets and one with two opaque plastic bins that fit inside each other. See the graphic for how to put your bin together. The opaqueness is important in selecting bins because the worms do not like light. Red wiggler worms, those best suited for vermicompost, can be purchased online or given to you from a fellow vermicomposter. Composting is so easy with this method—each day, you add new food scraps in a circle around the edges of the bin and into the middle, and in about two weeks' time you end up back where you started and the worms have eaten through all the scraps (again, see graphic). Avoid citrus, dairy, eggshells, or meat—the worms don't like the citrus, they can't break down eggshells, and the dairy and meat rot before the worms can break it down, causing odors. The worms love fresh vegetables and fruit, coffee grounds, and grains. If you add regularly to your composter, in a few months you'll have amazing worm castings for growing anything from indoor potted plants to large garden beds!

WORM COMPOSTING

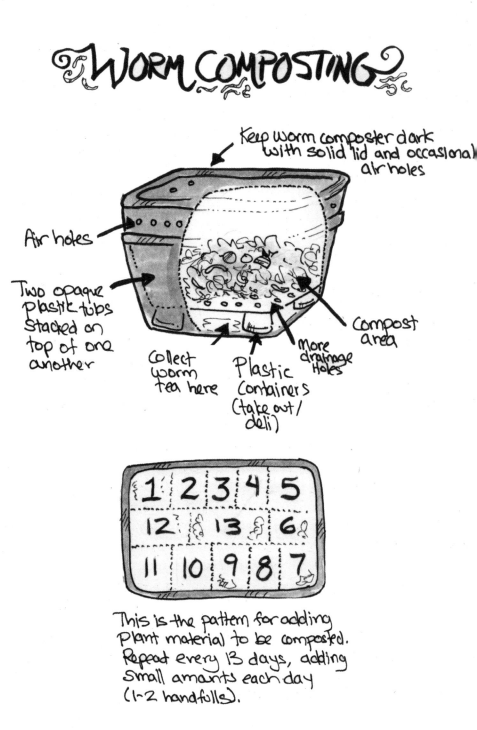

Keep worm composter dark with solid lid and occasional air holes

Air holes

Two opaque plastic tubs stacked on top of one another

Collect worm tea here

Plastic containers (take out/deli)

More drainage holes

Compost area

1	2	3	4	5
12		13		6
11	10	9	8	7

This is the pattern for adding plant material to be composted. Repeat every 13 days, adding small amounts each day (1-2 handfulls).

Animal-assisted composting works beautifully for those who have a flock of chickens, pigs, or other farm animals who enjoy eating scraps. Just throw the compost scraps (green and brown of any amount; meat and dairy are also fine) into the run. Chickens, for example, will happily eat any scraps you offer. If they don't eat the food scraps, it will draw flies and worms, and the chickens will eat the flies and worms and be fat, happy chickens. Throw in some brown material (such as fall leaves) and garden scraps and they will turn it all into a beautiful, rich compost. Chickens make beautiful compost faster than any other method I know.

Sheet mulching (or lasagna gardening) is a composting strategy that can be used to create and re-create garden beds and use up lots of yard waste. This method is described in more detail in chapter 6.

Mushroom composting can be done if you have an excess of fresh coffee grounds and cardboard boxes; if so, mushroom composting might be a good choice for you. You can readily purchase oyster mushroom spawn (brown or white oysters work best for this). Layer wet cardboard, mushroom spawn, and fresh coffee grounds in buckets or 2-liter bottles with the top cut off. Make sure you leave plenty of air, and don't fill the bucket too tightly. In a few weeks, the mycelium will permeate the boxes and coffee grounds and you will have tasty oyster mushrooms! After composting, the mycelium "bricks" can be dried and used for building projects or composted themselves.

The best thing about composting is the sacred lessons it can teach us in our lives—that transformation is a key to spiritual growth. One lesson composting offers is that we take what is essentially refuse and garbage, that which we want to discard, and, with the help of nature, process this into beautiful soil ready for new plantings. Through the physical act of composting waste, we are taught the inner lessons of transformation. Meditating on these practices and watching them unfold is a powerful spiritual act. Composting is truly alchemical process, aided by the elements and the microbiological soil web of life—and one well worth participating in for its lessons within and without. This is the essence of spring cleaning and the spring equinox; one of transforming those things that no longer serve us—those wasteful things in our lives—into something productive and useful.

Our Own Waste: Humanure and Liquid Gold

No discussion of waste can be complete without mentioning a few unmentionables. It is often the case that any "waste" our bodies produce is left out of discussions of waste and how to handle it. And yet, like any other waste, our own waste can be a resource. I realize this isn't for everyone, but the information is certainly useful for those who are determined to use all of their waste as a resource and live a zero-waste lifestyle!

Let's follow the path that one flush takes to see the problem with our handling of human waste—and where we might intervene and divert those waste streams to more-productive uses. First, obviously, you begin by doing your business. Most people in the Western world are doing their business into a gallon or more of *perfectly acceptable drinking water*. After flushing, your waste can take two routes: a typical city or town dweller sends their flush directly into a municipal sewer system. In a more rural area, waste likely enters a private septic system, a type of holding tank, where it can partially break down but eventually fills up. Then someone with a big truck comes and pumps it out, moving it into a municipal septic system.

Municipal septic systems are not just carrying human waste. They take human waste and combine it with many other kinds of material, including stormwater runoff (more of that perfectly good and clean water running into the septic system, often mixed with roadway pollutants such as oil), industrial waste from various factories and processing plants (much of which can contain poisons, heavy metals, and chemicals), and hospital waste (which can contain disease, toxins, caustic cleaning agents, and so on). Often present in this combined waste, from the many nonhuman waste streams, is something called "dioxins,"[37] which are one of the most toxic chemicals on Earth. Dioxins are currently not regulated or tested by the EPA for *sewage sludge that is applied to farmlands*. Even radiation is now being found in this sewage sludge. Regulatory issues with dioxin and radiation aside, on the basic level we take perfectly good material (human waste, stormwater runoff from roofs, water from flushing) and mix it with toxic waste and then process it with chemicals and energy. One of several underlying problems is that modern industrialized society treats human waste like a toxic substance, when it is not.

We can work to keep our waste out of the municipal septic system and instead cycle it back into the ecosystem in careful and mindful ways. The idea that human waste is a resource is not a new concept. For millennia, humans collected and used their own waste as a resource. When I spent two weeks living in an ecovillage and completing my permaculture design certificate, I remember telling my friends and family that I hadn't flushed a toilet the entire trip. This led to a wide assortment of responses: some thought it was reprehensible to compost feces, while others were intrigued by the idea. But what this did was align me, really effectively, with my own waste streams. Each time I made any kind of deposit into the ecovillage system, I knew I was producing a resource used by the ecovillage, returning to nature. And for that, I was grateful—I felt realigned with the land in a new and exciting way. And so, I worked to take that lesson back home by building my own compost toilet system. So now let's consider some options for using our own waste.

Liquid gold: Human urine, also called "liquid gold," has high amounts of nitrogen—so much that if you pee directly on plants (or pour your urine on them undiluted), it will burn them due to the high nitrogen content. Urine also has potassium, phosphorus, sulfur, magnesium, and calcium. Nitrogen is one of the key elements of plant growth. Our urine is perfectly safe to use as a direct foliar spray on plants and trees with a 10% dilution (10% urine, 90% water). I usually use it just like a fertilizer in the water that I'm using to water the plants.

It is possible to collect urine in the simplest ways, such as by using a wide-mouth canning jar. It doesn't necessarily take a long time to collect enough to be used for plants (indoor, outdoor, or seedlings)—a few hours of saving urine can provide a weekly watering of indoor plants and no need to ever buy plant food again. And you don't need to use the liquid gold every week—I usually use it every two to three weeks, and my plants are very happy.

Humanure: The modern term for human feces that is properly composted is called "humanure." Humanure is similar to other kinds compost—it contains microorganisms, organic matter, and carbon for the benefit of plants. It can be created and used no differently than other fertilizers if composted properly (two years, minimum). Most people that I know use it only on perennial trees or simply return it to the forest. The process is really simple, and not much different than other forms of composting.

Most humanure systems begin with a composting toilet, which is essentially a collection system for urine and feces. There are many models of composting toilet—choosing one depends on the codes and regulations where you live. Sometimes, the easiest way to do this is to keep the regular toilet and septic tank there in your house (legally required), but to have a simple alternative system.

Alternative systems are not complicated or expensive. The simplest is a 5-gallon bucket with a toilet seat (you can get both for about $25) and a second bucket full of wood chips, sawdust, shredded paper, or other absorbent woody/carbon-rich material. Some people use peat moss for the absorbent material, but I don't recommend it due to sustainability issues; find a local resource instead if possible. For my own compost toilet, I use a combination of sawdust (all natural, no treated wood), partially composted mulch, and shredded paper from work (for good absorbency).

The management of the collection is simple enough. You use the bucket, and each time you do, you add one scoop for yellow and two scoops for brown. Outside, you create a closed compost area out of the way and add material to it until it's full (which may take up to a year), then allow it to naturally compost down for two years. You can turn it to speed up the process. A thermometer inside the pile can let you know if you are getting to a temperature necessary to kill any pathogens (above 130 degrees). Much more elaborate, permanent systems can be built or purchased—these systems run upward of $6,000–$8,000 but are self-contained and odor free and do most of the work for you.

Humanure and liquid gold as offerings: As humans, we have a symbiotic relationship with the living Earth. When we make an offering as part of ritual—say, a shiny penny or maybe a bottle of wine—that offering is often symbolic, not physical. Given this, I have begun making different kinds of intentional offerings when I go into the forest. For solid offerings,[38] I bring a small trowel and make a hole 6 inches down. For liquid offerings, I make sure not to pee directly on any plants, but I do offer liquid gold near the base of trees or directly on the ground, since they can take a direct application of rich nitrogen. Nitrogen as an offering to the land is very welcome! (We will explore sustainable offerings other than liquid gold and humanure in much more depth in chapter 8.)

As this first part of this chapter has explored, reducing and recycling waste is a wonderful practice for sacred action, and one of the practices that each one of us, regardless of our living circumstances, can participate in. I have found that as I've eliminated waste from my own life (and have worked to reduce waste in areas that I have influence over), it not only made me feel more energetically "clean" but also has helped me become part of the solution.

Materialism and Eliminating Excess Stuff

Now that we've considered waste streams and how to eliminate or transform them in a variety of ways, we get to the heart of what creates waste streams to begin with: a consumerist system that promotes materialism. Let us now consider these issues from the ethical system that we explore in this book: through Earth care, people care, and fair share.

As we have already begun to explore, excessive consumption and materialism causes issues connecting to our ethic of people care, to humans and their communities. The most-recent research into materialism suggests that materialism not only correlates with but causes detrimental effects on people's well-being. In an article in 2012,[39] published in *Psychological Science*, Monica Bauer and colleagues found that high amounts of materialism heightened people's negative emotions, increased competitiveness, increased selfishness, and reduced social involvement. In this study, even for people with lower levels of materialism, when they were exposed to a materialistic environment they became more materialistic and demonstrated the negative effects. The ramifications of the Bauer study should be taken seriously. Even for people who aren't materialistic by nature, materialistic cues (such as the hundreds of ads that people in most industrialized nations are exposed to every day) trigger materialistic behavior and its detrimental effects. But materialism also affects people on a much more specific level: millions of people globally are forced, particularly in developing nations, to live in developed nations' trash. The electronics industry as well as the recycling industry exports almost 90% of waste to developing nations, where some of it can be recycled, but much more of it sits in the landscapes of everyday people.

Materialism has tremendous impact in terms of Earth care. As described in the opening, materialism and consumption demand much from the land. Resources are extracted and then waste streams from those goods—many of them hidden throughout the manufacturing process—damage ecosystems and pollute around the globe. Finally, materialism and consumption affect fair share. Most "ecological footprint" estimates suggest that as a world, it currently would take 1.7[40] Earths to fulfill demand. If we look at developed nations such as the US, if the entire world consumed like US consumers did, it would require between 5.0 and 7.0 Earths. Thus, certain planetary citizens are taking way more than their fair share of the Earth's resources. This is habitat, clean water, and natural resources needed not only by other humans but by all of the animals, insects, fish, amphibians, reptiles, birds, plants, and more that live here. Part of how we can reduce this consumption is by looking at materialism and habits surrounding "stuff" we consume, and by seeking a better way.

Eliminating Stuff and Reducing Clutter

Just take a moment now to survey your belongings: Do you feel you have too much stuff? Does stuff come into your life unannounced and kind of get "stuck" there rather permanently? Or maybe it's someone else's stuff causing you the difficulty? Physical clutter is a burden, in more than one sense. As we explored above, physical clutter is emotionally draining and can sap one's motivation and energy and disrupt one's inner spiritual life. Just walking into a cluttered space gives one a feeling of helplessness and being overwhelmed—and if you are living in this space constantly, it is damaging to your health and well-being.

I have a friend who kept so much stuff in her house and garage that it was difficult to even move through certain areas. The process of decluttering not only brought joy to her home life, but she said it helped her with mental clarity. She described it as if her physical excess was bogging her down emotionally. As my friend's story illustrates, the energetic side to having too much stuff is powerful, and our magical adage "As above, so below, as within, so without" connects here. Stuff holds energy, and, very frequently, not energy you necessarily want in your life. If you've ever tried to do a spiritual house cleansing, even a simple cleansing with some salt, water, candles, or smudge sticks, you probably know how hard it is to energetically clear a space that is full of stuff. Further, other people's stuff holds their energy, and that can be a real problem. Others have stuff from loved ones who have passed on, and by holding on to that stuff, they are holding on to their loved one, which prevents healing and release, both for you and for the loved one who passed on.

Further, given current industrialized manufacturing processes, that stuff also holds the energy of the processes used to create it. So much stuff is created through exploitation and suffering of humans and nature. That stuff still carries the energy of that suffering. It cannot be divorced entirely from the energy that went into its production. This is all to say that stuff can influence you on multiple levels, not all of them conscious.

Working to reduce the clutter and excess in your life and prevent more from entering can have direct spiritual benefits: just like working in a clean kitchen rather than a filthy kitchen, it can be hard to practice a dedicated spiritual path when we are so overwhelmed with our daily surroundings.

What to keep: Rather than thinking about what you want to eliminate, think instead about what you want to keep—and the rest can go. I began by listing the things I valued and that I needed for daily living; I put those in a list, and I worked to eliminate anything that didn't hold that kind of value. This made the decision process much easier. Once I realized what was important to me now and what was actually used, I was able to find better homes for the rest.

Giving as a blessing to others: When people get overwhelmed with stuff, the most likely thing that they do is turn to the automatic behavior of disposal: they throw it away, which perpetuates the cycle of consumption and disposal. Our stuff may not be wanted by us, but it can still be used in a great many ways by others, and tossing it in a dumpster creates a different kind of problem, as I discussed earlier in this chapter. Instead, I would suggest using the excess stuff as a way to practice sacred action and an opportunity to engage in people care. Thinking about eliminating stuff ethically, then, leads us toward "alternative" streams that don't end up in the landfill.

For example, when I was in my big process of decluttering, to give away household goods and clothing, I was able to find a local community center that runs a "free store" that takes donations and gives stuff freely away to anyone who is in need. This is a much-better option than a typical thrift store, which ends up throwing away (or shipping off to other countries) a lot of what is donated. If you have no such local center, you can also use Freecycle and Craigslist. Giving stuff away for free is an easy way to meet new friends, give someone something they need, and remove stuff from your life that you no longer need. You may also think about friends or family who need the stuff you have: when I cut down my art studio by 30%, my stuff went two places: a local community center for children and a good friend who was looking for some new supplies. Musical instruments I had had since I was a teenager also went to the community center. I had difficulty initially letting go of them, but when I heard they would be used to start a band to keep the kids off the streets, it was joyful to give them away. Similarly, I gave a large TV away to a friend who is a caretaker for a disabled person with very limited mobility.

What options you have to reduce your stuff really depends on your circumstances and local area, but do ask around. You may be surprised how many people are in need of something you may have to give. And when you can make a difference with that stuff, it makes the process all the more enjoyable. Stuff no longer needed in my life turned out to bless others' lives.

Create a "staging area" for letting go: Because stuff can be overwhelming and because we often have deep energetic connections to it, I found that it helped to create a "staging area" where the stuff could sit for a time while I mourned. Stuff I was planning on eliminating would go into a room, and I would have time to let it go before moving it off to its new home. There were things in my life that I would never use again, but I couldn't bring myself to let them go for many years. But when I had the staging area, I could let them sit there for a while until I was ready and then pass them on to someone else who could make use of them. This is especially a useful strategy for things that you have either had a long time or things to which you have a deep emotional connection.

Ritual of energetic disconnection: A quick ritual also helped energetically disconnect from the stuff. The ritual is simple. Envision your energetic connection to whatever the object is—typically, this is a small line of energy or light between you and the object. Visualize that connection and then, gently, sever that connection some way. For example, you can imagine the line being cut, or pull your energy back from the object. Further, you can also use energy work to send the stuff on with a blessing to its new home; Reiki or a simple elemental blessing is useful for this.

Enlisting help: Other people don't feel the way you do about your stuff, so finding the right friend or family member to help you eliminate it is a good idea. You don't want someone who will talk you into keeping anything—rather, you want someone who is ruthless and firm. It may take a few tries to find the right friend, but when you do, he or she will be invaluable in helping you eliminate clutter.

Building momentum: After you have started this process and given away your first large lot of stuff, you'll find that subsequent reductions of clutter are much easier, and it is easier to work to reduce the lure of the materialist and disposable mindsets much more effectively. Think about this like a boulder sitting at the top of the hill—once it is rolling, it is easy to keep it rolling. The key is in moving it to begin with.

Addressing the Flow of Stuff into Our Lives

The ultimate goal is to prevent too much stuff from flowing into your life, and this takes serious effort in a culture awash in excess stuff. First, Western culture makes it difficult in separating our wants from our actual needs, and many "wants" are recategorized as "needs" (or "must-haves"). I have found that Maslow's hierarchy of needs[41] is a good place to start: actual needs for human survival are food, water, air, basic clothing, and shelter. Above the base needs we have safety, love and belonging, self-esteem, and self-actualization (which connects directly with spiritual practices). It is these basic things that are needed for happy human living. Consumerist culture tries to replace these needs with stuff, and it fails miserably, with people surrounded by tons of stuff but largely unhappy and unfulfilled. So, when we take a few steps back to think about what we need vs. what we want, we can start making priorities in our lives.

While my mindset shift concerning stuff came from a lot of places, it was highly motivated by my teaching of a university service-learning course in Pontiac, Michigan, where many people live without basic needs (adequate food, warm clothing for winter, sanitation, adequate transportation, meaningful work, or shelter). Seeing children in our program without gloves or knowing they were getting their last food for the day with the "snack" at 5:00 p.m. really shifted my own view about wants and needs. The goal of my course was to help improve children's and adolescents' literacy skills, but more than once I saw that kids couldn't work on their reading or writing when their basic needs, such as adequate food, weren't met. This led me to a long series of meditations on wants and needs and eventually resulted in physical changes in my life with regard to stuff, consumption, and materialism. Here are some other suggestions we might consider.

No-new-stuff policy: I have found that a great deal of the stuff that takes up clutter comes not from my own decisions but, rather, the seemingly kind gestures of friends and family. Another mindset shift, and a series of conversations that can really be helpful, is to gently but firmly tell friends and family that you have a "no new stuff" policy. There are different ways you might go about it. The most extreme is to tell them that you aren't interested in any new stuff, and to refuse to take stuff when it's offered. Less extreme is gently reminding people about your no-new-stuff policy when they do give you something, but accepting it the first few times as everyone is adjusting to your policy. You can also set up meaningful alternatives: for example, if they want to give you something, baked goods, handmade things, or natural things (e.g., beautiful shells) are welcome, as is a helping hand around the home. I have found that this has really led to some interesting and productive conversations. It was also met with some serious resistance depending on whom I am trying to talk with (and for some, especially older family members, it takes years of conversations to make it work). Having alternatives to gift giving at holidays and birthdays is a really helpful way of helping others make this transition.

Reframing gift giving: Another option to help eliminate excess stuff is framing "gifts" in a new light—our consumerist culture suggests that it is most appropriate to purchase a gift, but a gift can also be seen in a new light. A trip to a state park with a thoughtful picnic lunch, tickets to see a local play, a kayak trip, dinner at a local farm-to-table restaurant, a fun afternoon working in a friend's garden, a massage, a poem, something handmade: all of these can also be seen as gifts.

Another option here is making **conscious purchases of higher quality**. Unfortunately, materialist culture works hard to make you believe that stuff you have is no longer relevant, useful, or functional. There are two related concepts worth understanding here. As discussed earlier in this chapter, perceived obsolescence is when stuff is purposely designed to feel obsolete, even when it is still totally functional. The clothing industry is particularly notorious for this issue—last year's styles are no longer to be worn, so you must buy new. Planned obsolescence is when things are designed to fail, such as an older but still-functional cell phone no longer being able to make calls due to software changes. Considering these two concepts when purchasing is helpful, since they can help us make better decisions: How do we buy "timeless" clothing (that is, clothing that doesn't go out of style)? How do we buy things that will last? Further, purchasing carefully and consciously can help slow down waste streams. I try very hard to purchase things that do not have planned obsolescence; rather, I purchase things of higher quality (and usually higher price) that will last longer. For example, iron skillets are a great investment, as are a good pair of leather boots that can be cared for over the years. Some companies offer lifetime warranties on their products, and these are well worth seeking out. Higher-quality stuff means it lasts longer and needs to be repaired less often.

Slowing down your purchasing: For a lot of us, purchases are often done at a whim, and with the internet it is easier than ever to purchase more than ever before. Given this, and to resist too much new stuff, I work to create space and reflectivity in my purchasing. For example, I consider my purchases carefully before buying. I try to plan purchases in advance and, when possible, allow several days or weeks between a decision and the actual purchase. There are exceptions to these rules, of course, but they are good general principles to follow for daily living.

Making stuff last and taking care of it: When stuff is cheap and plentiful, it has less value. By making fewer purchases and making them carefully, your stuff takes on more value to you. You can also make a conscious effort to better take care of what you have so that it doesn't wear out or break easily. Learning how to patch clothing and socks, for example, is a great way to get more time out of them and was a common practice throughout most of human history. Learning how to do small repairs, upholstering, and other such things also helps. Again, if we think about the source of stuff—the living Earth—we can treat it with more respect and make it last longer. I like to remember this when I'm using anything—these things, all of them, came from the Earth's resources. It is up to us to care for them effectively.

Moving to simple and smaller living spaces: The more space we have, the more space we have to fill. Choosing to live in smaller spaces, with fewer gizmos, gadgets, and clutter, can lead to more-fulfilling lives. I experienced this firsthand—moving to a smaller rental space meant much less consumption of energy for heat, less to repair, and less of a footprint on the Earth. It also allowed me continue to be conscious of my space and storage, which will allow me to have a smaller environmental footprint and live a more meaningful and simple life. I still have my books and art supplies—but I no longer feel like I'm living among piles of junk! A good friend took this idea to the extreme—selling off 95% of her possessions and quitting her retail day job opened up many new possibilities for her. She lives in an 8-by-13-foot camper, which she can travel anywhere with. She says she is blessed with no mortgage and very few bills. She produces her own electricity and recycles her own waste streams, and she lives life adventurously! These kinds of ideas are becoming more mainstream, since the move to simple living is appealing to many.

Holiday gift-giving alternatives: Since the holidays and birthdays produce an excess of stuff, and usually stuff you really don't want, eliminating that stream of unwanted stuff makes a huge difference. For the holidays, for years, my family has done a Secret Santa exchange. The exchange is simple: each person creates a list of things they would like, and names are secretly exchanged by one "coordinator." Each person gets a name and a list and buys exclusively from that list, spending no more than $50. Handmade, repurposed, or found gifts are also welcome. This means that nobody goes broke at the holidays, each person receives a few nice gifts, and all gifts are "wanted" gifts, things that people will use and cherish. We also have used old cloth to make beautiful gift bags that can be reused year after year.

Reseeing existing stuff: It is helpful to directly confront perceived obsolescence and avoid the idea that stuff has a shelf life. Electronics, automobiles, and clothing are two areas where some creative thinking can help you extend the life of something that is still quite functional.

Engaging in larger actions: We have only a small amount of individual control over waste streams, so this is where awareness raising, information gathering, and community action come in. By learning about what waste steams flow through (and into) one's community or workplace, we can take action, raise awareness, repurpose waste, and generally make our communities better places to inhabit. It's surprising how small initiatives make big differences, both for people's consciousness and in actual action. For example, communities can band together to take on food waste, garbage cleanup in a local area, or many other things.

Conclusion

When we begin to shift our mindsets, we will see how trash picking, upcycling, composting, closed-loop systems, mental decluttering, and other forms of creative repurposing allow us to become alchemists, agents of transformation and change. As I've described in various ways in this chapter, I've done much in my own life to shift away from a consumer lifestyle and consumer-based identity. While I have felt the tangible benefits of doing so from the perspective of health and freer living, it has also made me alive, aware, awake, and, most of all, reverent and thankful. If everything can just be purchased easily, it has no real meaning. When we start living simply and with less, the things we have take on much more meaning because they are not just bought, but found, made, adapted. We begin to seek out those joys that cannot be bought and that don't have mass market appeal, realizing that those are the best things in life. This opens up richness in our inner and outer worlds. The possibilities are simply endless!

Exercises and Rituals

House-Cleansing Ritual

Using some of the decluttering strategies above, plan to do an inner and outer house cleansing.

Outer cleansing: Begin with the outer cleaning and clearing work. If cleaning the whole house is too much for you at once, clean one or two rooms that you frequently spend time in, such as the kitchen or living room. Set yourself clear goals for cleaning—for example, in addition to scrubbing the floor and washing the windows, get a large box and make it a point to fill it with stuff to take to a local thrift store or homeless shelter. When you clean, use the principles above to clear material—make a goal for how much you want to be rid of! Add some essential oil (lemongrass or lavender) to have the plants' assistance with the cleaning process.

Inner/energetic cleansing: House cleansings can be done in a wide variety of ways. Here are some options for you:

- **House smudging.** Take a smudge stick (such as one of your own creation; see chapter 8), and go around your home, smudging each room. It is a good idea to make sure you get the smoke into each of the corners of the house, into closets, etc., for a thorough cleaning. As you go through the house, say, "May this home be cleansed and blessed," or some other simple statement. If the temperature permits, opening the windows and "airing" out the house can also be a wonderful cleansing in addition to smudging.
- **Elemental cleansing.** For a deeper cleansing, take representations of each of the elements around the house. Start with air and go around the house, using incense or a smudge stick, and do each room. Then repeat the process with fire (a candle), water, and, then, salt for Earth. As you go through, chant a blessing (e.g., "Let this home be cleansed and blessed with waters from the sacred pool").
- **Candle cleansing.** Get a fireproof candleholder and a plate. Put a

small chime candle (the four-hour burning candle) in the space you want to have cleansed. If you've made some of your own blessing oil (again, see chapter 8), you can "dress" the candle with the oil, dipping your finger in the oil and running your finger along the candle, starting at the bottom and bringing it to the top of the candle. Then, leave the candle to burn down.

- **Sonic cleansing.** Music or sound can also be a great cleansing for a space. Ringing a bell or singing bowl three times in each room or drumming a steady beat in each room can provide a good cleansing.

Creative Repurposing

Go to your nearest trash or recycle bin at home or in the office and pull out one item for which you can find a new purpose. Challenge yourself with this each week, if possible. Old mint tins or other small containers can be repurposed into a mini altar travel kit, old cat food cans work great as tea light holders for a labyrinth or altar, or an old milk jug with a hole cut in it can be used for berry picking!

Zero-Waste Lifestyle

An activity that radically helps you move into the direction of "spring cleaning" is working toward a zero-waste week or zero-waste month. This is a serious undertaking, and even if you aren't 100% successful, it is certain to help you engage with your own waste. First, figure out ways to eliminate plastic waste from coming into your life: this may mean changing buying habits (and shopping for bulk foods over prepackaged foods, for example) and also eating habits (avoiding takeout containers, straws, etc.). Second, it may involve monitoring other kinds of incoming waste streams and making choices that reduce waste (cloth diapers rather than disposable ones, a handkerchief rather than tissues, etc.). It may also involve you monitoring other kinds of waste streams: food waste, water waste, and so forth. Many people who work toward a zero-waste lifestyle make ecobricks (see earlier chapter) to address any waste that is nonrecyclable and nonavoidable. As you do your zero-waste week or month, keep a journal of your experiences and meditate upon them. When journaling, consider not only your successes and struggles, but also your emotions and mental state.

CHAPTER 4

Beltane

Sacred Actions in Our Homes

As the light comes back into the world, and as the celebration of the fertility of the land and its inhabitants draws near, we think about the many things that are birthed in our homes and everyday lives. It is fitting, perhaps, that at this sacred time of Beltane we consider the role of our immediate surroundings, our homes, our hearths. It is at Beltane that the fires burn brightly to usher in another abundant growing and harvest season. It is at Beltane that flocks and homes were traditionally blessed, recognizing their sacred role in the Wheel of the Year. It is at Beltane that considerable emphasis was placed on bringing in fertility to our homes and hearths. Thus, this chapter explores sacred action in our daily living spaces, dwellings, and everyday activities. A triad that sums up many of the material covered in this chapter is as follows:

Three principles for our homes and hearths:

1. Slowing down
2. Getting creative
3. Reducing dependency

This triad illustrates the themes of this chapter—the need to slow our lives down and live more fully, the need to get creative to stretch resources that we do have and to consider solutions for our own living spaces, and the importance of reducing our dependency on nonrenewable resources, particularly on fossil fuels.

This chapter offers a broad variety of different sustainable living techniques centered on our homes and hearths. This choice of breadth over depth in this chapter specifically was made due to the wide variety of living circumstances that readers may find themselves in: the sacred actions done by someone living in a shared apartment in the city may not be appropriate for someone living in a big, empty house in the country. Thus, as a general suggestion for this chapter, I suggest that you first read through the many options presented. Then, make a choice of a few key things that you'd like to try over the next six weeks. The goal, overall, for this chapter is helping you consider more-sustainable options for things that you do and use regularly in the home: that is, replacing easy-to-wear-out things with more-durable things, using more-sustainable methods for our daily needs, and seeking better alternatives. The material in this chapter has tremendous sustainable power: making a lifestyle change in your regular activities can considerably reduce your ecological footprint over a period of time.

The Home as a Sacred Space

As I described in the introductory chapter, each day, each moment, and each choice we make can be sacred. Rather than separating our magical and our mundane lives, we can see our everyday living as an extended magical act, a larger ritual that we can cultivate through sacred awareness and protection of the living Earth. One way of establishing this idea powerfully as part of your own spiritual practice is by creating a permanent sacred grove around your house and land where you are engaging in sustainable, sacred action. Beltane is a perfect time for such a powerful ritual of beginnings and shifts.

I found that this technique was very helpful to get me into the "sustainable mindset" I was seeking; the idea of being in ceremony while doing it was a very powerful way of helping motivate me in my goals. After all, what does the act of opening up a sacred space do for us? It puts us in a different mindset and shifts our energies so we can focus on the magical work at hand. Why not use this same strategy longer term for sacred actions through sustainable living? Energetically and mentally, creating my home as a sacred space created a profound shift. Knowing that I was living in a sacred space changed every interaction I had with my land, every choice I made in my home, and encouraged me to go the extra mile of making the sustainable choice. And what I found was that it changed not only the way I lived, but how I treated others and how I decided to spend my time, all of which helped facilitate sacred action. Exercise #1, at the end of this chapter, offers a ritual for how to set up a permanent sacred space in your home to focus your energies in specific directions.

The Problem Is the Solution

Much of the driving force behind writing this chapter was the electrical-power instability I experienced while living on my Michigan homestead. In a growing number of places, southeastern Michigan being no exception, power instability is a frequent occurrence. In the six years I lived there, electrical power would go out with nearly every major storm, often for days. Because I lived on the edge of a metro area with poorly maintained power infrastructure, the areas with higher population density would often be targeted first for power renewal, meaning that once the power was out in my area, it often stayed out for a few days. My neighbors opted for the conventional solution: fossil-fuel-driven generators. My solution was rooted in the permaculture design and the design philosophy "the problem is the solution," in which one sees a problem as a unique opportunity for change. So, I

used the power outages as an opportunity to live a more Earth-friendly life, to experiment with much of what I cover in this chapter—candlelight living, solar cooking, food preservation, hayboxes—and not consume more fossil fuels to keep my lights on. Even when I moved to a new state that had a much more stable power grid, I realized that working to do more with less was a powerful principle for us engaging with sacred action in the home and hearth. Further, electrical-power instability helped me understand how wedded our homes and everyday lives are to fossil fuels—and how it can be rewarding and enjoyable to try some alternatives. Most of these alternatives, but not all, do focus on moving away from fossil fuels, which are not only the driving force behind climate change, but also the most-destructive practices in terms of exploiting the land (mining, oil extraction, fracking, pipelines, refineries, etc.). Each opportunity to reduce our dependency on fossil fuels allows us opportunities to tread more lightly upon the Earth. Earth-friendly home living helps us think about how each day and each moment might draw us deeper into a mutually beneficial relationship with the Earth and live each day as sacred.

Cooking

Cooking and heating are central "hearth" activities, and certainly ones to consider at a time of a fire festival such as Beltane. Cooking and heating are also often dependent on fossil fuel: natural gas or electricity (much of which is generated by coal- or biomass-burning power plants). While we consider methods of more-sustainable cooking here, we consider seasonal foods and food rituals in chapter 5.

Cast-iron cookware: One of the things to think about is the "magic" of the hearth. We think about the hearth at the center of the home, as the center of home, and in ages past, in the time of many of our ancestors, this was true. The hearth offered us warmth, nourishing food, and magic. Many of the cooking strategies presented here are a way to bring a bit of that ancestral magic back into our home. Most of them take a lot longer and, yet, offer us powerful cast-iron cookware. Cast-iron cookware is a sustainable investment for your cooking needs—well tended, it can last for generations and requires very minimal maintenance. Many of the other cooking methods described in this chapter (solar cookers, hayboxes) also depend on cast iron. A lifetime of use of cast iron is superior in every way to the shoddily constructed pots and pans you can purchase today, those that are intentionally planned to last only a year. Further, most nonstick cookware today is toxic and, if burned, can kill pet birds and harm human lungs. Cast-iron cookware is often easy to find at yard sales and flea markets for reasonable prices (less than $10 a pan) and, if well taken care of, works better than any other kinds of cooking vessels. Cast-iron cookware is very effective both for conventional kitchens as well as unconventional cooking options I discuss in this chapter, including solar ovens and hayboxes. Cast iron holds heat longer, requiring you to use less fuel, and can keep food warm longer. For everyday cooking, I would suggest at least one 8-inch skillet and one larger 12- or 14-inch skillet for one to two people as a minimum investment.

Learning how to care for and adapt to cast-iron cookware is important. Cast iron takes longer to heat up than other kinds of cooking equipment, and it holds heat longer. This changes cooking times slightly. I turn off the heat five minutes before my food will be ready, for example, if I'm cooking with it on a stove. The other big thing about cast iron is that with use, it will develop "seasoning," which is a black, nonstick coating. The longer the seasoning develops, the better the cast iron becomes in terms of its nonstick surface. It's important to care for and maintain your seasoning (you can scrub it off with a scouring pad if you aren't careful). For everyday use, to clean your cast iron you can just let the pan cool, add some warm water, let it sit for a minute, and wipe it out or scrape it with a small plastic pan scraper. Then rinse, dry, and coat with a light oil (such as olive oil), and it's ready to go for the next use. Once in a while, you may need to "reseason" it: coat it with a thick layer of cooking oil and bake it in the oven at 350 degrees for thirty minutes.

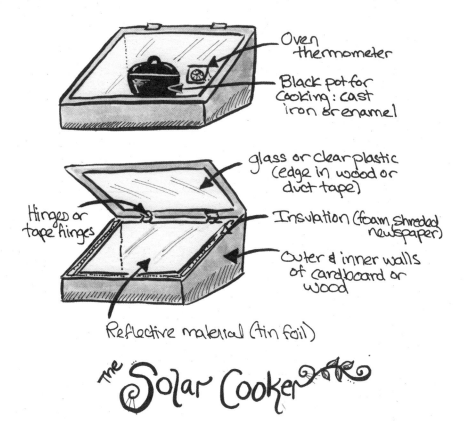

Oven thermometer

Black pot for cooking: cast iron & enamel

glass or clear plastic (edge in wood or duct tape)

Hinges or tape hinges

Insulation (foam, shredded newspaper)

Outer & inner walls of cardboard or wood

Reflective material (tin foil)

The Solar Cooker

Solar cooker: Harnessing the energy of the sun has long been a sustainable practice worth considering—the sun's light and heat are frequently available in most parts of the world, especially in the summer months. Solar cooking is one way to quickly reduce your dependency on fossil fuels, although, like everything else in this chapter, it takes some adjustments! While you can purchase expensive ($200+) solar cookers, you can also make really simple and effective solar cookers from everyday materials: black acrylic paint, cardboard boxes, tin foil. The easiest way to make a box is to get a large box and paint the inside black. Tape the flaps of the box so that they stand up at a 45-degree angle out of the box. Then, add tin foil to the flaps to reflect even more light into the box. Cover the box with a piece of plastic (thicker clear plastic) and then put a heat-holding, dark-colored pot in the box. The graphic offers a drawing of this simple setup for a solar cooker. I have used a solar cooker like this to cook food as well as help process excess wax from my beehive. Solar cookers benefit from an internal thermometer, so that you know how hot the cooker is getting (anything above 200 degrees Fahrenheit is a very good cooker!) Cooking times take a lot longer in a solar cooker (consider this a kind of "slow food"), but what you cook is no less delicious!

Lid with Insulation →

Hot cast iron

Insulation: Cotton, Old Comforter, Straw, etc.

HayBox

The haybox: Another old method of low-energy cooking is called a haybox. Quite simply, it's a box with some kind of insulation—traditionally hay; hence the name. Into this box, food that has already been boiled is placed; the insulation traps the heat and allows for a long, slow cooking time. You will want at least 8 inches of insulation for your box. You can make one with a large cardboard box, hay, cotton batting, and old pillows or old blankets as insulation. Into this haybox, you use a heat-holding pot, such as a cast-iron Dutch oven. The way this box works is simple: you bring food up to boiling temperature in the cast-iron cookware, then you put it in the haybox to finish cooking. It takes about three times longer to cook in the haybox, but you cut your fuel use (electricity, gas, etc.) down by half or more.

The Dutch oven: A cast-iron Dutch oven is another old-style cooking method that is extremely effective and sustainable for the right person. You can sometimes find Dutch ovens at yard sales—even one that is rusty can be cleaned up with a bit of elbow grease and some good metal scouring pads. There are different kinds of Dutch ovens—some are able to be used in the oven and may be cast iron with an enamel coating, while others have three little feet for outdoor use over coals.

Cast Iron Dutch Oven

The Dutch oven with feet allows you to cook with hot coals in an outdoor setting. The basic principle of this kind of Dutch oven is to apply heat, in the form of charcoal or coals from a wood fire, on the top and the bottom of the oven to cook your food. Adjusting the number and amount of coals you add allows you to do different kinds of cooking and achieve certain temperatures within the oven. Coals are added on the outside edges of the lid and the outside bottom of the Dutch oven. If you add the twelve to sixteen standard coals (or the equivalent), only to the bottom in a circle, you will end up with an excellent frying surface to cook eggs, vegetables, or whatever else you want to fry. If you add eighteen around the top and six around the bottom, you will end up with an inside temperature of 350 degrees, which will allow you to bake pretty much anything. The way you can tell the inside temperature quickly is through a "hand test," where you can put your hand inside and see how long you can keep it there: one second means it's above 500 degrees, two seconds means it's around 500, three seconds is about 450, four seconds is 400, five seconds is 350, six seconds is 300, and so on.

Do note that the conventional charcoal that your purchase in the store is nonsustainable, and its production is linked to increased carbon emissions and deforestation in addition to having a host of chemical additives. See if you can find a more sustainable option for charcoal, such as an organic lump charcoal that uses sustainable forestry methods.

Heating and Cooling

Another area that we expend tremendous amounts of nonrenewable energy is in the area of heating and cooling our homes. The very warmth of our bodies is a form of magic—there is nothing more magical than a warm fire on a cold winter or early spring day. This section explores some more-sustainable options for heat and cooling.

The wood cookstove: On the more permanent side of cooking and heating options are wood cookstoves. Wood cookstoves allow you to heat your house, cook on a hot surface, and bake in the included oven, and many also offer a food-warming area. If you plant to install a wood cookstove, make sure you are installing an efficient one that uses little fuel—carbon emissions from cookstoves are also of concern (and in the US, the Environmental Protection Agency has released new guidelines for woodstove emissions). A nice wood cookstove can allow you to cook, bake, and heat your house all at the same time. The wood cookstove is a magical presence in your living space that allows you to have heat, bubbling pots of goodies, and bread baking all at once! Real fire cooks differently, and it has a different kind of heat, one that warms you to the bones. When you are near one, you can feel—and taste—the difference.

The rocket stove and rocket mass heater: Rocket stoves and rocket mass heaters are an ingenious design that have been around for a number of years in various forms—they use an L- or J-shaped design to maximize the use of fuel. They burn very cleanly and can be used both for heating and effective cooking. My first introduction to rocket stoves was at a sustainable-living center called Strawbale Studio in Oxford, Michigan. There, my friend has a rocket stove made of cob (a mixture of sand, clay, and straw used in various natural building applications) that she used for heating a teaching space at her sustainable-living center. One day, during a natural-building class, it was my job to keep the rocket stove going. I brought in twelve to fifteen pieces of wood from the stack outside, certain that I hadn't brought in nearly enough for a full day. At the end of the day, I had added only five pieces of wood over an eight-hour period; the whole stove was blazing hot, and everyone had a delightfully warm place to sit. Since that time, I've experimented with a number of designs. They are simple and extraordinarily effective and can be made in a number of ways: from bricks, from concrete blocks, from cob, from old barrels. The key to an effective rocket stove is in properly cycling the heat and in insulating the whole stove (see the graphic). One of my favorites was a simple stove I used for outdoor cooking, made from old concrete bricks. It was like my "outdoor grill" but not dependent on fossil fuel![42]

When we think about sustainable heating, one aspect to consider is the principle of heating bodies, not spaces. It's extremely inefficient, in general, to heat spaces, since air is a very poor retainer of heat. Poor insulation in many houses, and heat loss through such things as windows and doors, makes this even more of a problem. If you instead use the principle of heating bodies and focus your efforts in that

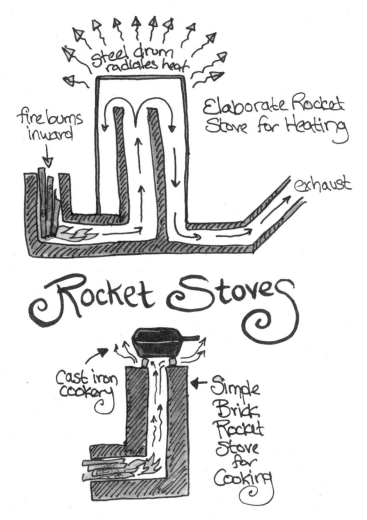

steel drum radiates heat

fire burns inward

Elaborate Rocket Stove for Heating

exhaust

Rocket Stoves

Cast iron cookery

Simple Brick Rocket Stove for Cooking

direction, you can heat more efficiently. In fact, this is the driving principle behind the rocket mass heater—the rocket mass heater usually has some kind of elongated bench, made of cob, that retains heat extremely effectively. This kind of heater allows a person to sit or sleep on a warm surface and stay comfortable, even if the ambient air is colder.

Heating frequently used spaces: When you are heating spaces in the winter months, consider heating or cooling only spaces that are frequently used. I think we have in our minds that our whole houses need to be heated or cooled all the time—but this is not so. When I lived at my homestead, I heated only about 900 square feet (of the 2,600-square-foot home): my art studio, bedroom, kitchen, bathroom, and den where my woodstove was. This allowed me to efficiently save on heating, use less wood (or gas, depending on whether I was using my woodburning stove or not), and not heat areas that I wasn't working in. Sometimes that meant using a small space heater to keep one room comfortable while the other sections of the house were more chilly, and often it meant turning the heat way down and depending on my woodstove, which I would sleep by, to stay warm and happy.

Hot bricks: Another strategy that I learned as part of my "electricity instable" living tied to heating bodies, not spaces, was the principle of the fire iron or hot brick. I had read about this in a Laura Ingalls Wilder book and wanted to try it out—and it works beautifully. This principle is quite simple: you use a fire, an oven, or some other heat source to heat up something that has a lot of thermal mass to hold heat, such as an old red brick or even a small iron skillet. You wrap this in a towel and then keep it close to the skin, taking it to bed with you or wherever you are going. In addition to being a wonderful way of keeping yourself warm, it has the added benefit of allowing you to make it through outdoor, cold, overnight vigils during the winter solstice, a technique that I used on more than one occasion![43]

Trees and shade: Many of our houses are extremely inefficiently designed, and that has real implications for winter heating and summer cooling. If you own your house, a few well-placed delicious trees or a vine on a trellis along the south side of the house are a perfect way to address heating-and-cooling issues. The principle is simple—you want shade in the summer and warmth in the winter. A vine with leaves or a thick tree in the summer offers shade; the tree or vine that loses its leaves allows the sun to warm the home in the winter.

Water and Water Usage

Our waters are under duress worldwide, and these include the waters flowing into our homes.[44] Water is a resource that is growing more precious by the day. I write this as a good part of the western US is in a serious drought, and, within the last five years, nearly half the country has experienced some form of severe drought. Rethinking our water usage is a critical part of lessening our impact on the land. This is also important for another key reason—the more water we consume, the less water there is for living creatures, rivers, and the rest of life. A good friend of mine who is a fellow druid and an ethnographer shared with me how the water usage and drought in California were literally killing all the native plant life there, leaving the natural areas barren. Humans were taking all the water for irrigation, showering, and watering lawns. Stories like this, in a time of growing water scarcity, are prime encouragement to reduce our water usage and seek localized, sustaining solutions. If we start viewing water as the precious resource that it is, it will help us shift our thinking and our actions so that we consume less. Focusing on reducing our water consumption activities also helps us develop a deeper relationship with the element of water.

There are basic activities for reducing water consumption that many folks know already: shorter baths or showers, less frequent showers, installing low-flow showerheads, not watering the lawn ever (see chapter 6), not brushing teeth or doing dishes with the water running, and so on. I would encourage starting with these simple solutions, and being mindful of water use in the home. This section explores some less well-known options.

Avoiding plastic and bottled water: Bottled water is an environmental nightmare. First, plastic water bottles contribute considerably to waste streams, so seeking alternatives is a good initial course of action. (Of course, if you can get enough plastic bottles from other people, you can also build a water-bottle greenhouse!) Plastic bottles substantially contribute to plastic in oceans, landfills, and more (see chapter 3). But more than this, it seems quite silly to ship water anywhere that there is already water. Further, many bottling companies in the US, including most of the readily available brands, are stealing water either from public/municipal supplies or from state parks, national forests, and local communities or are bottling water in the most-drought-stricken areas.[45] It's an all-around problem, and eliminating these from your life is a great start to rebuild your own sacred relationship with the local waters around you.

Any number of other options are available: metal water bottles, drinking fountains, mason jars—anything that is local and reusable is a step in the right direction. If you are concerned about the quality of your drinking water, other regional options can usually be found if you look around.

But here, I also want to push back on the idea that there is something inherently wrong with most municipal water supplies and that bottled water is somehow safer or better. This is another misleading advertising tactic that has manipulated us into buying something we could otherwise have for free or extremely low cost. In fact, most municipal water supplies are local water sources that are extensively tested and publicly owned, and only 25% of bottled water comes from non–tap water sources. This means that most bottling companies are simply selling you, with branding and packaging, exactly what you could get out of the tap anyway.[46]

Sacred wells and springs: When I moved back to Pennsylvania, I was delighted to find that right on my drive to visit my parents (which I took at least once a month), there was a fresh roadside spring. Because I live in an area that has substantial amounts of fracking wastewater, agricultural runoff, and mine runoff, I was very unsure about my local water supply (despite everything I just wrote in the last section!). But I obviously didn't want to drink bottled water. The spring proved to be a delightful win-win situation: it was in the direction I was frequently heading (so I was not expending additional fossil fuel or going out of my way), it was a local clean resource, and I was able to reuse jugs and not create any waste. You might not have such a convenient spring; however, I do encourage you to look at your own options and try to eliminate or reduce waste in this area.[47]

Showers and baths: Two other options exist for those wanting to reduce their water consumption further, beyond shorter showers or low-flow showerheads. One simple method called the bucket bath was used by my grandmother when water didn't easily flow from pipes. You fill up the bucket, get a wash cloth, and clean yourself thoroughly. If your bucket is big enough, you can also easily wash and rinse your hair—all for only a few gallons of water, rather than the 20 or so gallons a typical shower takes. So let's do some quick math here—let's assume you use 20 gallons of water each day, and you bathe each day. That's 7,280 gallons of water per year. If you switch to a bucket bath one day a week, consuming only 3 gallons of water, you will save over 150 gallons of water a year. If you switched a bucket bath to two days a week, you'll save over 300 gallons a year. Of course, you could also skip the daily bath or shower and move to an every-other-day model.

Solar showers and solar hot-water heaters are another way to engage in sacred action and to help reduce your dependency on fossil fuels, especially for those in temperate climates in the summer months or tropical climates year-round. Solar showers can be a very simple camp model (put the 3–5 gallons of water in it, sit it in the sun to warm, and have your shower). More-permanent solar showers are often custom built and placed on the roof; they all involve some kind of black pipes or hoses, usually in a black-painted box, that can cycle water through (and store it in a hot-water heater).

Graywater: Finding ways of diverting water from the waste stream is another way of treating water in a more sacred manner. One such method that has been around for a number of years is graywater catchment. The basic principle is simple: A lot of the water that flows through our sinks is not really that dirty and can be used for a second purpose. If you are using chemical-free laundry detergent (*see below*), washing your dishes, taking a shower, or brushing your teeth, the idea is that water is still very much usable. A graywater system built into your bathtub or kitchen sink will divert the water from these applications and use it in some other way. The ways it can be used are many: some systems include small wetlands behind a house that automatically purify and store massive amounts of water. Other systems use the graywater for crop irrigation or reuse the water for further indoor use with filtration. Believe it or not, primitive graywater systems are very easy to install in your home (even in one sink) and use effectively—this could be as simple as a diverter and a 5-gallon bucket under your sink. Once a week you use it to water your plants or water local trees!

Stormwater runoff: Another aspect of daily living surrounding our dwellings is that of stormwater. Stormwater refers simply to water that runs off houses, pavement, sidewalks, and other nonabsorbent surfaces. In fact, municipal systems are designed to "remove" water as quickly as possible rather than seeing it as a resource and retaining it on the landscape. In a natural setting, this water is absorbed into the ground; shade from trees keeps this precious, sacred resource deep within the rich soil and roots. You might notice that plants that have extra water grow just a bit greener—a bit bigger. I'll end this paragraph with a caveat—in some parts of the world, it is illegal to store or sink rainwater, so my suggestions in this section may not be appropriate for all places.

In permaculture design terms, we often say that "the problem is the solution," and in the case of stormwater, that is certainly so. The water off our asphalt roofs may not be safe to drink, but it is wonderful for trees and perennial plants. Even if you aren't in a position to build a stormwater system where you live, often these can be proposed and built in public places to raise public awareness. Being aware of the laws is one way to get involved with stormwater protection. You can see more about doing public sacred action in chapter 7.

Rain gardens: A rain garden is a garden designed to fill up and hold water after major storms. They are gardens in a true sense of the word and are planted with a variety of water-loving flora (some of which can be medicinal or edible, depending on the nature of the rain garden, runoff, and plants). Rain gardens have several parts: the mechanism to get the water into the garden itself (usually some kind of

Swale

rainspout with a diverter); the main rain garden, which is calculated to hold a certain volume of water (and may or may not include a pond feature); and finally, an overflow option for severe storms or multiple recurring weather events. Keys to successful rain gardens are (1) understanding how many gallons of water surface area you have from a roof or other space, (2) accounting for that rainfall in your design, (3) accounting for overflow, and (4) planting the right kind of plants.

To calculate the amount of water, you can start by calculating the square footage of your roof and converting it to inches. So, a 20-by-50-foot roof would be 240 by 600 inches. Next, multiply the roof dimensions by the number of inches of rainfall (a really major storm may have 3 inches, a typical storm 2 inches, and a light rain 1 inch; in our case, a light rain = 144,000 cubic inches of water). Finally, you divide your total cubic inches of water by 231, since a gallon of water is 231 cubic inches. In our example, this gives us just over 623 gallons of water. If we wanted to design a good rain garden that could handle that flow, we should design one that can hold at least one major storm's worth, or about 1,900 gallons, and account for overflow (where is the rain going to go if the rain garden gets full?).

In terms of plants, water-loving plants are a must for rain gardens. Research local plants in your area. For many temperate parts of North America, good plants include cattails, sedges, sweet flag, blue iris, blue vervain, marsh marigold, and swamp milkweed.

Swales: Another system of harnessing water is called a "swale." It's a simple ditch that holds water and sinks it in place rather than letting it run off. Usually the swale is dug "on contour," meaning it is dug along a slight incline/hillside, at the same elevation, for a wide area. Then, when it rains, the rainwater pools in the ditch and sinks in slowly rather than running down the hillside. When vegetation is planted on the mound just downhill from the ditch itself, you can harness all that water for growing food and nurturing diverse ecosystems—fruit trees do very well with this setup. A swale, combined with excellent mulch and plant cover, can divert huge amounts of water into productive growing spaces rather than into municipal sewer systems (or nearby polluted rivers).

Rain barrels: Rainwater catchment systems, including barrels and larger cisterns, are a wonderful way to store up water that can be used later for a variety of purposes (most commonly, for watering plants or wetting down compost piles). I personally prefer swales or rain gardens, so that good design takes care of most of my watering needs; however, rain barrels are the best option in certain circumstances. Rain barrels can be of very simple design. If they are properly elevated, they can provide enough pressure to use as a source of water for a hose, soaker hose, or even drip irrigation system for growing plants. Again, I encourage you to measure the rainfall off your roof and consider what happens if the rain barrel (or larger cistern) gets full. If you have one 50-gallon rain barrel and you have 144,000 cubic feet of water, your rain barrel can hold only one-twelfth of the rain coming in a typical 1-inch storm!

Sanitation and Cleaning

Sanitation is perhaps not the most popular subject, but if we are going to talk about daily living and sacred action, we have to talk about what keeps us clean (and how to manage our own bodily waste, which was covered in the last chapter). I have been really excited to see where sustainable living practices have been leading in this direction—and I encourage you to explore many of them.

Detergents and cleaning supplies: Many homes are more polluted inside than out, and it has a lot to do with the kinds of cleaning supplies, air fresheners, and other chemical products we use in our homes. Eliminating the use of chemicals in our homes has so many benefits, both in terms of people care and Earth care. Here are two my favorite recipes that are easy to make and use, and that provide alternatives to basic cleaning needs.

I have used the following simple laundry detergent recipe successfully for years. It cleans my clothing better than commercial brands, contains no phosphates that are destroying rivers, and is very cost effective (less than five cents per load); it is also perfectly safe for a graywater system.

Ingredients: 1 bar of soap,[48] 1 cup borax (purchase in the laundry aisle), and 1 cup of washing soda[49]

Materials: 5-gallon bucket with lid, 1 cheese grater, 1 large stock pot, measuring cups, gallon jug as a second measuring tool (or you can approximate; precision is not necessary for this recipe), and a stirring mechanism with a very long handle (I prefer a whisk wired to a paint stirrer or stick, since it breaks up the clumps better).

Instructions:

1. Grate up your bar of soap with the cheese grater into your stock pot and add ½ gallon of hot water into your pot.

2. Put the pot on the stove and bring your soap to a boil. Stir it up with the whisk, making sure that your soap gratings are fully dissolved. Be careful not to let it boil over, or you will have a soapy mess.

3. While your soap is dissolving, add to your bucket ½ gallon of cold water, 1 cup of borax, and 1 cup of washing soda. Mix these well. You should always pour the borax and washing soda into the water (rather than the water into the powders); this avoids creating a dust cloud.

4. After your soap has dissolved, add in your ½ gallon of soapy water. Mix well, again using the whisk. Be sure you don't touch the stuff at this point, since the soaps are a bit harsh. This is an appropriate time to add about 30–50 drops of lavender essential oil, or another skin-safe oil, to your mixture.

5. Add the last 2 gallons of water (cold) to the bucket. Stir everything carefully.

6. Now, over the next twelve hours or so, everything will cool and you'll see the detergent starting to gel. As it gels, stir it up to prevent too much clumping. As I mentioned before, the amount of gel is based on the soap you use, so some require quite a bit of stirring.

7. Add 1 cup of your detergent to each load of laundry.

A simple all-purpose cleaning solution: A combination of baking soda and vinegar will clean most things. For cleaning the toilet, for example, I add ¼ cup of baking soda and 1 cup of vinegar and use a toilet brush. For cleaning the tub, I start by scouring with baking soda and then wipe the surfaces with vinegar as a disinfectant. For removing stains, white vinegar applied with a sponge will get out many stains, including those in clothing, teapots, and carpets. An all-purpose cleaner and disinfectant for surfaces can be made with ½ cup of vinegar, ½ cup of baking soda, and ½ gallon of water. You can store it, put it in a spray bottle, and use to clean surfaces, mirrors, and more.

Castile soap: I want to mention one more of my favorite cleaning strategies—and that is using castile soap. Castile soap cuts through grease and grime really well and can be used in almost any way—washing dishes, hand-washing clothing, diluting it and using it as shampoo or body wash, scrubbing the floors, and so many more things. Once, my car was splattered with oil on the highway, and oil was all over my windshield. Castile soap worked like a dream, completely cleaning up my windshield and car. I always have a few bottles around my house and won't travel anywhere without it. Castile soap is very environmentally friendly and breaks down readily in the ecosystem—it is also safe for graywater systems.

Lighting at Night

Another common aspect of modern dwelling is our use of electric means of lighting our homes at night. One of the simplest, and yet profound, shifts we can make is to move from electric lighting to natural lighting—lighting a living space by using oil lamps or simple candles. Besides being an Earth-friendly practice, it's not that hard to do at all, and most people can quickly adapt to this lifestyle. Our eyes adjust, your rhythms change, and the world seems to slow down. Peace and tranquility are present in these candlelit evenings. Sleep comes much easier and stays much longer. It's almost hard to put into words how profound of an effect this can have on living. A lot of sustainable-living movements talk about "slow" things, and introducing candlelight is certainly a way of slowing down. I would suggest giving it a try for one evening a week to see how you like it. I first started doing the candlelit evenings occasionally, and now I do them nearly every night, since they have really improved my quality of life. I have even done some painting and artwork in candlelight, and that has given it a really different kind of quality than artwork done in full daylight or electric light. The candlelight allows for more conscious, Earth-centered, and sacred living.

Further, carefully managed resources can be more sustainable and less draining on the land than other forms of fossil fuel (which is likely keeping your electric lights going). Candles made of local beeswax from local hives support beekeepers and bees. Oil burners made from oils that have gone rancid or would otherwise go unused are a great way to "produce no waste." Both these options, along with several others, are presented in this section.

Candles, candleholders, and reflecting light: A good stock of candles is a necessity, and it is wise to source them carefully. I wouldn't go buy new candles, because the cost can quickly add up and that creates additional demand for more new stuff. Thrift stores, yard sales, and auctions are all places to get large amounts of candles for low cost. A few years ago, I found a huge box of candles of all sorts at an auction. Be aware, however, that some really old candles have leaded wicks. I recently discovered one such candle in my stockpile and quickly put it out after it started dripping little molten-silver balls into the wax.

If you have a local beekeeper (or are a beekeeper yourself), beeswax blocks or candles are a wonderful investment. Beeswax is extremely efficient and burns beautifully when compared to paraffin or soy. It also smells amazing, giving you an even more delightful experience.

To maximize candlelight for reading or delicate work (such as painting), you might need more light than a typical candle can provide. First, tea lights produce almost no light compared to tapers. A few tapers can give ample light for reading, however, I would suggest an alternative to the "lots of candles" technique. Instead, look for an old-style candle lantern or wall sconce that directs the light all in one direction by using a mirror or set of three mirror panels. These are very readily available. Avoid the ones that are partially or fully wooden (a fire hazard) and instead go with ones that are solid metal.

Likewise, good candleholders are a must, but make sure they are not made of wood! Wooden candleholders are easy to forget about, and once the candle burns down, such a candleholder itself burns. A good candleholder has a handle so you can take it with you and a dish for catching wax so that you don't make a mess all over your floor. The thin ones that are meant

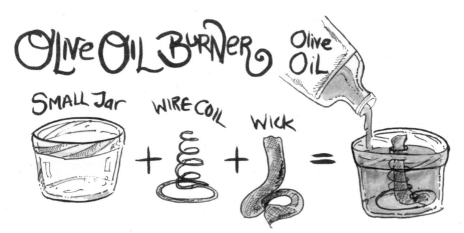

Olive Oil Burner
Olive Oil
Small Jar + Wire Coil + Wick =

for dining tables are much less useful when you are walking around your house and using the candleholder functionally day after day. Glass candleholders can easily break if the candle burns too low, and they will burn low, so I try to use metal or ceramic ones when possible.

Traditional oil lamps: Old oil lamps are not hard to find and are worth having around. I got to know these well with the countless power outages I experienced while living on my homestead in the Detroit metro area. However, the issue that I have had with these practical lamps is that they burn kerosene or lamp oil, and both these fuels are derived from fossil fuels. Further, these fuels often smell bad when they burn. Kerosene is extremely noxious, but even the more "refined" oils burn with an odor that is not pleasant. Other oils for these are not easy to use in a traditional lamp—vegetable oils aren't as flammable and don't draw well through the wick.

Crafting an olive oil lamp. Alternatives to the standard oil lamp are olive oil or vegetable oil lamps. You can easily make your own vegetable lamp (*see image*) by using some wire, some wicking, and a mason jar. Because I practice herbalism, sometimes I have older jars of infused oils that go rancid. I use this rancid olive oil in my simple olive oil burners quite effectively. These simple olive oil lamps make really wonderful options for lighting for rituals and altars. I would suggest keeping a lid on your olive oil burner when not using it (or place it somewhere that it can't get knocked over). You might think about how you can use this lamp not only for mundane purposes, such as reading, but also for sacred purposes, such as on an altar or in ritual.

Electronic-light mitigation: If you are going to use screens (TV, computer, phone, etc.) at night, there are better ways of using them to allow for low-light living and save energy. Various dimmer programs exist for computers—they adjust your color and brightness as the evening progresses, so even if you are on your computer later at night, it's offering a soft red or yellow glow, rather than blazing blue light at you. I'd also suggest not using any of these devices within an hour or two of bed.

Lightbulbs: It's worth paying attention also to the kind of lightbulbs that you use: the older ones often are more yellowish or cast a yellowish hue that is better on the eyes and allows sleep to come more readily. Lower-wattage bulbs and lampshades also help. I also have an old-school lava lamp that creates really diffused light on the yellow spectrum; I often use this for providing some low light to my main living area, and I supplement it with candles or oil lamps for moving about the house. It's not much different than a good oil lamp, and it has only a 40-watt bulb.

Slowing down at night: All these lighting issues also speak to a deeper issue—that of stillness, quietude, and really "slowing down" to live in a more intentional and sacred manner. I have found, since switching almost entirely to candlelight evenings, that my sleep is better, my meditations are deeper, and I am in a different mindful space at night. It's quite remarkable.

People Power

In science classes, a common definition of "energy" is the "ability to do work." Our civilization has heavily, and entirely, depended on fossil fuels; that is, deposits of combustible organic life, concentrated by the pressure of the Earth's crust for millions of years. That these fossil deposits happen to be combustible changed human civilization and brought us to where we are now. We use these fossil fuels to do a tremendous amount of work for us: moving goods and people around the world, transporting us to our jobs, keeping our lights on at night, building our homes, and more. Life without dependence on fossil fuel power is unthinkable to many in this age, but in the many millennia that proceeded our own, energy by other means was necessary. Even as some countries and regions now invest fossil fuels in alternative technologies, much of the current predicament we find ourselves in is rooted in our use, and abuse, of fossil fuels.

Another movement toward Earth-friendly living that has its roots in antiquity is the "person-powered home" movement; this people power helps us move away from fossil fuel dependence and its problems. The idea is simple enough: a shift away from fossil fuels means that if we want power, we need to power machines ourselves and can do so through simple technology. For example, the "treadmill" was literally a device that humans or animals would walk on that would produce energy that could be used to mill grains into flour; in the nineteenth century, a treadmill was used to put prisoners to work grinding grain. I think it's ironic that today's treadmills require energy input rather than producing energy output!

Rather than going to the gym or investing in an expensive treadmill, find something in your house that you could power. Typical machines that people are using today include human-powered saws, lathes, and other common woodworking tools. A friend of mine created his own foot-powered woodturner and is producing beautiful bowls with human power! A kick wheel for pottery, for example, is a fossil-fuel-free artistic opportunity. Another friend created a pedal-powered wool carder from an old bicycle, which is very effective and gives her some exercise at the same time. Plans also abound for human-powered washing machines (note that without fossil fuels, washing clothing is one of the most labor-intensive tasks humans have done throughout the ages), human-powered grinders (for your morning coffee), and human-powered water pumps (for moving water from your rain barrel into your garden), among many other things. I am currently working on a design for a people-powered grinder for my herbs—I often use an electric grinder, but it recently stopped working, and now I'm designing a hand-cranked alternative that will be more effective than a traditional mortar and pestle. I love the idea of hand-grinding my herbs and building in love and positive energy into the process.

If you want to pedal to produce energy, the best use of that pedal power is directly engaging in the task at hand (so pedaling to turn a fan, for example) rather than trying to pedal to store energy in a battery or generator. The idea behind this is simple: batteries and other electricity storage devices are extremely inefficient, and their mechanisms are unsustainable. By using your own human power to directly complete the task at hand, you are the most efficient.[50]

Radical Living

Many of the above options assume that you are staying stationary in a traditional kind of house, and since that's probably the option that works for the most people, I spent the bulk of the chapter exploring those possibilities. But for some, that kind of living is not necessary. If you are willing to build your own house or live in a smaller portable dwelling, other options for regenerative living are open to you. These kinds of dwellings offer a very minimal ecological footprint and incredible options for recycling and reusing waste, living off the grid, and more. Radical living options really help us embrace all three ethical principles; people care, Earth care, and fair share. We are better cared for in structures that are not full of toxic materials and are designed and built by us to suit our needs. We care for the Earth by sourcing materials locally and sustainably, and we are able to take only what we need, reducing waste. We take a fair share by demanding less square footage and have a minimal footprint. Here are a few of these more radical possibilities:

Cob and straw bale structures. For many years, I took classes and spent a lot of time at the Strawbale Studio in Oxford, Michigan. This sustainable-living center is run by a delightful person, Deanne Bednar, an artist, teacher, and natural builder. I learned how to do many of the things I'm sharing in this chapter from Deanne's careful teachings—from hayboxes to rocket stoves, from solar cookers to humanure. The bulk of Deanne's classes, however, focused on how to construct real dwellings by using materials found primarily on-site or locally—timber framing, straw bale construction, making and using cob, Earth plastering, thatching by using local reeds, and more. Although an in-depth discussion of these techniques needs its own book-length treatment (and has many such treatments, such as the *Cob Builder's Handbook*[51] and *The Hand-Sculpted House*[52]), I wanted to introduce them here as possibilities. More and more people are choosing to avoid conventional mortgages and instead build their own homes with sustainable materials—and this is doable for anyone with the time, patience, and enthusiasm.

Tiny living and mobile living: Another movement gaining a lot of traction is the tiny-house movement (which includes houses usually of 300 square feet or less, built on movable platforms). This movement is also connected with other small alternative-living spaces in vans, buses, and campers, and with other such lifestyle choices. Some tiny houses are in one place, and people who live in them just treat them like a typical home. But other structures are much more mobile. One of my best friends has lived in a small camper (13 feet long) and van for over a year and a half. She has traveled the country, seeing the sights and picking up work where she is able (there seems to be no shortage if you are flexible). Her friends and family thought that she was mad—and she laughed and told them, "No mortgage, no rent, seeing the country; what's not to love about it?" She ended up seeing many parts of the US, living as a "work trader" at various campgrounds and selling her crafts.

As we wrap up our chapter of sacred living within our homes, I encourage you to think about what sacred action you can engage in at this moment, what might need careful planning, and what may not be attainable at this point. Every step, however small, is a step in the right direction!

Exercises and Rituals

A Home Sustainability Audit

With the members of your family if at all possible, take a careful walk around your home. Make a list of things that you could do to live more sustainably. Explore waste flows, water flows, heating and cooling, storage, lighting, and more. Here is a list to get you started:

- Look at your roof in the winter. Do you see places where it melts first? Do you have icicles? Those may be signs of poor insulation and heat loss.
- Check your windows for drafts. Apply a film cover to any windows that are drafty.
- Check your light switches and electrical outlets to see if they are properly insulated.
- Check for leaky faucets.
- Look for "phantom" power draining by electronics in "standby" mode.
- Pay attention to electricity usage for lighting.
- Consider the flows of waste in and out of your house. Is there a way to recycle more? Compost?

Additionally, many municipalities and utility companies offer resources and even free or low-cost consultations that you can use for home energy audits. Once you've compiled the list of possible changes, consider the impact of each action and create a plan to change three things in the next six weeks.

An Exercise in Light and Darkness

For one week, try out candlelit evenings. If you have other family members or children, see if they are willing to try the activity. Keep track of things such as the amount of sleep that you get, how well rested you feel, and what kinds of activities lend themselves well to candlelight living. Consider how you might build candlelight evenings into other activities, such as a family game night, ritual and meditation, and more.

Your Home as a Sacred Space

If you want to turn your entire home into a place where you live and work in a sacred manner, as the opening of this chapter suggested, here are some suggestions for doing so. Instructions are in plain text; spoken words are in *italics*.

Outer symbolism: Symbols in the material world are important reminders to help us reflect inner realities and understand patterns upon the world. Creating some outer symbols to designate your sacred space is an important part of the work at hand. You can create any symbols meaningful to you and your tradition, of course. In my case, since my druid tradition works with the four elements in the four directions extensively, I created and fired small clay symbols depicting the four elements, and put them on four trees in each quarter of the edge of my property. Then, I painted small elemental banners for inside of my house and placed them on four separate walls, each showing the different directions.

Opening the space: You can also use a modification of a sacred-space-opening ritual to establish your home as a permanent sacred space for you to engage in sacred action. Here is one such method for doing so:

Set your intentions aloud for the space. *Let the powers be attentive that I am setting up a sacred space in my home. Spirits of this place, I ask for your wisdom and guidance on my ceremony.*

Call in the four elements. Hang elemental symbols (or place your other elemental representations) and speak aloud intentions that aligned with that element:

Air. *Spirits of the air! Spirit of the robin, nest builder, and bringer of spring! I call upon you this day to create a sacred space in my home. Powers of the mind, of my rational self, and of the wisdom of the ages, guide my path and help me live in a sacred manner that nourishes and regenerates our great lands. May the knowledge of my ancestors guide my path each day!*

Fire. *Spirits of the fire! Spirit of the fox who uses wit and cunning! I call upon you this day to help create a sacred space in my home. Powers of passion and creativity, guide my path and help me live in a sacred manner that nourishes and regenerates our great lands. May the force of will and the flow of Awen and creativity guide my path each day!*

Water. *Spirits of the Water! Spirit of the beaver who works the waters and the Earth! I call upon you this day to help create a sacred space in my home. Powers of emotion and intuition, inner gifts and guides, guide my path and help me live in a sacred manner that nourishes and regenerates our great lands. May the blessings of peace, joy, and gratitude guide my path each day!*

Earth. *Spirits of the Earth! Spirit of the turtle who carries home wherever she goes! I call upon you this day to help create a sacred space in my home. Powers of the home and the hearth, guide my path and help me live in a sacred manner that nourishes and regenerates our great lands. May the blessings of grounding, stability, and perseverance guide my path each day!*

Cleansing and blessing the home: Cleanse and bless the home with each of the elements, going through each space with a smudge stick (air and fire) and a sprinkle of salt water (Earth and water). You can continue to speak your intentions.

Maintaining the space: I found that it's good to reflect and reempower your sacred space on a regular basis. Once a month, perhaps on the full moon, strengthen and evaluate your own work as part of "sacred living" for that month, noting what you are able to accomplish and where you are heading. You can rebless the space at this time as well.

The Home Shrine and Home Book
To conclude the opening of a sacred space in the home, I set up a small home shrine dedicated to this work. On this shrine, I placed a small book, and this book was essentially a scrapbook or day book. As I went through each of my days and made my shifts pertaining to my daily actions and life, I added thoughts, images, photographs, and more to the book. When people came over, they, too, added things to the book, and it allowed me to track my journey and remember many wonderful experiences during the shift to more-sacred living. This "home book" became a very magical part of my journey. You might try creating such a book to chronicle your own journey and to inspire you by seeing how far you've come.

CHAPTER 5

Summer Solstice

Food and Nourishment

A few years ago, I received invitations to two Thanksgiving dinners. One Thanksgiving dinner was hosted by a family of homesteaders who had raised and slaughtered their own turkey; the rest of the meal came from the gardens at their homestead. The second Thanksgiving dinner was no less expertly prepared, but all the ingredients had been purchased from a big-box store. Both cooks were skilled and considered good cooks by their families, but there was nothing the same about these two meals in terms of flavor, satiation, or energy. The flavor of the homesteader's meal was incredible—everything was colorful because of the beautiful seasonal vegetables, the turkey was tender and flavorful, and the fixin's were divine. The homesteaders' meal was satisfying, and I was full for hours, my energy levels were higher, and I felt really good after eating it. The homesteaders had a sacred relationship with their food—they treated it with respect, they talked about raising their turkey and that experience and about raising the veggies that were growing, and you had a real sense of the cycle of life present in their meal. Despite the tremendous skill of my second set of friends as cooks—one can work only with the materials available, and they had used typical grocery store ingredients. The biggest issue was energetic: the food did not have that same vitalizing quality. And if we think about the conditions under which this food was produced, this makes perfect sense. The turkey was raised in a factory farm, where it spent all of its short life suffering; the plants were genetically modified and growing only with aid of chemicals; all the food was shipped hundreds or thousands of miles away from where it grew and was handled by who knows how many people prior to it landing on our table. Certainly, we see here that the nourishment our bodies take has a direct impact on our physical, emotional, and spiritual energy and that this connection reflects on our spiritual paths.

This chapter gets at a practice so central to being human that we cannot exist without it—eating. Food is a critical piece of sacred action for one simple reason: everybody eats, and every person has the opportunity to change his or her relationship with food, even if that change is only energetic. My story of two Thanksgivings illustrates on multiple levels some of the challenges with our current food system. I'll start by examining some of these challenges to make the case that we can enter a sacred relationship with our food. Our triad that helps encapsulate this chapter is as follows:

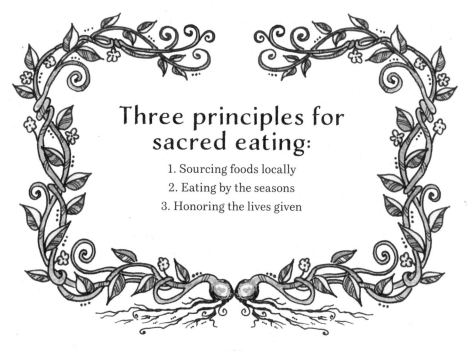

Three principles for sacred eating:

1. Sourcing foods locally
2. Eating by the seasons
3. Honoring the lives given

Our discussion of food comes around the time of the summer solstice, when seeds are planted, plants are beginning to mature, and the early harvests of the season are starting to be enjoyed. Plants take the light of the sun into their own bodies, and we take those plants into our bodies, and so the light of the sun drives all life. It is for this reason that the solstice, with its time of culinary abundance and radiant vitality, is a perfect time to consider the role of food in our lives.

On the Nature of Abundance and Scarcity

One of the most important lessons I've learned in the process of engaging in sacred action surrounding my food is the lesson of abundance and scarcity. Consumerist society, with its grocery stores full of perfectly chemical-ridden produce, is seasonless and contextless. In my lifetime, with the exception of a few extreme weather events where frantic people cleared the shelves, the grocery stores have always been abundant. Strawberries are always in season in my grocery store. I can pretty much have whatever I want, when I want it, and as much as I want, provided I can pay for it. And the food is contextless because I rarely know where it came from or who grew it—the system is designed to mask origins of food. When you always have access to something, such as strawberries, those things become commonplace, everyday, routine. The strawberry that is always available loses any sacredness it has—all you have to do is to go to the store and put a plastic container of strawberries in your cart. You aren't connected to the strawberry in any way: you didn't plant the plants, you didn't watch them flower, and you didn't pick them. Or, you didn't meet the person who grew your strawberry. The cost of the strawberry and the look of the strawberry are typically the only issues that matter at the grocery store—flavor, production ethics, or care is not part of the profit margin.

Never at any other time in human history have people been so disconnected from their food. Strawberries, and many other foods, always being abundant in the grocery store setting masks the circumstances in which they are produced, the manner of the production, and anything out of balance that might be problematic. The current conventional food system also disconnects us from the seasons and cycles of our landscapes, when strawberries aren't, in fact, abundant in December in most places. But the deepest problem is that we assume that the strawberry is always going to be there when we want it, and if it's not perfect, we can throw it away and get more because the cost to us is so minor. If food isn't valued or sacred, it ends up going to waste (and nearly 50% of the food in the US is wasted).[53] The strawberry isn't sacred; the act of eating and communing isn't a sacred act.

The simple strawberry also is hiding some dark secrets. Most of the food we eat today is the product of genetic manipulation (GMO). Many GMOs are bred to withstand chemicals, or to increase shelf life, or any other number of modifications—the long-term effects of which are still unknown and largely unresearched. GMO foods are literally changing the face of our world—and bee populations and many others in the ecosystem are suffering because of this. In addition, billions of tons of chemicals are dumped on GMO crops each year, which end up in streams, lakes, rivers, and eventually the oceans (where we have dead zones spanning hundreds and thousands of miles).[54] The ever-abundant strawberry is picked by immigrant and migrant farmworkers, who often work under terrible conditions and suffer routine exposure to chemicals that cause birth deformities, cancers, and more. And finally, there is the flavor and nutritional value of the strawberry itself. At one time, the strawberry may have been wholesome and delightful, but today, very little of what you buy really is nutrient dense (even vegetables themselves are much less flavorful and nutritious than those of fifty or a hundred years ago, due to current agricultural practices).[55] And, as is expected, that abundant, grocery store strawberry has very little strawberry flavor compared to a homegrown strawberry.

Permaculture's ethical triad further helps illustrate a food system where the only goal is profit and providing a false sense of abundance. In a food system emphasizing profit, care for people is not a concern: not the people producing the food, not the people living in areas where food is produced, not the people who are eating the food. Care for Earth, likewise, is not a goal of this food system. Whereas farmers of previous generations knew that to care for the soil was to care for oneself (as we explored with Wendell Berry's[56] concepts of nurturing and exploitation in chapter 1), today's farms farm primarily in soil with no web of life or any nutritional content. The lands are stripped in order to farm. Fair share, likewise, is not being enacted: the profits are concentrated at the top, and those producing the food often don't get a fair share, not to mention the serious problems with hunger and food waste in the current system.

Supermarket abundance is propped up by fossil fuels and industrial agriculture—things that are destroying our lands, poisoning our waterways, and poisoning our bodies. And understanding that the land, and our food, also has cycles is a critical distinction to make. Abundance in our immediate landscapes is different than perceived supermarket abundance. Abundance propped up by fossil fuels isn't sustainable in the long term because fossil fuels are limited. The land has limits. Supermarket abundance isn't real abundance.

What, then, does real abundance in the land look like? A few years ago, I had a prolific strawberry harvest out of my little strawberry spiral I planted in my Michigan homestead. The strawberries didn't do much their first or second years. Then, in their third year—magic happened. The strawberries crawled over the spiral stone path. Strawberries bloomed and burst forth with delicious fruit. These were the best strawberries I had ever eaten, the most incredible food I could ever have imagined. The work to put in the patch, and maintain it, was quite minimal, but the rewards were incredible. I harvested and canned almost 40 pounds in that third year, and then friends came over, harvested, and canned strawberries themselves. Other friends wanted strawberry plants, and the strawberries were so abundant that they took hundreds of plants without making a dent in my patch. Even when the little patch was covered in snow, I had jars and jars of strawberry jam, strawberry rhubarb jam, and strawberry vanilla jam. Years later, I am still enjoying those strawberries.

Because of this experience, I appreciate the abundance of the strawberry and recognize that it will once again be scarce. The strawberries taught me a true lesson of abundance, a powerful one, and I don't think I can ever look at a grocery store strawberry in quite the same way again. And now, I take some of those abundant strawberry plants with me and stick them into the ground in places, hoping that they'll take root and that someone else will benefit from the lessons they teach of abundance and scarcity.

The lesson of scarcity is a critical one, and one we've completely lost. In the foraging and organic-gardening world, scarcity is also what makes things special, magical, and full of value. It is scarcity that allows me to savor every bite of the strawberry jam I made, because my strawberries taste better than anything I could buy, but I have only a limited quantity.

I also recognize my position of privilege with regard to food and scarcity—if my crops fail, I can always find a farmer or go to the grocery store, because I have enough money to pay for food. Not so for many of our ancestors, or even for many on the margins in industrialized societies. Food scarcity is a lived experience of so many around the world, including plenty of people in industrialized nations. For those with privilege, it's possible they have never experienced scarcity once in their lives.

Scarcity teaches us about limitations, the ethic of fair share. Despite the way that humanity is acting toward this planet, it is finite, precious, limited, magical, valuable. When we understand the limitations and what scarcity does, it teaches us to be mindful and aware of what we take from the land in terms of food. Scarcity gives us a sense of appreciation for what we do have. If we can get into this mindset taught to us through the experience of scarcity, we can apply it broadly in our lives and understand that everything is precious, valued, magical.

If we can understand the nature of abundance and scarcity, these principles allow us to make better choices about all things, but especially about our food and where it comes from. We can live simply, better, within our limits, and more healthfully by learning these lessons. And that is of benefit to ourselves, our communities, and our world. Now let's move to the practical work in this chapter— developing a sacred relationship with food.

Energetic and Ethical Dimensions of Food

As my tale of two Thanksgivings and strawberry has illustrated, there is an energetic aspect to food. For many cultures, food was a sacred experience, an experience connecting humans to their land. The breaking of bread was a ritual and magical act, used often in ritual ways. Industrialization has taken this sacred relationship and reduced it to a matter of profit and efficiency, with what I consider to be disastrous magical consequences. When we eat food produced in a manner that causes suffering, we eat of all the energies that produced it. When we eat industrialized food, we are taking unknown energetics and processes into our own bodies. That food, if it comes from a big grocery chain, is likely hundreds if not thousands of miles removed from the land one inhabits, which creates energetic distance. Further, one's relationship with that food is often a constructed image, a brand-name product, and we are buying the brand rather than the nutritional content. The conditions under which the food was produced are, to me, the most serious energetic issue— if suffering took place in the production of that food, the food still holds that suffering, and whoever eats that food will be taking that suffering within. The sacred relationship with food is lost, and our sacred relationship with the land is weakened. Of course, this puts us in a conundrum, since so much of the food we may want to buy is inaccessible—but fear not, we'll work though these and many issues in this chapter.

To show the other side, we might again look to various traditional cultures from around the world and our own past. From the time the soil was prepared for the seed till the time of harvest, humans had a sacred relationship with their food. Sowing and harvest were marked with celebrations—and in many rural places, still are (around here, we have an abundance of pumpkin, maple, and peach festivals each year). These are some of the same celebrations that we celebrate as pagans, many centuries removed. Spiritual and religious practices surrounding food are often a big part of the religious life of a people. Offerings are made to trees or fields to ensure good harvests (such as the Wassail tradition for apple orchards); elaborate rituals are designed to bless the crops, the animals, and the land (Beltane) or celebrate the harvest (Lughnasadh). Spiritual practices surround the food: prayers are said before food is eaten; food is left as offerings for deities, spirits, and ancestors; families gather around the table for their meal as a daily ritual. Growing, honoring, and eating food is at the center of so much of human culture. The modern Wheel of the Year, which so many Earth-based spiritual traditions follow, is really a set of holidays devoted primarily to agricultural production. It wasn't till I started growing my own food that I really understood these holidays or their sacred relationship to food. This is why so many of our pagan holidays are agricultural: food is literally our embodied relationship with the living Earth.

In the remainder of this chapter, I'll examine some ways—beyond growing your own food, discussed in chapter 6—that we can work to cultivate a sacred relationship with our food and engage in sacred action. Given that not everyone is in a position to grow a good deal of their own food unless they have land and time, we can still cultivate sacred relationships through food in other ways and make sustaining choices, including selecting an ethical diet, purchasing food that was growing in a nurturing manner, honoring our food, and more.

Sacred and Social Diets

The politics of selecting a personal diet have been tenacious and challenging for as long as I can remember—now seemingly more than ever before as food is intimately tied to identity. There are so many diets that are promoted as the most ethical / best diet to eat. And many well-meaning people take on diets that restrict certain foods for health reasons, ethical reasons, or both. Unfortunately, many common dietary restrictions don't consider either the overall environmental ethics or the sustainability of the diet but instead focus on one or two glaring areas that their particular diet addresses (such as animal welfare or fat intake). I believe that if we are considering an ethics-based diet, the overall environmental impact of our diet and how sustainable that diet is in the long run should help guide our choices. We can again apply permaculture ethics to this problem.

Many diets that have removed animal products cite animal welfare concerns. And, certainly, animal welfare is a critical issue that we need to care about, with regard both to meat and dairy products. But placing concern only on animal welfare ignores a huge amount of other critical issues with our food system. We have issues with fossil fuel use, land use, poisoning of workers, the monopolization of seed crops, deforestation, agricultural runoff, genetically modified crops, pollinator abuse and die-off, the loss of genetic diversity, the destruction of the soil web of life, the loss of plant species, poisoning of community water supplies; the list goes on and on. In fact, the whole food system is rife with horrors and ethical violations; animal welfare is perhaps the most known and one of the more egregious, but it certainly isn't the only violation. Do we really want to eat another conventional tomato after learning how immigrant tomato workers in the US routinely have babies with fatal birth defects because of tomato pesticide exposure?[57] Can we feel good about your Earth Balance vegan spread when a main ingredient is palm oil, the production of which is directly responsible for hundreds of millions of acres of rainforest destruction?[58] How about the impact on childhood hunger that quinoa causes? Even the so-called "good guys" promoting ethical products are often not so great (as the battles in the US over GMO labeling laws have attested).[59] Further, many "ethical" diets are often based on exotic ingredients and don't frequently align with sustainable, seasonal, local eating patterns. In the end, even ethical diets have major challenges.

What I hope this is illustrating is that the problem with ethics is not just with any one part of the system (such as animal products); the problem is with the whole industrial food system. The entire system exploits and destroys. Whether it's a big, juicy steak or a big, juicy pineapple makes little difference: in both cases, lives have been lost, suffering has been caused, and we are meant to be kept in the dark about it. In the case of the conventional steak, the cow herself has suffered substantially. She was likely grazed on land that was once a forest (assuming she was able to graze at all). She was also fattened up with waste products from other parts of the system before her short life ended in a factory. Her entire life, from beginning to end, was filled with suffering and pain. In the case of the pineapple, it was likely grown on land that was once a rainforest full of abundance and life. To grow perfect pineapples, the soil is sterilized with chemical cocktails fourteen to sixteen different times for one season. The chemical mixes are carcinogenic, persistent in the soil, and frequently banned in other countries—these chemicals poison local aquifers, streams, and groundwater, killing off fish and wildlife. Humans, too, suffer when pineapples are grown. The pollution is so bad in parts of Costa Rica that villages near pineapple plantations[60] cannot drink or use any groundwater and instead have their water shipped in on trucks. When the imported water is scarce, the villagers are forced to use contaminated groundwater, leading to a host of chronic illnesses and childhood suffering. The workers on the plantations work twelve-hour piecemeal jobs and are purposefully kept in poverty. In visiting Costa Rica, I spoke with a man who lived in one of these villages. He told me that he became a tour guide to avoid what was happening in his home village.

What the story of the steak and the pineapple illustrates is that any diets dependent on the industrial food system are full of hidden ethical challenges that are not in line with Earth care, people care, or fair share. Rather, these diets are about marketing, meant to define a particular consumer base and then sell a set of products to that consumer base. It is a systematic problem and a problem on every level of production for nearly every different food produced.

Can we have diets that embrace people care, in terms of nutrients, those who produce the food, those who prepare/distribute the food, and those who eat the food? Can we have diets that embrace Earth care, including animal welfare, as well as agricultural practices that restore and regenerate the land rather than degrade it? And can we think about food that encourages a fair share, where 50% of the food we grow isn't wasted—where only what we need is grown, where we preserve ecosystems and still can obtain a yield, and where all who need to eat have what they need? I think we can, and there are both short-term and long-term ways to get there.

Local, Sustainable, and Seasonal Diets

To think about how we can eat more sustainably, we can look to our ancestors and the past for guidance. All of our ancestors ate locally, and seasonally, on the basis of what they could grow, raise, catch, forage, or hunt. While diets varied considerably between groups and regions, there is still a great deal of consistency in how food was produced and where it came from. Human ancestors used hunting/gathering, agriculture, animal husbandry, or some combination of these as primary methods of food procurement. In temperate climates, many preserved the harvest to survive the winter, especially the "hunger months" just before spring, when many of the root cellars and cupboards were close to bare. They also engaged in bartering and trading locally, regionally, and globally. Since ancient times, exotic foods and spices brought on ships or caravans from faraway countries were available to at least wealthier parts of the population in many parts of the world. It's not that exotic foods weren't available—it's that they were scarce and therefore, I'll argue, sacred.

I'd like to offer an alternative for those who are concerned with the ethics of eating, of applying the ethical triad to our plates, and those who want to engage in sacred action: a locavore diet. Rooted in the practices of our not-so-distant ancestors, a locavore is someone who focuses on local, sustainable eating and who supports local growers as they are able or provides some of his or her food directly. The locavore diet is a seasonal diet that changes as availability of food changes, with the goal being to minimize the distance from food to plate, and eating what is growing at the moment. It encourages building relationships with local food producers and farmers, as well as taking on some of the responsibility of producing food yourself, even in minor ways. It tries to source as much as possible from as close as possible, to reduce reliance on fossil fuels. Some locavore diets include animal products, although, in line with sustainable practices, when they are consumed they are consumed in limited quantities and raised/purchased from ethical farmers. Other locavores choose not to consume animal products and eat only vegetarian or vegan. Locavorism takes on different forms depending on your location: for example, I purchase as much as I can from within 100 miles or less—this is based on what is grown where in my geographical region. I also make sure I am eating non-GMO, organic produce as often as I can afford to do so. I select food that is as close to its natural, unaltered state as possible (e.g., fresh vegetables). I purchase a lot of food in-season and use traditional storage methods (canning, root cellaring) to extend the harvest.

I've seen several arguments against locavorism made, one of the key being that in order to feed the whole world, we need industrialized agriculture. However, a report from the United Nations titled *Wake Up before Its Too Late* from 2013[61] surveys the food and climate crises side by side and provides evidence that the only way to address both food and climate is to transition away from industrialized agriculture into "mosaics of sustainable, regenerative production systems" that include livestock, agroforestry, composting, climate-friendly food distribution, soil ecology, and sustainable farming practices. If this model is going to be adapted, we need to create economic demand for many more farms that are embracing this model, which is one of the benefits that a locally based diet provides.

Finally, I see locavorism as a critical part of my sacred action and Earth-based spiritual practice in the sense that this diet brings me closer to the seasons, aligning with the energies of my landscape and the foods that grow where I live. I enjoy fresh foods when they are in season, and enjoy dried, canned, and stored foods in the winter months, making all foods more sacred. I really feel that this diet helps me establish a deeper spiritual awareness of the turning Wheel of the Year, because I begin paying attention to what is growing when.

Principles for Local Eating

The following is a list of suggestions for how to make a transition to more-local eating, rooted in the ethics that help frame this book. It's important to understand that our eating and food choices are part of our lifestyle, so we transition our lifestyle while also transitioning our eating.

See what is already easily accessible and available. Start by seeing what you can easily and readily access nearby, so that local foods can be easily and readily built into your life patterns. Do you have access to a CSA (community-supported agriculture) share? Good farmers' markets? Local farmers who sell produce from their land? Friends who garden and need some help?

Identify challenges: You also want to identify any challenges you have: time, a limited budget, harsh winters with no fresh veggies, no good growing space, lack of local farmers, and so on. Start by mapping out resources and challenges so that you can begin to move forward.

Educate yourself about food: As you are staring to formulate your plan for transitioning to more-local eating, you will want to spend a lot of time educating yourself about food. You might do some reading on what is in-season for your region, as well as how various foods are produced and what can be grown locally. A local diet can be extended by learning various preservation methods: canning, root cellaring, dehydrating, fermenting, smoking, brewing, and more. Some of these methods will be discussed later in this chapter.

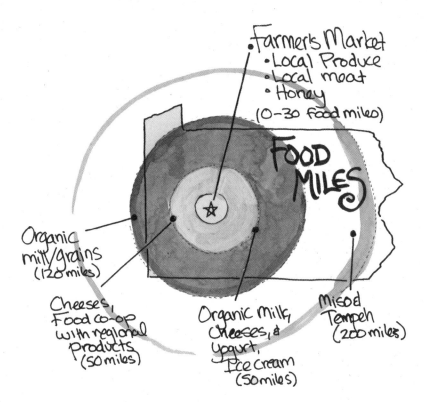

Observe your current practices: Applying principles from permaculture, you can observe and evaluate your (and your family's) eating habits. Keep track of the things you buy and consume most often—and how much. This will allow you to formulate a plan that targets certain kinds of foods. For example, I realized that I eat a lot of tomato products, so I began growing as many of my own as possible and buying tomatoes in season in bulk from farmers. Then I canned them for year-round use. I also ate a lot of cereal products, so I worked to find alternatives (such as getting local oats and making my own granola with berries).

Create a plan: Having a plan in mind is good to set goals and to think about your targets. In making the transition to local foods, you are making a pretty substantial lifestyle change, and this change takes time and patience to enact. You may also have to deal with family members who aren't as committed to the change as you are, and find good alternatives that satisfy even the pickiest eaters.

Target easily accessible local food: Obviously, you want to make obtaining local food as easy as possible—as easy as a trip to the grocery store. Why? This will help you sustain your shifts in eating, especially as life gets busy or unexpected. My first big shift was seeking out any easily accessible sources of local food. I rejoiced when I found a year-round collective of farmers that offered online ordering and weekly drop-offs just 5 miles down the road. These farmers carried veggies, fruits, locally grown and milled flour, cheese, vinegar, eggs, teas, local meats, herbal remedies, garden supplies, and assorted other wonderful things—and in the five years I ordered from them, their inventory grew from fewer than a hundred options to over five hundred! The online local market combined with our seasonal farmers' market (and my own reduction of food waste, to account for my increase in food cost) immediately allowed me to shift close to 40% of my eating year-round.

Identify weak areas: Snacks and convenience foods are rarely local (although there are exceptions), and so you'll really have to think about how to address snacking. The good news was that in this process, you can cut out a lot of the junk food. I usually, now, snack on local popcorn (some of which I grow myself and some of which is grown nearby), homemade kale chips with a really good dressing, or dehydrated or fresh fruits and veggies.

Slow solutions: Mountains are not climbed in a day, nor will you make the transition to local foods in one day. Be realistic with your goals, and remember that a small, lasting change is almost always better than a drastic fast change that you are unable to continue. Each year, I take on a "project" that assists me in making the transition. These projects help my local eating and lifestyle changes "stick" long term. "Tomato independence," learning to can, root cellaring, and so on all were yearly projects I undertook.

Make it enjoyable: We all have our favorite foods, and one of the challenges in making the transition to local eating, especially with children or picky family members, is making sure that the favorites are still accessible, perhaps with a local twist. Local eating does require more preparation and foresight. Often, working with locally available ingredients means learning new recipes, expanding one's horizons, and thinking creatively. Old recipe books can be a wealth of information— in my area, I look for Mennonite cookbooks and older cookbooks from thrift stores, and many contain high-quality recipes that use ingredients that can be found locally or are part of "from scratch" cooking. Other cultures may also serve as inspiration: I grew sick of vegetable soup and decided I would try to make some recipes from India. One of my very favorites was palak (or saag) paneer—imagine my surprise when I learned I could make it all locally (except for some of the spices and oil). I make the paneer fresh from local milk, and I use tomatoes I canned myself along with onions from the root cellar and fresh spinach (or spinach frozen from the garden) or even stinging nettle in place of spinach. Delicious!

Declare independence: Another big shift for me was targeting a particular food and declaring independence. After observing my eating habits and recognizing how many tomatoes I consumed, in my first summer of local eating I aimed to be 100% tomato independent. This meant that in August and September, I spent time canning and drying tomatoes (which is really an enjoyable way to pass an afternoon). I am pleased to say that since declaring tomato independence all those years ago, to this day, almost all of the tomatoes I have consumed at home have come either from my garden or from local farmers and all were consumed or preserved in season. The flavor is so amazing!

Affordability

One of the big challenges of local eating is that it can be more expensive at first glance. But when we dig into the issue, many ways exist of making it much more affordable. Industrialized agriculture in the US, particularly corn and soy, are highly subsidized, artificially lowering the price of many foods. Convenience foods and fast foods which containing practically no nutritional content are extremely low priced but still high profit for the producers. When you purchase food from a local farmer or producer, you aren't benefiting from those subsidies. You are also paying your farmer a living wage, as opposed to an illegally low wage, and this also is part of the cost. Given these circumstances, local food can cost a lot more—especially meat. A huge part of the challenge in making the shift to local eating is how to make it affordable. One way of thinking about the issue is that you are eating healthier, which saves long-term healthcare costs. But even so, the cost can still be prohibitive. I've found ways of making local eating much more affordable, which we will explore in the next paragraphs.

Eliminate food waste. Industrialized nations waste anywhere from 30–50% of food that is grown. A typical statistic for a household is 30–40%—that's 30–40% of what you have purchased that ends up in the compost bin. It used to be that I would go to a farmer's market or grocery store and purchase whatever I felt I wanted to eat on a whim. Now, I go in with a meal plan—I know what I want and how much of it I want to purchase, because I know what I'm planning on making that week. Further, I have developed lists of all of the food in my house and the dates I need to use it by—including my canned goods, freezer goods, dry goods, and more. This allows me to quickly survey what I might need to use up or what I already have, avoiding unnecessary purchases. While working to eliminate food waste requires a bit more forethought, it can go a long way to making local eating more affordable. I actually think the higher cost of the local foods (or the amount of work involved in preparation) is actually a good thing in one sense because it asks us to use the food carefully and not waste any of it. This gives us a better sense of the sacred with our food.

In-season bulk purchasing and processing. The first thing I do is work with my local farmers to buy their produce in bulk. I ask to purchase beans, tomatoes, or cucumbers in bulk and then spend that day or the next day canning, freezing, or drying those vegetables, especially in August and September. Some farmers will sell you what's left at the end of the day. Others will not—but nearly all will allow you to make a bulk purchase when requested in advance (by the bushel or half bushel; a bushel of tomatoes is about 55 pounds worth). Tell them you are willing to take food that may be odd shaped, have a little damage, or otherwise be less than perfect for selling (farmers call this "farmer food" and are often delighted to sell this at a discount). This actually is much cheaper in the end than grocery store purchases. If I pay $25 for a bushel of organic tomatoes, I can make 12–15 pints of soup and 12–15 pints of sauce, plus dried tomatoes, all from that bushel. Compare this to a $5 jar of organic sauce in the grocery store or $2.99 for three organic tomatoes! This bulk buying ends up being not only more cost effective but also more healthful because I can control exactly what goes into sauce.

Eat more vegetables and grains: Meat and dairy are much more expensive on this diet; there is no getting around that. However, this gives a wonderful opportunity to eat lots of healthful vegetables, fruits, and grain. And when they are in season, they are abundant and quite cheap or free from your garden. See "bulk food buying" in the next section for more information.

Buy meat or meat substitutes in bulk: If you eat meat, consider purchasing meat in bulk rather than by the pound. This will require you to have a dedicated freezer for such a purchase. While the going rate of many meats (such as sausage, hamburger, ham hocks, bacon, and so on) range upward of $8–$10 per pound for locally produced free-range organic, I can purchase half a pig or a quarter of a cow at only $3.00 per pound. This bulk purchase assumes that you eat enough meat for this to be worth it. Still, the option is very economical if you eat meat.

Learn to use different cuts of meat and stretch meat further. A lot of meat that is considered subprime can be had at a bargain. For example, farmers sometimes sell stewing hens at a quarter of the price of their regular chickens for sale. Why? The stewing hen was a laying hen for many years, and so she is a bit tough, requiring extra cooking time. I purchase stewing hens (who have had long, healthy lives) and then pressure-can them in the following way: Put the stewing hen in a crock pot with a tablespoon of vinegar, herbs, celery, onion, and carrot and let cook for at least eight to ten hours till the meat is falling off the bone. Remove the meat and broth and strain the veggies. Put the carcass back into the crock pot and add fresh veggies and other nutrient-dense wild foods (such as nettle, hen-of-the-woods mushrooms, and burdock), cooking for another eight hours. Strain a second time. Combine the broth and the meat and pressure-can at 15 pounds per square inch (psi) for seventy-five minutes for pints. This method often yields 5 pints of broth and another 5 pints of meat and broth—that's material for ten meals out of one stewing hen! Other kinds of meat work in the same way. Bones or even chicken feet are cheap for broth, and a good broth with fresh veggies or rice is super satisfying. Occasionally, I will go for the more expensive cuts of meat, and then my goal is to stretch them to as many meals as possible. Just like with everything else, the more that we can conserve, the better off we are.

Go foraging, fishing, or hunting: Another way this diet can be more affordable and enjoyable is to go foraging, fishing, or hunting. Once you start gathering free, abundant food, it is hard to return to the supermarket. One particularly abundant summer, a friend and I gathered almost 75 pounds of berries—I canned them all and, years later, am still enjoying the fruits of my labor. In another summer, I found incredibly abundant wild mushrooms that ended up in many of my meals—and in my freezer.

Ecosystems and Food Purchases

Obviously, you can't purchase all the food you want to eat locally. But you can choose to purchase foods that support healthy and diverse ecosystems and that treat their workers with respect. I think this is another facet to sacred eating—when we are consumers, we should be critical consumers and make ethical choices.

One of the things I like to do is purchase foods that require a diverse ecosystem to grow. Chocolate requires a diverse ecosystem for growth and pollination, and eating chocolate supports healthy ecosystems. If it is grown organically and fair trade, all the better! Other foods that fit in this list include coffee, oils, tea, sugars/sweeteners, produce, and certain herbs/spices.

I also work to carefully purchase foods that are based in new agroforestry models rather than those that are monocropped. Nuts are a great example of this—some require diverse ecosystems. New farms based in perennial agriculture and soil regeneration, such as Mark Sheppard's farm discussed in *Restoration Agriculture*,[62] offer a wide range of crops that are grown in a healthy ecosystem. This is a model that uses perennial tree, fruit, and alley crops combined with rotating pasture for various animals (producing hazelnuts, acorns, berries, vegetables, honey, and free-range meats from one ecosystem). Given the potential of such regenerative systems, I would purchase hazelnuts or walnuts over almonds (which are sprayed and monocropped).

Finally, I also consider where I shop. Even if I end up buying something I need that isn't made locally, at least I can purchase my food from companies and businesses that are either locally owned or treat their employees with respect and pay a living wage. This gets into the people-care part of the ethical triad.

All the suggestions I have been making take extra work to research and learn about what foods are produced and how, but this sacred action can be part of our spiritual practice. This work results in better decisions about our food, supporting better companies and practices and creating a better world. This also puts you in a much-better relationship with your food from a sacred perspective.

Bulk and Abundant Foods: The Root Cellar and Pantry

In addition to the skills and suggestions above to help make local foods go further and to buy nonlocal foods ethically, one of my absolute staples for local and sustainable eating is establishing and using a pantry and a root cellar. Root cellaring and pantry establishment are skills largely forgotten. A pantry is a place where we can store bulk dry goods and canned goods. In the earlier part of the twentieth century and in earlier centuries, all households had such pantries. The larder is a cool place to keep dairy and other perishable goods (modern refrigeration handles most of what was once in a larder). A root cellar is a cool, damp place for storing root vegetables, ferments, and home brews. While you may not be lucky enough to have all three kinds of spaces in a more modern home, a cool basement or unheated room in the winter offers root cellar possibilities. A nook tucked under the stairs or a closet in the back of a kitchen is a good place for a pantry. Even a bucket buried in the backyard can function as a root cellar.

Partially, I use a root cellar and a pantry because doing so is another way to cut costs with a local diet—buying dried goods in bulk is more economical. So even if we are purchasing more-expensive fruits, vegetables, meats, cheeses, and dairy, if we are buying the other goods in bulk, we are finding ways to save. Furthermore, a pantry and root cellar can help us store things away when they are abundant for when things are scarce—this allows us to live and eat closer to the seasons and live more sustainably.

The other reason that establishing a pantry is important is because of food security. Having food security means that we have enough food tucked away to be secure against any short-term or long-term disruptions in the typical food distribution system. People both in industrialized and nonindustrialized nations face food insecurity. The symptoms of it are clear—anytime in my area when we

Bury bucket in a north-facing hill

5 Gallon Bucket FOOD GRADE

Strawbale for insulation

Store root vegetables without washing them

Holes for moisture & temperature regulation

Root Cellar Barrel

have a major snowstorm or other forecasted major weather event, the grocery store shelves go bare. Why? Because few people have enough food in their houses for any long-term disruption; in fact, few people have enough food in their houses to eat a balanced diet for more than a week or two. This doesn't mean stockpiling five years of food, but it does mean buying in bulk and having enough food for a few months. If you lose your job and find yourself without enough money to buy food, if a natural disaster or snowstorm strikes, or if we have disruption in the food distribution system resulting in empty grocery store shelves, establishing a pantry and root cellar means you will have literally months of food tucked away in the pantry and root cellar. You will likely have enough not only for yourself, but for some friends and neighbors if things get rough. And that, my dear readers, offers some serious peace of mind.

So where do we begin in establishing a pantry and root cellar? Let's look at what they might contain. A modern pantry would certainly be based on what you and your family actually eat. It might contain the following:

- Rice
- Flour(s)
- Noodles
- Dried beans
- Nuts/seeds
- Sources for micronutrients (such as kelp meal, seaweed, dried stinging nettle)
- Dried fruits
- Dried vegetables (tomatoes, corn, carrots, onions)
- Dried mushrooms
- Commercially canned goods
- Home-canned goods
- Dried milk
- Other baking goods
- Extra food for companion animals (wet or dry)

Likewise, a modern root cellar might contain these:

- Potatoes
- Onions
- Carrots
- Apples or pears (don't store the apples too close to the potatoes)
- Winter squash (butternut, acorn, etc.)
- Other root vegetables (turnips, radish)
- Pumpkins
- Ferments (sauerkraut, miso)
- Home brews (dandelion wine, elderberry wine, hard cider, etc.)
- Garlic
- Wild-foraged root foods, such as burdock

Stocking your pantry and root cellar and learning how to eat from it requires paying attention to the timing—and it will take a few years to get it right and learn what can be stored and how long it can be stored for. As I mentioned above, having a full list of what is in the pantry or root cellar and when you placed it in there will ensure that everything gets eaten and not wasted. If you do decide to stock up, always make sure to eat the oldest food first—a new bag of rice goes behind the old bag of rice, and so on.

Stocking Your Root Cellar

Obviously, if you have your own garden, this is the first place to go to stock your root cellar. You can plant "keeper" varieties that are good for long-term storage (look for these in heirloom seed catalogs—either they will be called "keeper" in the name, or the description will list them as "keeper" or "storage" varieties). But with or without a garden, you'll find that you will likely need to supplement your root cellar stores.

Here are a few of my methods for building up the stores in my root cellar. A local farmer will sell you food at a discount when it's in abundance (especially if you ask about slightly blemished "farmer food"). Each year, I'm able to purchase about 75 pounds of potatoes and 50 pounds of onions by using this method—and these last me well into the winter, happily tucked away in my root cellar. In the fall, farmers sell winter squash and pumpkins quite cheap, and you can stock your root cellar with these delightful treats that store for up to six months. Then you can sit back and enjoy the winter snows with wonderful soups of squash and potato, all sourced locally, long after the farmers' market ends!

In the fall, go out in search of free apples, pears, and nuts. Most people who have fruit trees in their yards simply let the fruit fall on the ground and see it as a nuisance; ask them if you can pick their fruit, and perhaps even bribe them with a jar of homemade jam or preserves. Once you've established these relationships, you can come back each year and pick their apples and pears and have a store of lovely fruit through the winter. You can also look in parks and other wild areas for apple and pear trees—they are quite abundant in some parts. In addition, if you get enough of either, you can make hard apple cider or perry (a pear-based hard cider). Nuts, likewise, can be abundant if you know where to look: hickory, walnut, acorns, hazelnuts, and more! Hardwood nut trees typically produce a bumper crop every three or so years. At my university where I worked in Michigan, we had huge apple orchards with dozens of trees. After work, I'd head over to the orchard, check on the apples, and pick them in abundance when they were ripe. Many of these I'd turn into cider, applesauce, apple pie filling, and apple chips, but others I would simply tuck away in my root cellar room for eating during the late fall and winter months.

Storage in Your Root Cellar

Root cellar storage is an art in and of itself. One key is knowing which foods cause other foods to spoil. For example, apples and potatoes are incompatible and shouldn't be stored together; apples produce a gas that makes potatoes go bad faster. Another key is knowing how and when to store your foods—the saying that one bad apple ruins the whole bunch refers to the fact that if you just stack your apples up and one underneath is going rotten, it can make the whole basket go rotten. I have found that in storing any foods, I want to have them on shelves where I can clearly see them and monitor them every time I'm in the root cellar. In the same way, knowing when to store things is important. For example, potatoes should die back before you dig them up for storage (when they die back, the skins toughen a bit); garlic should be hardened off in the sun for a few days to help it form an outer layer that will hold in the moisture, and various roots can be stored in sand or wrapped in newspapers. For more details, I refer to Mike and Nancy Bubel's *Root Cellaring: Natural Cold Storage of Fruits and Vegetables*[63] for complete lists of how to prepare and store foods.

Stocking Your Pantry

Pantry buying is usually only partially local or regional, depending on where you live. If you have access to any pantry foods, such as dried beans or a local mill, obviously you will want to start there. For the rest, you will want to seek out a traditional bulk food store and make it a point to visit this store a few times a year. This bulk food store is very different than a Sam's Club or Costco—I'm talking about a store that sells bulk dry goods, doesn't require a membership, and can get you bulk goods at a steep discount. In both Michigan and Pennsylvania, where I've lived, these kinds of stores were run by members of the Mennonite community, and both were kind of out in the middle-of- nowhere farm country. Once you've found your bulk food store, you can stock up on whatever you want in great quantity. I really enjoy a particular brand of organic short-grain rice grown in the US—it costs almost $4 per pound at regular stores, but I can purchase 25-pound bags of it for $1.68 per pound, and 25 pounds of it lasts me a full year.

All this excitement can lead you on a buying spree, but I want to stress that you should buy only foods you actually eat in bulk. I got a bit excited the last time we went to a bulk food store and purchased 50 pounds of black beans, only to discover that there was no way I could consume that many. My chickens ended up helping me enjoy the beans!

Storage in Your Pantry

The other thing to be aware of with this approach is the art of storing bulk foods properly and rotating your stores. To store bulk foods, I turn to a few methods. First, I purchase food-safe 5-gallon buckets: these store my white rice and many smaller packages of dry goods. Second, I purchase half-gallon and quart mason jars (also at that bulk food store): these are great for dried beans, dried corn and other dried vegetables, and even bulk flours. Some rice and flours (unrefined, brown) can go rancid over time due to the husks, so I store excess in a freezer or even a refrigerator, where it will keep for much longer. Once I have my food stored, I put a label on it that includes a date. If I purchase more food before the original food is used up, I make it a point to rotate the original stuff to the front and use that first. I like to keep my rice in the bucket; when adding new, I will pour the old into another container. Then I pour the new rice into the bucket and top it off with the old so that the oldest is used up first. These processes are all quite simple, yet effective for long-term storage.

Cooking from Your Root Cellar or Pantry

Unsurprisingly, like many other sustainable things you can do, cooking using dried goods and bulk goods requires a bit of shifting of recipes and mindsets. Many of us no longer know how to cook using the dried ingredients of old—for example, most of us learned to cook beans that were in a can rather than dried (dried beans require a soak and a much-longer cooking time). Many of us don't how to cook a lot of things from scratch. Part of the fun in shifting to more-local foods is working with a more limited palate of ingredients—and seeing how many interesting things you can make! It reminds me of my work as an artist—sometimes my favorite paintings are those with only three colors. Local food and bulk food work in much the same way: we may have fewer ingredients, but they are higher quality and can lead to a lot of really interesting dishes. As I mentioned earlier, older cookbooks and recipes, including those from previous centuries, assumed that you were cooking under certain kinds of conditions and that you always had an ample supply of certain ingredients. You'll also start to notice when cooking seasonally that certain ingredients are often paired because they are in season together (such as strawberry rhubarb pie or tomato basil sauce). I would highly recommend older editions (pre-1950) of *The Joy of Cooking* to get you started; this book offers great advice for cooking with basic ingredients as well as basic instructions in how to prepare foods for cooking.

Food Availability

Other than affordability, the other big challenge with eating locally and organically is availability. It's usually easy to find organic and local food in cities, which function like hubs for surrounding farms. But out in the small towns and rural areas (where land is plentiful), these kinds of foods can be much harder to find. For example, after moving to rural Pennsylvania, I went to two different grocery stores—a locally owned grocery store and then to a regional chain store. The locally owned store carried nothing organic at all in the fresh-vegetables section and very limited organics anywhere else in the store and no local produce. The regional chain had some organic food (much less than I was used to for a store of that size in Michigan), and it was all 25%–50% more expensive than I was used to paying in a larger, more expensive metro area. This was surprising to me, because normally everything there typically ran about 30% cheaper. Because many people in rural areas are on a very limited income, most people in the area couldn't afford the organic. This means there is less demand, and that keeps the prices high and the stock older and less fresh. The solution to the food availability issue is to keep our eyes open for new farmers and opportunities and support them—and to consider growing some ourselves.

Developing Seasonal Food Rituals and Honoring Food

So far in this chapter we've explored where we source our food and how selecting better sources can lead to sacred action. But even if we have less access to better food (such as being in a rural area, being financially unable, or renting and not being able to grow our own), we can still honor the food and the lives that have been given. The last few generations of those in Western societies have typically not lived in a situation where we have any knowledge or ability to physically provide any of our own food. This means we are dependent on a system that has prevented us from engaging in a critical part of our human heritage—developing a sacred relationship with food. Developing spiritual practices surrounding food can be enacted by everyone, even if you are not able to grow your own, obtain local food, or eat seasonally.

Everyday Prayer and Energy Blessings for Food

The tradition of praying over food is used in many religious traditions, and it certainly has a welcome place within Earth-based pagan traditions. Part of this is an act of gratitude, and part is an act of acknowledgment and connection. Prayers don't have to be complex, but taking a moment to honor our food acknowledges the life that was taken (either plant or animal) to eat that meal. I also think that simple prayers can offset the problematic energetics that accompany industrialized foods. Here are two simple prayers that I use to honor the food. This first prayer I wrote to connect to the elements as well as honor those who helped the meal come to be:

With the blessing of the Earth,
I honor the lands that sustained this meal.

With the blessing of the air,
I honor the hands that prepared this meal.

With the blessing of fire,
I honor the labor that produced this meal.

With the blessing of water,
I honor the lives that were given for this meal.

With the blessing of spirit,
I wish a safe journey to those who now move on.

In gratitude, love, and peace,
I recognize that all are part of the great web of life.

Another simple prayer was taught to me by Deanne Bednar, who runs Strawbale Studio, a sustainable-living center I described in chapter 4. She has people of many faiths and traditions visit each month for full-moon potlucks, and began doing a simple physical-energy blessing. Since nothing is said during this prayer, it's very appropriate for mixed groups.

Start by rubbing your hands together, generating heat and friction. After a few moments, when you feel your hands tingling, place your hands over the food and send the positive energy that you raised into the food. Then, move your hands outward to face any others in the room, sending positive energy in their direction. Finally, sweep your hands above your head and circle them down to the Earth below to bless the land and all its inhabitants.

Blessings for the Land That Produces Food

Even if we can't always eat in line with our principles, we can energetically lend our support. I think there are many places we can draw upon for inspiration to engage in land blessings—and blessing the land that provides our food is a way of honoring that food and that land, and bringing in a sacred awareness of our dependence on the soil, sunlight, rain, microbial life, plants, bees, and so much more. We can draw upon these ancient traditions of food-producing cultures for inspiration and even begin to enact them again ourselves and in our communities.

One traditional blessing ceremony associated with food harvests is a wassail. The basic wassail ceremony is quite simple (and many versions exist). Wassail derives from the Old English "waes hael," literally meaning "to be healthy." It refers both to a drink of mulled cider and the actual tree blessing, meant to keep evil spirits out of the orchard and ensure a good apple harvest. It takes place on the old twelfth night, which is January 17. Like many ancient traditions, wassailing recognizes the important, symbiotic relationship of humankind to nature. As a tree blessing, this tradition allows us, as humans, to express our appreciation for the fruits of the harvest and also our role in the physical and spiritual care of our trees and agricultural lands. Wassailing also recognizes that the physical realm and spiritual realms interact, and that we need them. See the "Exercises and Rituals" section in this chapter for a complete wassail ritual.

Many traditions had blessings specific to tree crops and harvests. For example, Native Americans blessed maple trees in the late winter before the sap ran to ensure a good maple sap harvest. Given that maple sap was one of their only sources of sugar, it was a critical harvest! In the United Kingdom and later the United States, wassail traditions were used to bless apple orchards; apple was a critical crop for both food and drink.

We can also create simple new traditions that honor the land and—by extension—the food we eat. An example of a very simple ceremony is putting out home-cooked food for the land as an offering. I like to put out home brew (wine or cider) with cakes that I bake especially for the ceremony. This can be done at any point, although you could time it astrologically to make an offering on the full moon (or another auspicious harvest day—any old *Farmers' Almanac* will provide all such days for the year). I like to make regular offerings in this way. Dancing and erecting a maypole are also wonderful ways of bringing fertility to the surrounding land!

Truthfully, whether or not you draw upon an ancient tradition such as the wassail or something right out of your head is not important. The important thing is to honor the land from which all of our food flows. I think we have a great opportunity to spread "Oak knowledge" by offering such blessings of the land and inviting others to do the same. The land today often gets no such honor. Through these kinds of celebrations, we can shift our consciousness and recognize the importance of maintaining a physical and spiritual connection with the natural world upon which our food systems and lives are based.

Ritual Feasts and Dinners

Feasting and partaking in sacred rituals surrounding food goes back before recorded human history. In the US, Thanksgiving is our traditional ritual feast, honoring our history and seeking to be thankful for what blessings we have been given. It's unsurprising that in this massive age of consumerism, the emphasis on gratitude and partaking a traditional, seasonal meal has been subsumed in the consumerist hysteria of Black Friday.

Given this, we can again draw upon ancient traditions or create our own traditions and rituals surrounding food. For me, at least once a year, I like to hold a ritual dinner, honoring my food, eating in silence, and simply being with it. This is usually done by cooking one of my last harvests of the year, right before I pull out the main part of my garden. I cook all my food from the garden, say prayers, make offerings, and generally just be thankful for the food and my opportunity to develop a relationship with it.

Another kind of ritual dinner that my druid grove has done on occasion is for Samhain, where we create a feast for the dead by using seasonal and local ingredients. We eat in ritual silence, making plates for ourselves and for our ancestors, and focus on eating the food and reminiscing. This is a traditional "dumb supper" that has been used in many traditions throughout the ages.

A friend of mine holds monthly "full-moon potlucks" at her sustainable-living center. These potlucks have no overt spiritual significance but are simply a time for the community to come together, break bread, and engage in conversation and connection.

Exercises and Rituals

Shifting Food Choices

Choose just one food that you eat frequently and that you would consider a staple food in your house. Research that food, how it is produced, and who is doing the producing. On the basis of this information, make a commitment to change one thing: growing it yourself, buying organic rather than conventional, buying local rather than conventional, learning how to preserve it, etc.

Sacred Recipes

For any seasonal celebration, starting with the summer solstice, create a locally based set of recipes based on what is in season in your area. Note that you might not have to look far, since many traditional recipes for holidays already connect. Cranberry sauce and turkey and potatoes all are in season in many parts of the US at Thanksgiving. These recipes can be tied to the eightfold Wheel of the Year or other kinds of celebrations. For example, a very traditional New Year's Day feast includes ham hocks and black-eyed peas (both of which would have been available during the winter in earlier points in history). You might also consider developing recipes for each full moon. See Jessica Prentice's *Full Moon Feast: Food and the Hunger Connection*[64] for inspiration and a series of recipes based on the phases of the moon.

Tomato Independence

One of the ways to shift into more-local eating is to try to shift one food at a time. As I mentioned above, for me it was tomatoes and tomato products. I decided I was not going to purchase any store-bought tomatoes again, and instead to focus on eating them fresh when I could grow them or buy them from local farmers, and to buy in bulk and seasonally and preserve them. I remember the year I declared tomato independence—it was such a triumph! So I'd suggest trying the same—find one food that you eat fairly regularly that you can shift into local eating or growing yourself—create a plan and declare independence!

Mindful Eating

A spiritual practice that comes out of Buddhism is the practice of mindful eating. The principle is simple: very often we live in our heads, rushing through our meals and not savoring our food. Mindfulness, as a general practice, asks us to live in the present moment and experience it fully. In mindful eating, you slow down, focus on your breath, and take a bite of the food. Put your utensil down and then focus on the taste and texture of the food, chewing slowly and savoring it. Don't do anything else while you are enjoying your food in this way. Even designating one meal a week as a mindfulness meal is a very helpful activity.

Traditional Wassail Ceremony

As mentioned above, the traditional wassail ceremony is performed in an apple orchard on January 17. Prior to the ceremony, a "king" and "queen" are chosen to make offerings. Needed supplies include mulled hot cider with mugs for all participants (cider is typically of the alcoholic variety), two pieces of toast, drums, or noisemakers.

To perform the ceremony, one tree is selected for the blessing; this tree receives the blessing, which is then radiated outward to the whole orchard. The ceremony varies considerably from region to region. A variant that a group of us used is as follows:

The participants gather around the main apple tree, each with a cup of steaming, mulled cider.

The "king" of the ceremony holds out a cup of cider while the "queen" dips two pieces of toasted bread. The queen then hangs the toasted bread on two branches of the tree as an offering.

Everyone then drinks the cider, and each participant pours a little on the tree's trunk and around its roots.

Participants bow three times, like they were picking up bushels of apples, hailing the tree.

Participants sing a wassail song (many varieties exist; here's one traditional song):

Apple tree, apple tree, we all come to wassail thee

Bear this year and next year to bloom
and to blow

Hat fulls, cap fulls, three-cornered sack fulls

Hip, hip, hip, hurrah! Holler bys, holler hurrah.

Participants dance and drum around the tree in a deosil (clockwise) position, raising energy for an abundant harvest for the year to come.

The formal ceremony is concluded. Participants break bread together and enjoy an apple-themed potluck.

The nice thing about this ceremony is that it can be done by many different people, including those not on the pagan path. I have adapted this ceremony to honor all the food-bearing plants on the land or specific food-bearing plants—and they very much appreciate the positive energy that this ceremony provides.

CHAPTER 6

Lughnasadh

Landscapes, Gardens, and Lawn Liberations

Behind a tall fence in a busy suburb of Detroit lies a friend's ½-acre permaculture garden: an abundant and magical oasis that you can literally eat your way through. Dwarf apple, pear, and peach trees form the tallest layer, while gooseberries, currants, raspberries, blueberries, and blackberries offer delightful treats. Herbs and nectary plants dot the colorful landscape attracting bees and butterflies. As you graze your way through the garden, walking onions and other perennial vegetable crops such as French sorrel carpet the ground. Hops and grapes trellis up the sides of the fence, and tucked in here and there are annuals: tomatoes, sunflowers, peppers, and more. The sunflowers stand over 10 feet tall, with beans growing up their tall canes. The paths weave in and spiral the space in circular rather than angular lines. A picnic table and hammock under the shade of the tree finish the picture.

The land on the other side of the wooden fence in all directions offers a very different tale. The typical monocropped[65] lawns that require constant mowing, chemical use, watering, and synthetic fertilizers. Here and there you see a neighbor with a backpack sprayer hitting the "weeds" with chemicals, or buzzing about noisily with a weed whacker, or pushing a guzzling, loud, smelly machine to keep the grass under control. There is little life, no abundance, and uniformity.

In both cases, humans have invested a considerable amount of time, money, energy, and resources (both financial and ecological) into cultivating a particular kind of space. In the case of the permaculture garden, this once lawn has been transformed into a space with many yields: food, forage, habitat, beauty, tranquility, plants for others, and a place for community outreach and education. The lawn on the other side of the fence offers little and instead consumes resources: the life energy of humans, the lifeblood of the Earth (fossil fuels), chemicals and fertilizers, and the funds needed to maintain it. Even if one were to go outside and enjoy the space, one would likely risk chemical exposure. Interestingly enough, both spaces take regular maintenance, but only one of these spaces offers food, joy, shelter, nectar, forage, and habitat to a variety of life forms.

And so, in the story of these two spaces we see the topic of this chapter being laid before us: inviting nature back into our immediate indoor and outdoor spaces as part of our sacred action. This chapter focuses on cultivating spaces that are closest to us: a 10-by-20-foot patch of land in front of one's house, an abandoned lot in our neighborhood, a balcony with pots, a warm windowsill, a ½ acre or more yard. Each of these spaces offers us opportunity for land-healing work and cultivating a sacred relationship with nature.

Some of us are blessed with access to a small—or large—patch of land. Others may be renters or have other situations that disallow us from getting our hands into the dirt. The goal of this chapter is to offer philosophies and opportunities for every person regardless of situation, to grow something, even if it's just as simple as sprouts on the windowsill or having a small raised bed at a family member's house or community garden. I have experienced both kinds of circumstances. From abundant full-sun growing space on my 3-acre homestead in Michigan to my container garden while renting in Pennsylvania, the lessons are the same—tending and growing things deepens our awareness and connection and allows us to engage in sacred action.

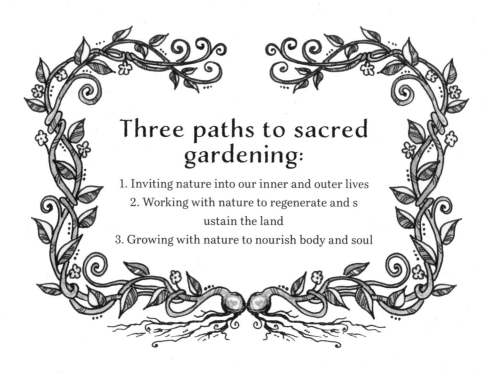

Three paths to sacred gardening:

1. Inviting nature into our inner and outer lives
2. Working with nature to regenerate and s ustain the land
3. Growing with nature to nourish body and soul

Sacred Gardening Principles

We begin our work into sacred action in our immediate landscapes by exploring this work in the context of the permaculture ethical system that frames this book: people care, Earth care, and fair share, and how we might use these principles in any gardens we cultivate.

Earth Care Principles for Sacred Gardening

Most typical "gardening" and lawn "care" practices are rooted not in the ethic of care, but in the immediate gratification, expediency, and convenience (and the ability of lawn care and chemical companies to make a profit). When we practice Earth care in our immediate landscapes, it is important to resist narratives that frame what our lands should look like, what our gardens should look like, what our gardening practices should be, and what our basic relationship to the land should be. Nearly all of these narratives have been framed for us by advertising and mass media to make a profit and sell us an image, not to cultivate a sacred relationship with nature. Instead, with each lawn maintenance practice, ask, "Is this caring for the Earth?" Some general principles under Earth care are as follows:

Reduce or eliminate fossil fuel use: Because so many of our lawn maintenance practices are driven by the unnecessary expenditure of fossil fuels, the first principle is to substantially eliminate or reduce such use. Redesigning outdoor spaces so as not to require mowing, using a rake rather than a leaf blower, or using compost rather than chemical fertilizers are three examples of practices that reduce or eliminate fossil fuel consumption.

Reduce, reuse, and repurpose: A lot of gardening equipment that is available for purchase is unnecessary, so be on the lookout for how to avoid gimmicks. Good tools are a good investment, as are high-quality, organic plants and seeds. I have dug many extremely good tools and pots out of trash piles from "spring cleaning" day (see chapter 3) and have found many others at yard sales. Beyond tools and seeds, nature can provide much of what you need: fallen logs for the sides of raised beds, sticks for trellising, stones for stone paths, materials for composting, and more.

Avoid chemicals, sprays, and fertilizers: Most chemicals and synthetic fertilizers are derived from petroleum and present severe problems for the ecosystem. Sprays and chemicals should be avoided at all costs (natural ways exist to deal with pests, as well as mentality shifts that can help us accept that vegetables won't always be perfect). Likewise, synthetic fertilizers certainly work, but they actually contain way too much nitrogen, and the excess nitrogen ends up in our waterways. The nitrogen travels to the ocean, where it creates giant algae blooms that make dead zones thousands of miles wide in our oceans. One idea for fertilizer was discussed in chapter 3 (liquid gold); cultivating good soil and cycling nutrients through compost are other ideas. You can also plant companion plants that "fix" nitrogen (legumes, blue false indigo) or that pull up nutrients into the soil (comfrey, burdock) to help build soil fertility naturally.

Consider the power of perennial agriculture: Annual agriculture is a human invention, and many who are interested in regeneration and sustaining lifestyles are now looking to perennial agriculture for its restorative and regenerative potential. Annual agriculture requires us to disturb the soil each year, cut back the plants at the end of the season, and constantly plant and replant each season—this all takes a lot of work! Perennial agriculture instead focuses on planting something once and fostering an ecosystem where it can thrive, while focusing on building and maintaining the integrity of the soil web over time. Perennial agriculture allows us to reap abundant harvests year to year! For example, perennial agriculture can include berries (strawberries, raspberries, blackberries, currants, gooseberries), nuts (walnut, butternut, hazelnut), and also perennial or self-seeding greens (sea kale, asparagus, horseradish, lovage, rhubarb, and fiddlehead fern).

Work with nature: Most of typical human interaction with our immediate landscapes (shrubbery, landscaping, yards, lawns) focuses explicitly on the repression of nature. Weed whacking, mowing, spraying—all these activities are restricting growth of plants, many of which are working to begin to repair damage and begin regrowth and healing. This principle encourages us to instead work with nature and allow her to return to being nature. Let things grow; see what will grow; bring in abundance and biodiversity. Above all, embrace life.

People Care Principles for Sacred Gardening

As much as our immediate landscapes need Earth care, they also need to foster people care. Permaculture's principle of obtaining a yield is helpful here. People care in this case is about cultivating sacred garden spaces that bring many yields.

Grow for nourishment and healing of the body: One of the primary reasons many people create a sacred garden, indoor or outdoor, is obviously to grow food. And, given the ethics of the food system (see chapter 5), this is one of the better shifts we can make to lessen your burden on the living Earth. Growing even a small amount of our food, such as greens in a windowsill, can take a burden off the land—and it will taste better than anything you will buy in a grocery store. Another common thing you can grow is medicinal or culinary herbs. Because I practice herbalism, I devote a portion of my growing spaces to key medicinal herbs that are hard to source or are rare in the ecosystem. I can find many delightful vegetables at the farmers' market, but my medicinal herbs are a bit harder to come by.

Grow for nourishment of the soul: When we engage in any kind of sacred gardening, we are growing a connection, growing nourishment for our soul. As we cultivate a sacred relationship with nature and begin to be responsible for the health of plants, we nurture that connection between nature and spirit. I have found that we can literally grow inner peace, and that the work of growing is the work of embracing the sacred within and without. You might find yourself drawn to particular plants—fill your garden with these plants to bring you peace.

Give freely to others: Sacred gardens, even in small spaces such as a patio or windowsill, offer abundance. Perhaps it is your lettuce in the pot going to seed and producing more seed than you can ever use! Perhaps it's your strawberry patch going wild and producing more plants than you will ever need. Or perhaps it is a boatload of tomatoes and extra beans just waiting for a good home. Fair share suggests that we have plenty we can offer others once we are living in the natural abundance of nature—and we should share, and share freely. This sharing also helps us build community and nurture relationships in our community (see chapter 7).

Grow for exercise: Another "people care" yield that we gain through sacred gardening is self care: the physical exercise and mental peace we gain in cultivating garden spaces.

Fair-Share Principles for Sacred Gardening

Sacred gardening also helps us embrace the ethic of fair share. This is especially true when we consider that the point of growing things isn't just about what we get out of it, but what others do too.

Make space for nature: If we return to the lawn described in the opening of this chapter, it has no room for anything other than the lawn mower, perhaps some anthills, and an earthworm or two. But by cultivating different kinds of spaces, we can create forage and nectary plants, habitat, and food for insects, amphibians, birds, and mammals. Even the patch of grass outside your apartment or home is part of the Earth. Inviting a bit of more of life back in can help us practice fair share. This means that when we make decisions about our growing space, it should be for the benefit of all life, not just ourselves. For example, on the edge of each of my 20-by-4-foot annual garden beds, I dedicate 3 feet of space for pollinator plants: borage, chamomile, poppies, mints, motherwort, milkweed, and many other flowering plants that support life.

Stack functions: One way to ensure fair share and ecological balance is to consider planting "multifunction" plants. For example, New England aster is a fantastic medicinal plant; it is beautiful and it also offers one of the last nectar sources of the season for bees and other wild pollinators. Bee balm is another wonderful medicinal plant that provides nectar during the "summer dearth," when many other nectar sources dry up. Beans not only provide nectar but also enrich the soil with nitrogen (especially if at the end of the season, the plants are cut and the roots are left in the ground). Nearly all plants can "stack functions," and this careful selection can create harmony and offer multiple benefits in your sacred garden.

Indoor Sacred Gardening

Now that we have the basic principles of sacred gardening, we will explore different possibilities for how you can begin to cultivate gardening as a sacred practice in your life. Growing indoors, in containers, or in other small spaces presents both challenges and opportunities. I love the brightness and life that plants bring indoor spaces! I saw this firsthand when I moved into a windowed office at work and decided to create a windowsill garden. My plants on my windowsill all had uses—a lemon-scented geranium provided an uplifting scent as well as delightful tea, and a mint, a wintergreen, and a small pine also offered fantastic tea and air purification. A mini orange tree flowered and produced oranges once a year. Bee balm, which offered antimicrobial qualities, completed my windowsill garden. When people would come to my office, they would be amazed to see the different flowers and edibles—students and colleagues would come in and stay because they enjoyed the energy of the space. It also helped me feel less "disconnected" from nature when I was at work. This was all done ish annual plants good for windowsill gardening prefer full sun (eight hours, so you'll need a south-facing window) or part sun (four to six hours of light a day). Ideally, a south-facing window is best for vegetable growing. Herbs and some greens can do well in eastern or western windows. Only low-light plants can handle northern windows.

In terms of what to grow, herbs are always good choice, particularly hardy herbs that can deal with a range of conditions: sage, rosemary, thyme, cilantro, parsley, chives, basil, and mints. If you want to grow a bit of food instead, there are a few good choices: carrots (with a deep pot), any kind of greens, dwarf fruit trees (I've had a lot of success with patio lemons and tiny sour oranges), peppers (especially little hot ones), or scallions. Some heirloom and open-pollinated vegetable varieties are specifically selected for their compactness and tolerance to small pots—so look for these when selecting your plants.

Any kind of container gardening requires you to ensure that your plants, in the long term, have the right kinds of nutrients. One big issue with any kind of container gardening is making sure that you are repotting at least once a year (for perennials) or rotating the soil for annuals, giving the plants nutrients and making sure that they aren't too wet (you'll see yellow leaves), nutrient deficient (pink or purple leaves), or dry (you'll see droopy or brown crinkly leaves). To keep my "closed loop" system going in my windowsill or container gardening, I will use liquid gold as a fertilizer (see chapter 4) and do indoor vermicomposting (see chapter 3) and use recycled graywater from my bathtub for watering (see chapter 4); these options provide ample nutrients and soil for my indoor plants.

Container gardening: Container gardening on a balcony or patio may offer some additional opportunities over just a windowsill, especially in the larger size of pots and the exposure to the elements (rain, light, pollinators). Container gardens can be big or small and often take place on a deck, patio, or open porch where you can grow an abundance of herbs, vegetables, fruit, and even small trees (such as figs!). When I first moved to Pennsylvania, I noticed that a neighbor was moving out, and she had about ten large plastic pots under her porch that didn't seem to be moving with her. She gladly gave them to me, and my most recent container garden was born. Because I moved halfway through the season, I focused primarily on herbs, strawberries, and a few quick-growing greens such as lettuce and spinach. Just like windowsill gardening, make sure to tend your plants carefully and monitor nutrient levels in the soil. Frequently, nitrogen and calcium are lost, so you will need to find ways of replacing it (crushed eggshells, compost tea, and liquid gold— see chapter 3—are good options). Since pots can dry out extremely quickly during the summer months, mulching the top of the pot with leaves or cut grass can help hold in moisture. Some specially designed containers offer a water reservoir that can hold extra water and let you water less.

Indoor aquaponics: Yet another opportunity for indoor sacred gardeners is to experiment with one of the ultimate closed-loop systems: an indoor aquaponics system. Most aquaponics systems use goldfish as pets or tilapia for fresh eating. Fish in a tank sitting below the tray of greens are regularly fed, and the water, including their feces, is cycled through plant roots. The roots sit in a soilless mix (of small stones, typically); this allows the roots to directly uptake the nutrients from the fish feces in the water and cleanse it, where it is cycled back to the fish tank. While you can purchase very costly aquaponic systems, you can also build one with used and repurposed materials for less than $50 (sourcing an aquarium and a rack for the system secondhand). A small air pump keeps water moving through the whole system, and electric lights or a nearby window provide necessary light. Fish can be fed fish food or a range of table scraps (remember that you are ultimately eating what they eat, so this matters!)

Plants that are growing in these systems grow much faster than in typical soil, allowing any aquaponic system to produce a lot of food in a very short period of time. Note that not all plants are ideal for this setup—greens (kale, lettuce, spinach, collards), tomatoes, and peppers all do well. The biggest challenge with one of these systems is regulating the pH of the water. But once you have the system set up and regulated, you literally just feed the fish, plant, and harvest!

Community and Friendship Gardening

Even if you don't own your own land, opportunities for gardening on someone else's property or community property can often be cultivated. First, if you are willing to do the legwork and be responsible across the full season, friends and family often have potential spaces for you to grow a few things. There are a few ways this can work out; the most effective is to have a set gardening time each week where you go and work on your plot or help in the garden (the last thing you want to do is to have your friend or family member shoulder a burden). At my homestead, I had three different families gardening with me—each of them had their own space to grow food and plant herbs, and we would have regular gardening days where everyone came to help out, learn, and spend time together. All the families were new to gardening, so I was able not only to offer them space, but to teach them the basics of my fossil-fuel-free, no-chemical, no-till, organic-gardening approach. And later, when I was the friend in need of land, I ended up gardening at a friend's house—my friend had a vegetable garden that went unused, and she welcomed me with open arms. I kept her supplied with a steady stream of veggies and herbs. I'll also mention that friendship gardening, in either direction, is a great way of being an Earth ambassador (see chapter 7).

Another option is getting involved in a community garden—this is a good option for anyone, even those who have some land. The community garden in my town offers not only individualized plots but also community growing spaces for herbs, fruit, and more. Anytime I wanted friendship and exercise, I could come down to the community garden and work my plot or other open community spaces. A community garden is not only a great place to grow vegetables but also an outstanding place to talk more about sacred action and everyday living. If there is no community garden in your area, you can consider starting one—see principles for community organizing in chapter 7.

Indoor Aquaponics

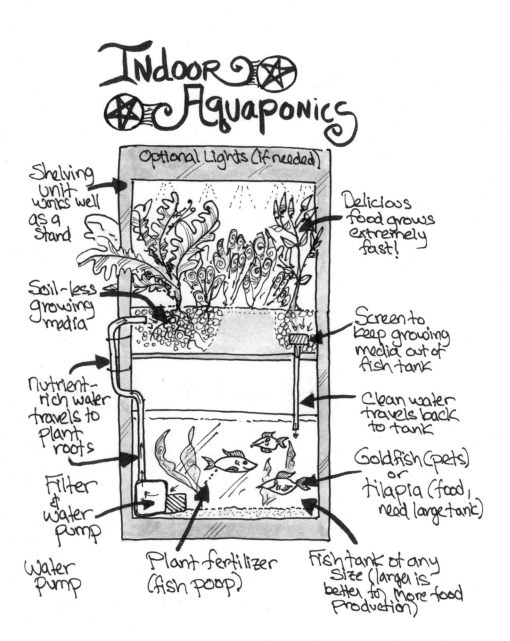

Optional Lights (if needed)

Shelving unit works well as a stand

Delicious food grows extremely fast!

Soil-less growing media

Screen to keep growing media out of fish tank

Nutrient-rich water travels to plant roots

Clean water travels back to tank

Filter & Water Pump

Goldfish (pets) or tilapia (food, need large tank)

Water Pump

Plant fertilizer (fish poop)

Fish tank of any size (larger is better for more food production)

Beyond the Lawn

A couple of years ago, I decided that mowing the front lawn violated my spiritual principles, and instead I was determined to let my front lawn grow, seeding it with wildflowers and pollinator-friendly herbs. I had assumed that nobody would bother me, since I had a very secluded yard out in the country. Truthfully, I ceased mowing without a great deal of forethought or planning. I simply got fed up one day and committed to stop mowing, to scatter seeds, and to see what grew.

It was magic. Grasses grew tall, flowers sprouted out of nowhere, and plants I had never seen before appeared. However, from a conditioned American eye, it looked like I no longer "cared" about my land and was neglecting it, eventually drawing the ire of my neighbors. Within a few months, as the lawn grew taller and taller, someone reported me. My township sent me letters threatening a lien on my property, to fine me $1,000, and to hire someone to mow it if I didn't get it "under control" within three days. What I hadn't realized in my haste to engage in sacred actions and regenerate my landscape was that I was working against a powerful cultural narrative. My own thinking had moved well beyond the lawn— but the rest of my community hadn't.

This experience taught me three things. First, it gave me a deeper understanding of the role of the lawn in our lives—the lawn directly ties to a whole set of powerful myths and cultural narratives, and none of these are particularly good for ourselves or our lands. Second, the experience made me realize that if we can transform the lawn and educate others in the process, we can transform our communities and ourselves. And finally, it made me think about things much more cautiously and long term, understanding that sometimes, change needs to come slowly. Since then, I've gotten a lot smarter about lawn conversions and have worked with a number of individuals and community groups on various lawn projects; I've also taken and offered various classes and workshops on tools for converting laws. During this process, I've given careful consideration to the spiritual implications of the lawn.

Because the lawn is such an iconic symbol of American (and larger Western) values and traditions, it is worth spending some time exploring here before we move to practical lawn alternatives. This helps us understand its origins and problems, so that we have an understanding of why and how it might be changed as part of sacred action. As Lois Robbins describes in *Lawn Wars: The Struggle for a New Lawn Ethic*,[66] early "lawns" in Europe in the Middle Ages and Renaissance were not much different than pastured fields, where livestock kept the grass clipped short. The birth of the modern lawn came about in the United Kingdom in the seventeenth and eighteenth centuries, where a velvety green lawn was a status symbol for wealth and power. The reasoning was simple: if you had enough money, you didn't need to use your land to grow food, and you could afford to pay someone to scythe it down or afford enough livestock to graze on it to keep it clipped. The lawn's dominance spread throughout Europe and America, where the wealthy everywhere began growing English-style lawns as a symbol of power. In the 1800s, a series of inventors worked to perfect the lawn mower, and then, beginning in the 1860s, the rising middle class was able to start keeping lawns. The passage in the US of an act mandating a forty-hour work week in 1938 gave people more time to tend their lawns on the weekends. During the war years, keeping a lawn was promoted as a hobby that relieved stress, firmly entrenching the lawn within the American cultural mindset.

By then, more people in the industrialized world had shifted away from growing their own food and instead worked in factories, mines, and mills. With the rise of industrialized agriculture and mass-produced food, there was little need to do much else with one's land but demonstrate one's status. By the time my generation was born in the 1980s, the lawn was so dominant in the industrialized world that it was difficult to envision a landscape without it. Keeping and tending a lawn is just what everyone does—a common practice of pride that people rarely question. Given this history, we can see the lawn as a product of the same thinking that drove industrialization: a radically disconnected and exploitative view of nature, and a concern for power and privilege.

Truly, I believe that the lawn epitomizes industrialized nations' dysfunctional relationship with nature, and it is for this reason that the lawn can be a very positive focus for sacred action. This dysfunctional relationship manifests in three directions: cultural, ecological, and spiritual.

Culturally speaking, the lawn itself is a physical representation of human wealth linked to the dominance and subduing of nature—the opposite of Earth care and fair share. When we cut our grass by using fossil fuels, we are dominating that space, demanding that nothing but what we want grows. Think about the lawn wars taking place in many upscale suburban neighborhoods—the person with the greenest, most weed-free, and perfect lawn is the person who commands respect in the neighborhood.

Furthermore, the lawn perpetuates the idea that humans are at war with nature; the lawn is literally a site of chemical warfare. This can be reflected in the language we use surrounding lawns and the advertising of lawn products ("Take control of your lawn!," "Destroy the invaders!," and so on). Also, the lawn causes suffering in humans. Pay attention to your neighbors as they mow their lawns or do any of the other "lawn care" behaviors such as spreading poison or spraying dandelions—very few people seem to be happy, yet they are out there doing the work once a week all the same. Finally, exposure to all those chemicals and toxins do take their toll on our bodies and health and can lead to direct deaths of pets and bee colonies, sickness and cancer, and more. Taking care of the lawn, then, is more than just a chore but a toxic battleground.

Ecologically speaking, the lawn presents yet another set of problems. First, the lawn is a site of consumption rather than production: it consumes fossil fuel, increasingly dwindling supplies of water, time, and space. Its existence speeds global climate change. The lawn, in the US alone, comprises more space than any other irrigated crop, taking up approximately 49,000 square miles (almost 40,000,000 acres), consuming 7.8 billion gallons of water (30% of all US water usage), and requiring people maintaining them to spend upward of $1,200 a year (a $28.9 billion industry, resources of which could be going to much-better things).[67] Those numbers are hard to imagine and put into perspective—but think if that was all forest, garden, or open field! The US Environmental Protection Agency (EPA)[68] indicates that a single gas-powered lawn mower produces, in one hour, emissions equal to eleven cars, producing 5% or more of carbon emissions (in addition to emitting other dangerous fumes such as sulfur dioxide and ozone). In the US alone, lawn maintenance consumes 800 million gallons of fossil fuel and an estimated 17 million gallons spilled when refueling (more than most major oil spills per year). This is all in addition to the billions of tons of pesticides and chemicals. On a massive scale, the lawn is causing pollution and harm to our Earth.

The second ecological issue is that the lawn is nature in a state of suffering. When we go into a forest, what do we experience? Wet, spongy ground, coolness, and an abundance of different kinds of life—an ecosystem where many parts add to the whole. The lawn is the opposite of this—it's dry, it doesn't cycle nutrients, it doesn't hold water, the soil is compacted, and it's a monoculture. The third ecological issue is the degrading of the soil, the compaction of the soil, and the loss of soil ecology. Dandelion, burdock, yellow dock, and many other plants that pop up have tap roots that can break up hard, compacted soil and accumulate nutrients to rebuild the soil so that other plants can grow. When these plant allies appear in the lawn, they are functioning like nature's first-aid team to begin long-term healing. And yet, these healing plants are targeted with ire and chemicals. The fourth, but by no means final, ecological issue is that the lawn is essentially a wasteland—there is no food or forage to be found in a lawn, not for people, wildlife, or pollinators.[69]

Spiritually, the ramifications of the practice of keeping a lawn are tragic. First, humans need interaction with nature—it provides healing, connection, regeneration, and soothing of the soul. Unfortunately, for many, the only interaction with nature they get each week is through their lawn maintenance. I see this firsthand where I live in a small town; my neighbors are invisible except for when they are mowing their lawns. The only interaction people have with nature is through chemical warfare and fossil-fuel-powered destruction. Second, by keeping the lawn as a lawn, we are also depriving ourselves of the abundance and healing that nature can provide, again disconnecting ourselves from the living Earth. Mowing the lawn is a violent act against nature—it kills insects and pollinators, it prevents plants from growing, it keeps nature in a state of suffering, and, I believe, from the human perspective, it dampens the soul. We cannot reconnect with nature if we are at war with it. We can do quite a bit to rebuild the relationship with nature. When we transform our immediate landscape through sacred action, we transform and heal ourselves.

A Vision of a Sacred Garden

A dear friend of mine and fellow druid was a certified organic vegetable farmer and horticulture teacher for over twenty-five years. Due to a set of challenging life circumstances, she had to relocate into the middle of a small urban area and went from farming 10 acres to having a tiny 50-by-50-foot front-yard growing space. In a period of months, she single-handedly converted her front lawn into an incredible, beautiful, and bountiful vegetable garden, and she couldn't believe how many neighbors loved what she had done and started to do the same. She used many of the principles discussed in this chapter: building good soil, not using pesticides and herbicides, selecting good seeds, and cultivating sacred awareness. Her lawn transformation helped her heal and work through a very difficult time, deepened her relationship to her immediate landscape, created ecosystems, created beauty and interest, and produced several thousand pounds of food in one season! Her garden also became the seed of change in her small community, growing into a giant oak and gaining news stories, regional attention, and much interest. She is now a certified permaculture designer helping other people design and enact their own front-lawn transformations—all because of her willingness to engage in sacred action in her front yard.

Lawn Laws and Restrictions

As my story earlier in this chapter demonstrated, visionary people who want to move away from the lawn often face the issue of restrictive laws or serious community pressure to conform. Restrictive laws can be found at the municipal level (e.g., town/city government, townships) or even at the county or state levels. These laws were put in place by well-meaning people to make their town or city look good— because "good looking" is essentially associated with well-tended lawns. So let's look at a few potential responses and consider the legal issues here.

Join the movement and find allies: A lot of people are realizing that the lawn is not serving them, and are seeking to rekindle their sacred relationship with the land, rip up the grass, and plants some veggies and fruit trees. The first thing I suggest you do if you are interested in this kind of sacred action is to find allies— find people in your community or neighboring communities who have converted their lawns or are considering it. Resources such as the "Grow Food Not Lawns" (growfoodnotlawns.com) movement and a local permaculture guild or native plant groups are also possibilities.

Work around restrictive lawn laws and loopholes: Even the most-restrictive laws can be read carefully and loopholes found. While these are highly situational and depend on the specific laws, I can give a few examples of things that worked well for others. One friend of mine lives in a town that has a really restrictive lawn code, but she found a loophole: a stipulation that allows grain crops of any height to be grown. And so, she grows buckwheat and oats in place of her lawn (she eats the buckwheat and turns the oats into milky oats tinctures for medicine). She's fully within her legal rights and is prepared when people ask questions or complain.

The farmer friend with the front-yard garden lives in a city with an ambiguous lawn law (it said simply, "No weeds," but we knew from experience that a "weed" is in the eye of the beholder; legally, there was no definition offered in the city code). She received verbal permission that she could have a garden in her front yard as long as there were no "weeds" that appeared out of place—and she has had no trouble with her alterative front yard in the three years since.

A third friend lives in a housing development with an extremely restrictive

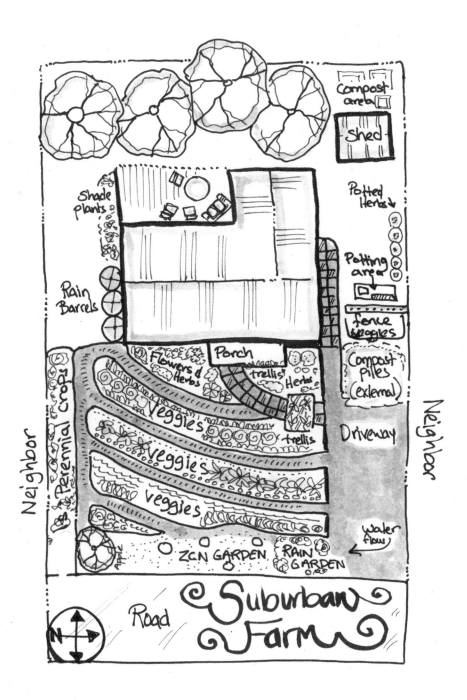

Compost area

Shed

Potted Herbs

Potting area

fence veggies

Compost piles (external)

Driveway

Neighbor

Neighbor

Shade plants

Rain Barrels

Perennial Crops

Flowers & Herbs

Porch

trellis

Herbs

trellis

Veggies

Veggies

Veggies

Water flow

Apple

ZEN GARDEN

RAIN GARDEN

Road

Suburban Farm

N

code that did not allow any traditional vegetable crops (a lot of housing developments have very restrictive laws). She got around this by planting ornamental (yet still edible) kale, planting serviceberry trees (a common ornamental), replacing shrubbery with blueberry and currant, and tucking in strawberries here and there. She's now working to replace the lawn itself with a low-growing clover that will also provide a great deal of nectar to pollinators. Even though she still has a large patch of lawn, she has worked to make her yard a place of abundance for herself and wildlife. These three stories go to show that reading laws and knowing what can and can't be done is a good first step.

Create harmony with nature through Earth care and fair share: Long term, we need transformation in the hearts and minds of individuals, and transformations in the laws and lawns themselves. Regardless of our ownership status, all of us can work to learn what is permitted in our communities and to bring awareness and positive change. We can do this through leading a task force on front-yard gardens to change the law, working with businesses and municipalities to convert lawns to gardens, spreading a positive image of front-yard gardens, and educating ourselves and others.[70] Sometimes, all it takes is one person to make a tremendous change in a community, and the only reason something hasn't been done is because nobody has yet thought to do it.

Understand alternatives and lawn education: Anyone can learn about the medicinal and edible foods that are grown in the place of lawns, and share that knowledge with others. It doesn't require owning a home to study an edible landscaping and permaculture design and offer knowledge freely to friends and family. This is, to me, the most powerful of the things we can do to help shift consciousness—simply have that "Oak knowledge" and share it. Many times a year, I find myself leading an impromptu plant walk through someone's yard, identifying mushrooms growing on someone's tree, or pointing out delicious berries. These are in addition to my regularly scheduled plant walks that I offer in the community. At my first plant walk of the season, I make a point to start with dandelion and cover it thoroughly and then conclude with a bottle of dandelion wine—this certainly had an impact on those who came to my walk! The power of Oak knowledge is the power to change our communities and heal our lands.

Engage in people care: Another group that is, in many ways, the most difficult to manage is resistant immediate family members, such as a resistant spouse who insists on pouring chemicals on the lawn. Remember here that given the deep-rooted cultural connection of status and privilege to the lawn, we have to be patient, kind, and loving with any change—that is, we have to practice good people care skills. Change can come slowly, but it does come, if we give it time and opportunity for open heart-to-heart discussions.

Work on education, outreach, and signage: Once you are ready to take the plunge and convert part of your lawn or all of your lawn back to something more nature focused, carefully educating and doing outreach is a very important step. I have found, specifically, that registering your lawn with one or more nonprofit organizations and displaying a small sign on a mailbox or in the yard are great ways to raise awareness. After my initial failed attempts at lawn conversion, I registered my homestead with Monarch Watch as a certified monarch way station, and with the World Wildlife Federation as a certified wildlife habitat.[71] These two certifications cost $50 each and came with beautiful signs; the signage provided a wonderful way to show people I was doing something intentional.

I see community work and lawn conversion as sacred actions we can have that directly improve the health and vibrancy of our lands and that heavily influence our relationship with nature. The lawn can be one of the primary sites of transformation and change for us in the Western industrialized world. Not only can the lawn be transformed from a consumptive space to a productive one for growing vegetables, herbs, and flowers to benefit humans and other life, but it can be a site of personal reconnection and healing with our landscape.

Creating Your Sacred Garden

And so, whether you want to transition your entire lawn, develop a patio garden, or start a tiny patch of garden somewhere, the next step in that journey is planning and visioning. A garden can be as big or small of a production as you can make it. I would suggest that you go for sustaining changes—those that you are able to maintain with your available time and energy rather than diving in headfirst in an enormous garden only to find out you are overwhelmed. Start small, with what you can manage, and build each year as you grow in your knowledge. Whether or not you are starting a small garden or doing away with the whole lawn, the following suggestions should help you get started.

Spend time visioning, observing, and considering possibilities for the space.

As permaculture design suggests, a year of observation will allow you to see the space in all seasons: when the rains come and the water table rises, where water lies, when the rains end and the dry season begins, where snow lies, where snow melts first, how much light everything gets. A lot of people get very eager and just jump in without doing these observations—and this is a way to end up having a problem that is harder to fix. To address the issue of light specifically, you can borrow or purchase something called a "solar pathfinder" that will tell you exactly how much light the space will get during any season and any point of the year. There are physical devices as well as mobile phone apps.

One of the biggest mistakes that people new to gardening make is to jump into converting the lawn or starting a veggie garden without a clear plan of what they are doing. Since gardening is often highly visible work that can be time consuming, make sure you have a plan. Consider creating your plan in stages over time. Make sure you can account not only for the size of the plants now, but the eventual size they will achieve after five to ten years or more of growing. One friend of mine lived in an upscale subdivision, and rather than convert her lawn all at once, she started by extending the beds from her house a few feet at a time, so that the neighborhood could get used to the idea. This process worked well. At minimum, your plan should include an understanding of how big of a space you have to work with, where the beds and plants will be placed, where the light is coming from, where the water is flowing from, what you will use for paths, and more. Sketching and drawing out your ideas is a fantastic way to help you vision what these spaces may look like.

I would strongly suggest visiting a number of gardens in order to experience how different people have laid out their gardens. Talk to them about the maintenance and upkeep, what they would do differently, what works well, and so on. Following are some additional tips and insights to consider during this planning stage.

Bed structure: You will want to carefully consider what kind of bed structure to use. Raised beds are wonderful to avoid weeds and also to prevent people from walking where you don't want them to walk. But raised beds dry out faster and freeze earlier than other kinds of beds. The taller the raised bed, the easier it is to work, but the taller bed requires more soil (and freezes/thaws faster). You can also use beds directly on the ground or even a slightly raised bed, lined with stones.

Bed size: The size of your beds is important. As a 5-foot, 3-inch woman, I simply can't reach across a 4-foot bed easily (although they are the "standard" size that

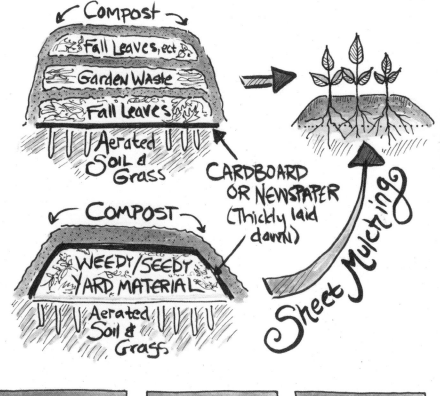

Compost

Fall Leaves, ect

Garden Waste

Fall Leaves

Aerated Soil & Grass

CARDBOARD OR NEWSPAPER (Thickly laid down)

COMPOST

WEEDY/SEEDY YARD MATERIAL

Aerated Soil & Grass

Sheet Mulching

B.B. Blueberries

Asian Pear

Dwarf Apple

Raspberries

Water

Herbs

Herbs

Annuals

Annuals

Annuals

Flowers

Herbs & Strawberries

Annuals

Annuals

Flowers

Arbor with Hops

Raspberries

Strawberry

Garlic

Straw berry

Herbs

Annuals

Annuals

Blueberry

Currants

Gooseberry

Ground Berry

Annuals

Annuals

Herbs

Herbs

B.B.

Strawberries

Dwarf Apples

Hazelnut

B.B.

Sitting Area

Herbs

Herbs

Berries

Annuals

Annuals

Grapevines

Pollinator Hedge

▨ Pathways ⊞ Sidewalk   **Three Garden Designs**

people usually create). Consider using either 3-foot beds, or "keyhole" beds for easier access. Keyhole beds are shaped like a horseshoe (*see graphic below*) and allow for maximizing growing space and minimizing garden path space. A garden in the shape of a leaf, with multiple keyholes, is a really a productive use of a small space.

Aesthetics: Aesthetics are an important component of gardens, especially ones visible to the community. How large your plants get is part of this, as are color, texture, and various angles. Consider carefully from the beginning how ecological succession happens, how large plants and trees will grow, and plan for those changes.

Walking paths: Walking paths, and clear indications of where to walk, are really critical for keeping people where you want them when they visit. Many people in the permaculture community make paths of recycled materials: for example, a thick layer of cardboard or newspaper covered in wood chips (readily available for free when someone nearby is getting tree work done). These paths need to be redone every two years or so. More-permanent paths would include stone, brick, or low-growing clover! You want to make sure you design paths carefully so that once your beds are in place, all work can be done from the path, and you don't step on the beds (compacting the soil).

Making space for nature: In my own garden and lawn conversions, I didn't just create a space for plants, but I focused on cultivating a sacred sanctuary for all life. This included water features for insects, birds, and amphibians; wild-bee homes (a chunk of log drilled with varying diameters between 2 and 10 mm); and carefully selected plants with varying bloom times. I certainly include milkweed, given the difficulty that monarch butterflies are facing with farming practices that have eliminated hedges and edges. You can do research on species that need help in your area, and work to cultivate spaces that will offer them a nice home.

Sitting areas: Consider places for people to sit and enjoy the garden. I like to put these kinds of spaces right in the center of the garden, so friends can come and enjoy a cup of tea and nibble on some berries with the abundant garden around them.

Design from nature: Consider the magic of the space: you can use designs inspired from nature (spirals, leaves, waves), designs from sacred geometry (circles, lines, pentacles, hexagons, and more), or other designs (Celtic knots, labyrinths).

Part of the reason I suggest to start slowly and build over time with sacred gardening is that it's not just the installation that requires effort but also the regular maintenance of the space. Part of what happens is that we have an initial burst of energy to get the gardens installed, and then we might lose steam. Anything that is perceived as out of control or disorderly can get us in trouble, given people's current mindsets. Gardens require commitment; we have to be willing and able to put work into it each week, with larger blocks of time set aside in the spring and fall, when, at least in temperate regions, a lot of planting and maintenance need to happen.

Attending to Your Soil and Mimicking the Forest Floor

The very first thing when you create a garden, before putting a single plant or seed into the ground, is to grow your soil. I would suggest beginning this with a soil test to understand what you are working with (in the US, most state extension offices offer free or low-cost soil tests). This will tell you what your soil profile is, and you can tailor your actions accordingly (e.g., if you have very acidic soil, wood ashes are good; if you have high-alkaline soil, you can use pine needles as a mulch). As I discussed above, most typical yards are nutrient deficient and compacted and have little organic matter—hardly ideal growing conditions. The good news is that soil can be rehabilitated in very straightforward ways!

One of my favorite strategies for getting any garden going is called sheet mulching or lasagna gardening. This is a process that mimics the land's natural method of building soil, creating successive layers of organic matter. It is best done in the fall months, when leaves and other resources are abundant, or when you have access to a large variety of organic matter (manure, compost, soiled straw from a nearby farm, leaves, weedy material, grass clippings from nonsprayed lawn, coffee grounds, vegetable-based food waste, etc.). The overall process starts with a bottom weed-suppression layer (to eliminate the grass itself), and then layering thin layers of organic matter.

To do this, you will need newspaper or cardboard in good supply (with tape or staples removed), a garden hose or other source of water, a garden fork or broad fork, a large supply of at least two different kinds of organic matter (I use compost and fall leaves most often), and some friends to help move materials around.

Start out by marking off the boundaries of your bed (using a rope, flour, or a hose). Then, in the bed area, aerate the existing soil with a garden fork or broad fork. Simply stick a fork in the soil and a tilt the handle a bit to offer aeration. A typical lawn is very compacted, and you want to make it less compacted so that the roots and worms can get down deep.

Next comes your first layer of organic matter, which includes anything that may have weed seeds. This can include manure, which often contains live seeds, or weedy material (in this case, we define "weed" as any unwanted plant). If you don't have weedy organic matter, manure, or seedy compost, skip to the next step. Take your weedy material (6 or so inches thick or more) and then wet the entire layer down. Wetting all the material down throughout this process helps speed up decomposition. If you are unable to wet it down, decomposition will still take place, but that decomposition will be much slower. If you have enough weedy material for multiple layers, spread a layer of compost or leaves and then add a second layer, continuing until all the weedy material is layered.

Now, add your weed-suppression layer—this is in the form of cardboard or newspaper. This is where you begin if you have no weedy material. Lay the cardboard or newspaper down fairly thickly, making sure that edges overlap by at least 6 inches. If you are using newspaper, use at least ten sheets at a time; a single sheet of cardboard is typically sufficient. Wet this layer down thoroughly.

Next, add additional layers of organic matter on top that are weed free. You can alternate among compost, leaves, coffee grounds, and whatever else you have. Leaves can mat together if you aren't careful, so make sure you layer them thinly (especially if they are oak) or shred them before you add them. Pine needles also work well here and break down very quickly compared to oak; however, they do make your soil slightly more acidic (you can counter this by throwing in some wood ash, but I'd do so only after you know if you have acidic or alkaline soil).

Keep adding successive layers of organic matter till your beds are at least a foot or two high. The beds will sink quite a bit over the winter months. I usually top mine with finished compost or more fall leaves and let them sit for a time. If you do this in the fall, your new bed is ready to plant in the spring, and the cardboard will keep the weeds from germinating. The bed will be completely broken down after about six months, and the whole thing will be an amazing place to plant. You can sheet-mulch new areas each year, adding a layer or two of finished compost, fall leaves, or mulch to your garden beds. If your beds ever get too weed dominant, you can repeat the sheet-mulching technique with a single weed-suppression layer and new layers of compost and leaves.

There isn't really a wrong way to sheet-mulch. The key is to keep layering, keep the weedy layers and grass beneath the weed-suppression (cardboard/newspaper) layer, and keep wetting the whole thing down. Other than that, the sky is the limit! In future years and seasons, you just add more organic matter on the top of the bed, just like in natural settings (*see below*). If you end up with some weeds or lose part of a bed later in the life of your garden, you can always do a second or third sheet mulch. You can also aerate the bed every few years with a broad fork or garden fork, if you feel the need and are planting annual vegetables. But you don't need to till it—just plant in it, and at the end of the season, cut the annual plants back at the roots (not ripping them out) to maintain the structure of your soil.

One way of building soil in any setting is by adding organic matter—preferably the "waste" materials of others. It is a time-honored tradition to use composted manure and finished compost to fertilize and condition the soil. Many municipalities offer free wood chips and finished compost to any who live in their area, and this is another great way to get free resources. Please note that some weed killers take two-plus years to break down and still might be present in composts produced commercially. Any friends who have chickens, rabbits, horses, pigs, alpacas, cows, goats, and so on also produce an abundance of manure that you can get, usually for free if you are willing to pick it up and do some shoveling. Let's not forget the fall months, when neighbors so graciously rake and bag up their leaves and leave them for you by the side of the road—gather these up in great quantities, mulch them if possible, and add them to your garden, around trees, and so on. If you have chickens, get a bunch of bags and add a bag or two each week to the run and allow the chickens to do the work of producing compost. A local coffee shop nearly always has free coffee grounds, which add nitrogen, phosphorus, potassium, magnesium, and copper to the soil. Vermicomposting (chapter 3) produces worm castings that are incredible for any garden.

Adding organic matter to your soil each year helps create stronger plants, and stronger plants produce more and better withstand pests and disease. Tilling your soil disrupts the microbial web of life, so add your organic matter to the top of your garden beds. As more and more people turn to gardening, organic matter is becoming higher and higher in demand. A friend in upstate New York recently told me that she was paying double for compost compared to ten years ago because of the increasing demand. Developing local and reliable composting methods of your own to include this organic matter is also a wise idea.

Visually Creating Sacred Space

In addition to plants, consider other garden features that can help visually create sacred space. A garden altar, a standing stone, a spiral, a circular pattern, statuary, large crystals, a labyrinth, a dolmen arch, a trilithon—all these features have historical connections to sacred sites and may be appropriate for the garden you are building. In one garden, for example, I have a water feature with a standing stone sitting in a sacred pool (drawing on the druid concept of the salmon in the sacred pool combined with the setting of an ancient standing stone). I also prefer flowing shapes and designing with patterns in nature (a leaf pattern, a spiral, a pentacle) rather than using squares and boxes for planting beds or sacred features. Flowing paths can help build a sense of sacredness. Consider your plans carefully and think about how you can best cultivate a space that has elements you find sacred and that link inner and outer worlds.

One friend has a "goddess garden" that includes various goddess statuary with carefully selected plants. Another friend did a medicine wheel garden with sacred herbs, using wood chips as the path (as described above). Another friend who has a container garden has statuary and a small fountain among his containers. In my community garden plot, I have a stone cairn and sacred stones tucked among the small vegetable patch. The possibilities are endless for creating a sense of the sacred in your garden.

Your sacred garden can become the focal point of your spiritual practices throughout the year. Each time I enter my sacred garden, it offers me new insights. Meditating in the garden or simply observing the plants carefully can be a source of great peace and spiritual connection. I do ritual in my garden each morning both as a blessing to my garden and as a blessing to myself. Sometimes, I take a blanket and hide in between rows of corn or tall blueberry bushes and just read, passing time slowly on a lazy afternoon. A central garden altar is a place for offerings.

Deciding What to Plant

Selecting what to plant is one of the most fun parts of garden planning. Your goals for what you'd like to create, and the kind of light you have available, should determine the path you take toward planting.

Perennial agriculture: There has been a large movement, inspired by permaculture, to replace annual crops (soy, corn) with perennial tree crops (hazelnuts, chestnuts, walnuts). For sacred-gardening purposes, this is a good idea, since perennial gardens are much less disruptive to the ecosystem and help promote a greater diversity. They are also less work on the part of the gardener! While perennials offer different kinds of food: nuts, berries, leafy greens, and herbs—there are some perennials that can replace annual vegetables quite effectively. Perennial agricultural systems take a bit longer to get established (you won't be getting much of a harvest in your first year). However, once they are established, you can literally eat your way through them and don't have to till, replant, and follow that more work-intensive annual vegetable cycle. This isn't to say that you should include only perennials in your sacred-gardening plans, since everyone loves a good tomato! But I encourage you to think about growing an ecosystem with perennials rather than a garden of annuals that you must replant each year. You can also start with more annuals during your first year and plant fewer annuals once the perennials begin producing.

Perennial berries: Many possibilities exist for berries, including those that you can't get at a local store! Some good berry crops include raspberries, strawberries, gooseberries, currants, blueberries, blackberries, goumi berries, and grapes—to name a few. Planting different varieties of the same kind of plant but that ripen at different times extends your harvest time and flavor possibilities. Look also for heirloom varieties. Alpine strawberries, for example, are a clumping strawberry that is ever bearing; they offer smaller fruit but are highly flavorful. Golden raspberries are ever bearing in the summer and fall months. If you put a dozen or so canes in, each day you will have handfuls of golden, succulent berries. The book *Uncommon Fruits for Every Garden* by Lee Reich has a wide range of unique possibilities. Perennial vines, including the vigorously growing hardy kiwi, grape, and maypop, also offer delightful treats.

Perennial fruit trees: Spend some time researching what fruit tree crops do well in your ecosystem without the use of chemicals and fertilizers. Where I am, peaches and cherries are often more difficult to grow than apples due to pests and climate. An easy way to find out what grows well is to visit your local farmer's market and talk with the farmers about what they are growing and how it grows, what the soil is like, and more. Asian pears are an excellent all-around tree crop because they are quick to bear and bear abundantly. Many fruit trees can be grown on dwarf rootstock so that they stay fairly small and compact, which is useful for smaller-space gardening. Look also into unconventional varieties such as pawpaw and beach plum.

Perennial nut trees: Perennial nut trees are a long-term investment, but a splendid one to consider. Most of the time, two nut trees are needed to ensure more-adequate pollination. I see nut tree planting as an investment in the future—they provide fabulous shade, erosion protection, habitat, and food for you and wildlife. Nut trees include chestnuts, hazelnuts, oaks, walnuts, butternuts, almonds, pecans, and many more. Hazelnuts are a good choice for a faster-growing and faster-producing nut tree (they typically produce in their third or fourth year if you plant them as a shrub (and are delicious, especially when made into a nut butter with cacao and maple syrup).

Perennial greens: Perennial greens such as French sorrel, ostrich fern, sea kale, and good king henry offer perennial edible greens. Certain plants we typically grow as annuals, such as kale, can be perennial if they can survive the winter where you live. Even many trees (maples, particularly) have young edible leaves that make good salad greens. And let's not forget dandelion here—a delightful, land-healing perennial that is excellent medicine and food. In fact, old *Farmers' Almanacs* used to include information on when to plant your dandelions!

Perennial nut/tuber crops: Perennial tubers such as ground nut, skirrett, earth pea, and Jerusalem artichokes offer hearty starch options. Jerusalem artichokes grow 6–10 feet high, are beautiful sunflower-like plants, and also offer abundant tubers in the spring and fall. There are many other options beyond potatoes, beets, parsnips, or radishes to consider.

Annuals: Nearly all the gardens that employ perennial agriculture include sections for annuals—sometimes tucked in among perennials, and sometimes in their own separate area. Most annual crops deplete the soil, so crop rotations and good soil management practices are critical. Annuals can help you produce a lot of food quickly, and usually that's the only goal for people. Heavy feeders such as the nightshade crops (tomatoes, potatoes, peppers) need careful rotation. Starting seeds indoors early with a simple light system or near a sunny window can allow you to develop a sacred connection with your plant through every aspect of its life cycle. I would suggest ordering a few good seed catalogs and browsing the descriptions (in the US, I'd recommend a variety of organic-seed companies: Fedco, Baker Creek, Fruition, and the Seed Saver's Exchange).

Helper plants: A number of plants don't offer direct harvests of food but do offer benefit to the ecosystem and overall garden. In permaculture terms, we see that many plants work together and grow better together; we call this grouping of plants a "guild."[72] Guilds usually include a dynamic accumulator that draws up nutrients deep in the soil and can be chopped and dropped where it grows as a "living manure" (comfrey is often used for this—but be warned, wherever you plant comfrey, it will be permanently). Guilds also often include some kind of nitrogen fixer—legumes, alfalfa, or blue false indigo are common ones. A guild may also include some kind of nectary plant (most medicinal herbs fit this category—especially butterfly weed, bee balm, mints, and sages).[73]

Sourcing plants and seeds: Not all seeds and plants are equal. Like most other things, big-box stores should be avoided at all costs, since they are usually selling almost GMO plants (see chapter 5) and spraying them heavily with pesticides and chemical fertilizers. These toxic plants are not what you want to be planting in a sacred garden; the more we purchase these plants, the more we condone these practices. For annual vegetable seeds and perennials from seed, I would suggest going with a smaller seed company that is committed to organic, non-GMO practices.

Dealing with Common Gardening Challenges

Most gardeners face a variety of challenges in their first few years of gardening. My biggest challenge was a groundhog, whom I affectionately called Bubba and who continually burrowed under my fence to eat my kale and greens. Eventually, creating an underground fence barrier solved the problem, but it certainly was a memorable experience. While you can't anticipate everything, talking to others in your community who are growing things can give you a good sense of what you are likely to face. If you know, for example, that you have groundhogs all over or heavy deer traffic, consider fencing, planting "sacrifice crops" to lure them away from other crops, or planting varieties of plants that they won't eat. If you know that rabbits are a problem, small clumps of dog fur (gathered from a local groomer) around the perimeter of the garden can be very effective. There are dozens more tricks just like these, and doing a little research, rather than reaching for a bottle of chemical spray, is really important here. Animals are part of nature too, and sometimes we get in our heads that we always have to harvest and keep everything to ourselves—remember though, a sacred garden respects all life, and we need to learn to adapt and live with all parts of nature.

Another common issue that people experience is pests eating their vegetables. A pest infestation indicates that the ecosystem is out of balance in some way. Potato beetles, aphids, slugs, moths, squash borers—all of these are common problems for annual vegetable gardening. A technique called integrated pest management offers some solutions. For example, by building a healthy ecosystem around your garden (including such things as a pollinator hedge), you will encourage predatory wasps, ladybugs, and other predatory insects to move in and keep your problem insect population under control. Sticky plates, changing planting times, and other nonchemical solutions can be very effective here. Each pest requires its own management system, but the pollinator hedge and habitat work well for any circumstance—so build your garden with this in mind.

Both pest and wildlife challenges also ask us to reframe our relationship with nature. Pests, in particular, show up when nature is out of balance, almost always due to human causes. Those bugs, beetles, or rabbits are still part of nature and, in my opinion, deserving of respect. I might not want them in my garden, but they are there, and I have to decide how to deal with them. Maybe, this year, you don't have a harvest of a particular crop due to the damage. Or maybe you have some holes in your leafy greens, or a few worms in your apples. These are all parts of nature too, and reframing problems in our own minds in this way reminds us that what we are trying to cultivate here is a sacred space for all life, not just for life that we like.

Your Sacred Garden and Broader Community

Depending on what kind of sacred garden you end up creating, and its location, you might find that people often are interested to know what you are doing. This is particularly true if you've decided on a front-yard garden that replaces a lawn. Another option here is getting wildlife certification (as I mentioned earlier in this chapter). Signage and education go a long way when you are doing something different.

My dear friend Linda of Nature's Harvest Urban Permaculture Farm in Lake Orion, Michigan, has done such outreach. After she converted her 50-by-50-foot front lawn in her small town, so many people were talking to her each day that we created an informational brochure. The brochure explained what she was doing, the principles of permaculture, the benefits of her approach (no mowing, but exercise, beauty, produce, habitat) and the kinds of things she was planting, and resources for their own gardening efforts. This pamphlet sits in a little "take one" box below her mailbox, and then, as people come by, they learn more about her garden. She also routinely invites neighbors to harvests and potlucks and offers free vegetables to spread goodwill and encourage conversations in the community.

Talking with others and doing outreach is sacred action. If we keep everything we know and experience to ourselves, the chance to reach others and make a more lasting change is lost. See chapter 7 for more details about how to do this work.

Planting and Harvesting by the Sun and Moon

Another sacred gardening technique is the age-old tradition of planting and harvesting using the sun, moon, or stars as a guide. The idea here is similar to other kinds of magical timing through astrology, the Wheel of the Year, and full-moon magic: certain times of the day, week, and month are better for planting or harvesting activities. If you plant by drawing on this energy, your plants will grow stronger (having the pull of the energy of the moon, for example), and if you harvest, your harvests will store longer.

Two primary methods exist for doing this: planting by the moon and planting by the stars. I have worked using both approaches, and I favor planting by the moon for its simplicity. To plant by the moon, you can use this simple chart:

New/Dark Moon	Waxing Moon	Full Moon	Waning Moon
Planting	Planting	Planting, harvesting	Harvesting, weeding, composting

The more complex approach is to plant by the stars, using astrology, also known as planting by the signs. Most farmers' almanacs offer some basic guidelines for planting by the signs; however, Rudolf Steiner's biodynamic gardening has the most comprehensive system. If you are interested in this, you will need to purchase a yearly biodynamic sowing-and-harvesting calendar. This method is much more dynamic, and it requires you to consider the position of the planets, the sun, and the moon, as well as the kinds of crops (roots, fruits, greens). The dynamic nature of this approach has a cost: you might have to wait until 12:27 a.m. on Wednesday night to sow your beans!

Conclusion

Gardens great and small offer us the opportunity to cultivate and extend our relationship with the living Earth. The experience of healing nature, building soil, planting seeds, and creating sacred space in a cultivated outdoor environment allows us to grow and extend our own relationship with nature. Truly, gardens can be some of the most magical places!

Exercises and Rituals

Visit a Garden

Before taking on a new garden project of your own, spend some time in other people's gardens. The more gardens that you visit, the more you will learn. Some towns or extension offices offer garden tours that will allow you to see different possibilities, to meet some plants and see how they grow, and to see how people have cultivated a variety of different spaces. I would also recommend trying to visit at least one garden employing permaculture principles; these gardens often look and feel very different than your typical vegetable garden!

Plant Some Seeds

Even if you are planting lettuce seeds in a pot that will sit on your window, I encourage you to choose one thing you want to grow, then plant seeds. Spend time daily with the plants, observing their growth and meditating upon them. Bringing this kind of magic into your life is an incredible opportunity to grow closer to nature and grow.

Convert the Lawn and Create a Sacred Sanctuary

Even if you start small and do only a few feet a year, consider converting part of your lawn into a sacred sanctuary for all life. Even setting a small goal, of a 3-by-3-foot area converted into herbs, is a great first step! If you aren't able to do so yourself, consider helping a friend!

Planting Ritual

This is a simple planting ritual that you can use in a variety of ways. You can easily adapt this ritual to a group setting or do it on your own. You can use this for planting a tree in your garden, or for planting out a whole garden (see revisions to the ritual at the end), or even planting seeds in a windowsill garden. The ritual uses a tree as the focus, but you can easily adapt it for other plants or for planting a whole garden.

Prior to the ritual: You should prepare the following items prior to the start of the ritual and tree planting:

- **Shovels for digging holes.** Begin by digging the holes for the trees or plants prior to commencing the rest of the ritual.
- **Trees or plants to plant.** After you dig the holes, you can place a tree next to the hole in preparation for the ritual.
- **A small bowl of hardwood ash.** If you have saved Yule log ashes or ashes from the Beltane fires, this is a perfect use for them. Otherwise, any hardwood ash will do. If you have neither, you could substitute a handful of compost, composted manure, vermicompost.
- **Watering can(s) filled with water.** New trees and plants need a lot of water, so make sure you give them a very good drink! (You can add a little urine to this water at 10% dilution to give an extra amount of nitrogen.)

Ritual explanation: If you are performing this ritual by yourself, perform all parts. If you are using this in a group setting, have everyone prepare the holes for the trees or plants. Then split into four groups (a group for Earth, air, fire, and water) and make your way around in a clockwise manner, eventually meeting back up to close the ritual. If you've already planted your trees or plants but still want to bless them, you can still use the bulk of the ritual below; just sprinkle the ash near the tree's roots (for fire) and put some high-quality soil, compost, or composted manure for the "Earth" part around the trunk. Note also that the ritual is listed as "tree," but you can easily substitute this for any plant you are planting in a sacred garden.

The Ritual

Begin by opening a sacred space, using your own method (or use the opening from chapter 1). Instructions are in plain text; spoken words are in *italics*.

Speaker: *The ancient druids celebrated in groves of trees and respected so many plants for their medicinal and magical virtues. Plants and trees are a vital part of all life on this planet—nourishing the soil and preventing erosion, creating oxygen, absorbing carbon dioxide, providing habitat and food, and creating shade. With each tree we plant and tend as it grows, we provide a blessing to the land and all its inhabitants. As these trees grow, so too does our connection with this land. Come now and welcome these trees to our sacred garden.*

Fire: Place a pinch of ash into the hole prior to the planting Say:

> *May this tree be nourished by this sacred ash, by the energy of the sun, the great stag of the summer forests, and the powers of the south. We thank this tree for the energy she will provide.*

Earth: Place each tree in the hole, filling the hole with Earth. As you are planting the tree, say:

> *May this tree be blessed by the soil web of all life and powers of the north. We thank this tree for the bounty and stability she will provide.*

Water: Water each tree after it is planted. As you are watering, say:

> *May this tree be blessed by the flowing waters and the salmon of the sacred pool and the powers of the west. We thank this tree for the wisdom she will provide.*

Air: Blow on the tree and say:

May this tree be blessed by the powers of the east and the air, by the hawk of May soaring high; we thank and honor her for the clear, pure air she will provide. I offer you carbon dioxide and breathe in your oxygen, recognizing our own symbiosis.

Speaker: After all trees are planted, all stand around the newly planted trees and say:

Spirits of this land, spirits of this sacred garden, we ask for your blessing and protection over these young trees. Dearest trees, we welcome you to the fellowship of these lands. In this sacred Earth will you grow strong. In the warm rains will you be nourished. In the wind in the air will your leaves speak to us as we listen. In fire of the sun will you grow and shelter our grove. You embody our core value of peace, for though you are strong, you harm none. And though you are mighty, you shelter all beneath your branches. We now sing/dance/drum in honor of you.

Close the ceremony with chanting, singing, or drumming.

CHAPTER 7
Fall Equinox
Earth Ambassadorship, Community, and Broader Work in the World

Acolleague walked up to me as I and a few students were scattered in the hallway, looking at some garbage cans. He said, "Hey, Dana, what are you doing?"

I responded, "My students and I are counting every garbage can and recycling can on campus. We are taking count of what's here in this building."

Just then, one of my students came up and said, "I counted all of them on the third floor. Do you have the numbers for the fourth?"

He looked at the two of us. "Why would you count garbage cans?"

I looked at my student and she responded, "It's really hard to find a recycling bin on campus. It is so much easier to throw things away. Why is that?"

He said, "Come to think of it, I don't even think there is a recycling bin anywhere on our floor."

My student responded, "Exactly! That's why we are counting them."

I added, "You might mention that to your colleagues and write to the Campus

Environment Committee. With more voices, we can hopefully get a better campus recycling plan."

He nodded and thanked me.

This activity was part of a course I was teaching. My students took on a class research project that they designed that examined the accessibility of garbage cans and recycling bins on campus. What we discovered was that garbage cans were much easier to find, and in some cases, several of the main classroom buildings had only one recycling bin per floor or none at all. The best recycling program was in the dorms, since student-led initiatives pushed for better recycling opportunities not available on other parts of campus. Our small project grew quite large and ended up being sent to various decision makers—and soon enough, more recycling bins with better signage started showing up on campus. One small group of students made a big difference in the overall waste flows on campus. This kind of project represents the kinds of simple, yet powerful, sacred action that you can do out in our workplace or community.

Thus far, in this book we've explored many aspects of everyday living: ethics (chapter 1), knowledge and skills (chapter 2), our consumption and waste (chapter 3), our home lives (chapter 4), our food (chapter 5), and our immediate landscapes (chapter 6). Almost all of these have been very personally focused on making more-life-honoring choices. With this chapter, we move into the broader world and consider how we might engage in sacred actions beyond our homes and move this work into workplaces and community spaces. Sacred action in the broader world can mean a lot of things to a lot of different people, but here I'm primarily going to be focusing on areas that connect our communities and our workplaces, how we move between those spaces, and how we bring others together. Our triad for this chapter is as follows:

Three paths for sacred action in our communities:

Being ambassadors for the Earth
Cultivating learning opportunities
Living quietly by example

Through considering our role in the larger world, we'll consider how to engage in people care, Earth care, and fair share. We begin this chapter with a framing philosophy that can help set our actions in the broader world: Earth ambassadorship.

The Practice of Earth Ambassadorship

One challenge we face today in the broader world is that our land and nearly all of the land's inhabitants are generally not legally protected. In fact, in most cases, laws instead protect those who would exploit that land. As such, our lands and their nonhuman inhabitants are subjected to exploitative decisions by humanity. It's not that every culture has had such a problematic relationship with nature; some have recognized the inherent sanctity of the land and her nonhuman inhabitants and included considerations of such in their decision-making processes. Other cultures could hear the singing of the trees, the sounds of the wind, and the babble of a bubbling brook and respect those voices. But in our current culture, we are very far from that way of living or being. Right now, it seems the land is in need of some ambassadors.

An Earth ambassador is a dedicated human who focuses on learning as much as she can about the Earth, sharing that information freely, and helping reconnect humans to their lands in a multitude of direct and more-subtle ways. Like the ancient druids of old, those who walk Earth-centered paths are poised to be leaders in our communities, offering a wealth of plant and nature knowledge, living by example, and offering methods of more fully and consciously inhabiting the Earth. Having "Oak knowledge" (chapter 2) puts us in a position to speak compassionately about the land and teach others of her magic. This may not be your calling, or it may not be something you are interested in right now—but it can be one outcome of this work if you feel you are called into the service of our living Earth. Earth ambassadorship isn't a glamorous thing; it can be small, everyday moments in everyday living when you can live by example or positively advocate for change. This kind of advocacy work is incredibly powerful in a culture that has so fully lost its connection with the natural world. What does it take to be an Earth ambassador?

Deep knowledge, Oak knowledge, and learning Earth care: An Earth ambassador needs to have intimate knowledge and direct experience with those whom he or she is representing. This is not just a surface knowledge, just an abstract idea that nature is "good," but rather an intimacy that is gained only over time and experience. If we want to be Earth ambassadors, we have to understand the land and live the sustainable practices we seek to promote. Ambassadors need to understand ecology, biology, the things that have potential to harm the land, and the things that can help heal it. To be an Earth ambassador, then, we have to dedicate time to improving our own knowledge base, setting aside our assumptions and recognizing how much we have to learn—through the practice of building Oak knowledge. We can do this ambassador work when we are still building and growing our knowledge, but the more we know, the better we are able to engage in it. Knowledge building is, as discussed in chapter 2, a continual process.

Nature immersion: To be an Earth ambassador, spending a lot of time in nature is really key. We can't be ambassadors for something that we admire from afar or set on a pedestal in our minds. We also can't be ambassadors if we stay on the perfectly paved paths of our state forests and local county parks or experience only the "tamed" areas that have been cultivated by humans for humans. Spending time in nature as an immersive experience that gives us the depth of awareness necessary to be ambassadors, to be insiders, to become part of nature and attuned to her rather than separate from it. Nature ceases to be a romantic thing in our heads and, instead, becomes real. When we slow down to nature's time, we align our energies to her rhythms and pathways, and that gives us more-conscious awareness of her needs and how to align ourselves with her needs.[74]

A nature-oriented mindset and lifestyle: It's one thing to know about nature, and it's a completely different thing to have a mindset and lifestyle oriented to nature. We can't be ambassadors for nature if we say one thing and do another. And for examples of this, I point to people such as Thomas Friedman (who wrote *Hot, Flat, and Crowded*)[75] and Al Gore (who created *An Inconvenient Truth*),[76] both of whom tried to encourage less consumption and new ways of living, and both of whom were called out publicly in many venues because of their personal lifestyle choices. Thomas Friedman lives in an 11,000-square-foot house and advocates for smaller dwellings and less consumption.[77] Al Gore lives in a 20,000-square-foot house and uses up $30,000 of electricity—that's 221,000 kWh—in a single year.[78] Please don't be these guys. It's important that we walk our walk first before we talk our talk in the community.

When doing any work in the community, I have found it to be very forthcoming about where you are in your own lifestyle shifts. I talk about my struggles at various points with areas I am still working to change. People such as Gore and Friedman live in the extreme opposite direction of what they are advocating; of course, this substantially damages the message they are attempting to send. And worse, the topics that they are talking about are discredited. Gore and Friedman *attempted* to be Earth ambassadors; despite all the knowledge in their heads, it was poorly received when it was obvious that they were telling others what to do but not embracing that lifestyle for themselves. A much-better strategy is to *live the lifestyle first* and others will come; they will seek your knowledge, and they will want to learn more.

A willingness to serve and seizing opportunity: Most of the work of an Earth ambassador is quiet work. Building knowledge and reading books, immersing ourselves in nature, making lifestyle shifts, putting in a sacred garden, making better eating choices, and just engaging in sacred action every day. But then an opportunity arises, and when it does, it is important to take advantage of it. Opportunities to be Earth ambassadors often come in unexpected ways or places. For example, a friend and druid in New Hampshire found himself in a leadership position fighting an oil pipeline and an oil compressor station and building an incredible Earth-centered community in the process. Having a deep awareness of the Earth helped him point out at-risk species in delicate ecosystems in the path of the pipeline. I'm pleased to say that after almost two years, his group won their battle against the pipeline and compressor station. Another friend, whom I spoke of in chapter 6, converted her front lawn to vegetables and now teaches others to do the same. When you have the knowledge and are living the practices, you can use it to strongly advocate for our land and help rebuild land-human connections.

Taking Up the Role of Ambassadorship

Let's start with some statistics for why being out in our communities and helping rebuild human-land connections really matter. According to the US National Human Activity Pattern Survey (NHAPS),[79] the average American spends 87% of their lifetime indoors and another 4% in enclosed transit (cars, buses, trains, planes, etc.). That means that over 90% of a typical person's life is not spent in nature. They don't offer statistics on this, but I wonder how much of the remaining time is spent doing lawn maintenance and other activities that disrupt and harm the living Earth rather than heal (or even just experience). When we wonder why our lands are under duress, these statistics are an obvious reason. People are almost never outside, and when they are, they are entirely disconnected from what they see. If people aren't going out to nature, we need to bring nature to them.

One of the most important keys to Earth ambassadorship is to be subtle, to let people come to us, and to give opportunities for people to learn in a nonintimidating setting. If we know anything about the land, we likely know more than most others. I have found that when it becomes obvious that I "know something" beyond the standard knowledge and when others see how I am living each day, I frequently find myself in a position to share that knowledge, often in nonformal settings. This is what allowed me to begin to fill an ambassador role. Now, on a regular basis, I have people ask me questions that can lead to good conversations: they ask about my beehives and we can talk about the dangers of pesticides, or they ask about my front lawn or they ask about herbs for various conditions and I point to the herb that is growing there in the sidewalk that could help them. I now lead plant walks where the proceeds are donated to charities all summer long—these walks allow people to learn about plants such as dandelion and drink some dandelion wine and reflect upon their own relationship with the dandelions in their yard. While I didn't get into this with the idea of being an Earth ambassador, as I grew in my own knowledge I started to realize how powerful this Oak knowledge is, and how hungry many are for learning it. And here's the key: each time I have this opportunity, I have an opportunity to educate people about the ethical principles of sacred action—Earth care, people care, and fair share. I have a chance to share with them the mystery and wonder of our natural Earth and help them reconnect with nature.

Creating Community Groups and Sharing Knowledge

Ultimately, Earth ambassadorship has to do with building communities and opportunities for people to learn and grow. As people start out on the path to regenerative practices, they are desperate for community and knowledge-building, and this is something else you might feel called to help organize.

Permaculture and Sustainability Groups

When I first became interested in sustainability and permaculture, I checked a bunch of books out of the library and began reading and studying the concepts. Then I applied what I learned at my own property and observed the results. I volunteered at a local organic garden that grew most of its produce for a local food bank.

Despite this volunteering, I still felt quite isolated—not just away from others who were like me who were doing similar work, but also from the localized knowledge that can't be found in any organic-gardening or design book (the nature of the local soil, what grows well, what are typical pests—the kinds of things I mentioned throughout chapter 6).

Then, a few friends and I created the Oakland County Permaculture Meetup group, a meet-up located in southeastern Michigan. Our goal for the group was to base a community in the principles of permaculture, to build a more "permanent culture," to talk about the host of subjects surrounding it, and to ask people to share their knowledge and to give opportunities for people to teach, learn, and share. These kinds of activities are particularly important because modern culture encourages us toward isolation. Groups come in all shapes and sizes, but a long-term group is likely to help enact the most positive change over a period of time. Our group, in the tradition of other permaculture meet-ups all over the world, used the following strategies to help bring people together and share knowledge.

Skill shares: During our monthly meetings, these skill shares are short lessons ranging from thirty to sixty minutes where one or more members share skills and information, usually in the form of a demonstration, discussion, and hands-on activity. We've had skill shares on fruit tree pruning and grafting, soil blocks and seed starting, vermicomposting, seed saving, root cellar barrels, chickens and permaculture, soapmaking, bread baking, fermentation, animal husbandry, natural building, composting, and much more. Hands-on activities are a critical component of these skill shares.

Special-interest groups: We established "special-interest groups" on the basis of members' interests, generally to take place at other meeting times. We originally had a number of special-interest groups, such as primitive skills, organic gardening, foraging, alternative energies, food preservation, and so forth. What we found is that the groups functioned effectively only with a leader. Special-interest groups can do a lot of different things, but only if the group is big enough, and devoted enough, to support them.

Permablitzes: One of the main functions of our group is the permablitz, an activity where a member of the group asks others for help on a particular project. It is part workday, part educational project. For example, when I needed help building a new chicken run, I invited people over to learn about chickens as part of a garden system, and then folks spent a few hours putting in the chicken run. Another permablitz established four raised-bed gardens for a new gardener, another put in a small pond and perennial garden where there was lawn, and so on.

Potlucks: Most of our meetings and permablitzes feature some kind of food; our regular monthly meetings feature a potluck where we share in the bounty of the local Michigan harvest. We have found that asking everyone to bring their own plates/cups/silverware (nondisposable), having compost and recycling setup, and asking everyone to bring an ingredient label allows for a great potluck!

Movies and speakers: Once in a while, we will offer a movie or invite a guest speaker from outside the local area to come and share their knowledge. Films such as *Inhabit: A Permaculture Perspective* are really useful for a group to see and discuss. Again, this offers opportunity for education and connection.

Sharing resources: Resource sharing is another great way to bring people together. Our group does a seed swap in the late fall, a plant swap in the spring, a "taste and trade" where people bring various items to trade (canned/baked goods, homemade laundry detergent, etc.) and food to enjoy, as well as a group barter day (anything goes).

The power of this kind of community is incredible. We have elders in the group who freely share their knowledge, and we have younger people who inject the group with enthusiasm and energy. We have those who are brand new, and those who want to learn, and all come together. The friendships that I've gained through the process of establishing such a group are important and meaningful.

Groves, Covens, and Spiritual Groups and Gatherings

Yet another great way of bringing people together and sharing is through existing Earth-centered spiritual groups. You can do many of the things I listed above in the context of nature spirituality. In some American druid groups, the term "firesides" has been used (a term I first heard used by Mystic River Grove of the Order of Bards, Ovates, and Druids). Again, these are opportunities for an activity, discussion, or talk about skills. In my first grove, we focused these conversations and demonstrations on sustainable-living skills: a grove member who knew primitive/survival skills taught us about fire starting and knot tying, I gave a presentation on seed starting, another member taught us about cooking with local ingredients from her garden, and so on. These activities usually took place before or after our main ceremony of the day. Tied to these groups are bardic circles, a chance for people to come together to share their talents and provide entertainment. These are yet another nice way of bringing people together, encouraging conversations, and sharing. In addition to regular events, then, sustainable practices can be built into spiritual group activities.

Reading Groups and Full-Moon Potlucks

Even something less structured offers many opportunities to engage in Earth ambassadorship and community learning. One option is a simple reading or discussion group that meets once a month to talk, share, perhaps read a book, or focus on a theme. A second option is for a regularly scheduled potluck. I'll turn here to Strawbale Studio's Full-Moon Potlucks as a powerful example of bringing community together in this way. Once a month, on the night of the full moon (whatever day that falls), Deanne Bednar hosts a tour of her property followed by a potluck feast where everyone brings an Earth-friendly dish with an ingredient label. The potluck offers a circle where people get to share something about themselves and the food they brought and then break bread together. These potlucks offer unstructured opportunities for sharing, community building, conversations, and study of natural building techniques.

Sacred Action in the Workplace

We now shift gears and discuss another potential outreach area that we often have direct access to: our workplaces. Regardless of what workplace setting we are in, we can make small changes that can help the workplace shift away from consumptive and Earth-harming behavior. Usually, initiatives for better recycling, composting, reducing food waste, reducing energy consumption, streamlining practices, planting a small garden, and other workplace practices are initiated by everyday employees. A good druid friend of mine works as an information technology manager for a local hospital. Despite the fact that hospitals are supposed to be places of health, they often aren't, and he had the idea of starting a small workplace garden. The only space they had available was a parking lot. They put in raised beds, using old horse feed bags for growing plants and focusing on hot crops (nightshades such as tomato, peppers, and eggplants) that would like the heat of the parking lot. They had a harvest in their first year, and the project is continuing now in its second year. Sometimes, these small projects have a way of getting much larger over time, and it's up to one or two people to provide the leadership and vision to make them happen.

Sometimes sustainable changes have to go through official channels (such as starting a garden in the hospital parking lot), while others are a bit smaller and can just be done (such as growing medicinal herbs in your windowsill in your office). Following are some broad suggestions for activities that you can try in your own workplace.

Workplace garden: Workplace gardens as sites for exercise and health education are growing in popularity, and employers see these as great ways to help employees stay healthy, possibly thereby lowering healthcare costs.

Reduce, reuse, recycle: Workplaces are all about efficiency, and if there is a way to make things more efficient or save on costs, then employers are interested. I've found good ways in my various workplaces to cut down on paper waste, to be more efficient in recycling, and even to encourage less food waste. Start paying attention to the various "flows" of waste in the office and look for ways to reduce your own and your workplace's waste.

Encourage conversations: Start a series of talks on various things that people share at lunchtime. Create fifteen-minute skill shares where people can talk about their own ecologically friendly living or have open discussions about shifting workplace practices.

Team efforts: There may be others trying to start more environmentally friendly practices in your workplace. Join together, lend your energy and enthusiasm, and get some positive changes happening. Often, these kinds of opportunities for collaboration stem from simply talking with others.

Workplace composting: Vermicomposting, even on a small scale, is a great way to encourage workplace awareness of waste, cycles, and repurposing waste.

Sourcing materials: Another big issue comes from how materials are produced and sourced. Often, better materials can be found; it's just a matter of one person asking the right questions and putting in the legwork for a better supplier.

Food waste: Each time you have a catered meal, whatever isn't eaten is often whisked off by the caterer to the garbage. What I've taken to doing is to keep a set of paper or to save plastic takeout containers in my office, which I can then bring to events and pass out to people. Then, the food goes home and gets eaten rather than in the trash. Chickens are always willing to eat day-old food that was left on the counter overnight.

Alternative views: When I was in high school, I was given the job of putting together craft activities for summer activities at a local park. I looked at the plan and, on the basis of that plan, made a few small suggestions to reduce waste and encourage more-renewable activities (such as finding sticks that dropped from trees rather than purchasing popsicle sticks). These sent a subtle yet powerful message to children and their families. I have found that there many small opportunities like this that you can use to shift small practices that, over time, can have a large impact.

Transportation

Another issue of being out and about in our communities and moving to and from work is transportation. Transportation in terms of sacred action is a tricky beast, primarily because of the issue of access. Everyone needs to get somewhere, and the sheer distances between people (especially here in the US) combined with the lack of good public transportation in many places often makes transportation a real hurdle. Even with these challenges, many people are embracing alternative ways of transporting themselves and are working on ways of reducing their fossil fuel use for transportation. Transportation is something to consider seriously when making potential shifts toward sacred action, since 92% of transportation currently in the US entails the use of fossil fuels.[80]

In my own life, I've gone through a number of different transportation challenges. I've both lived out in the middle of the country on a 3-acre homestead, where my workplace was 18 miles through traffic each way, and rented in a small town where my house was only eight blocks from my workplace. What I've learned through these two experiences is that transportation does matter and that our choices about how close we live to where we work shape how we decide to engage in sacred action in terms of transportation. A factor influencing my decision to make a big move to a new location was transportation—the Detroit metro area was practically devoid of functional public transportation. Even when I had lived less than a mile from my campus earlier in my time in Michigan, I wasn't able to bike to campus or walk due to the extreme traffic flows and lack of sidewalks and bike lanes. When I went out on my bike, I was afraid I would get killed (there was precedent). This is to say that even though some of us are stuck in the circumstances that we are in, we can still review our transportation circumstances and see what we can do to shift them.

Transportation does come down to a matter of choice. Right now, I'm considering my next stage of property ownership. The big tension in my mind is simple: I could stay in town, with limited land, privacy, and very restrictive laws, and live a walkable lifestyle. Or, I could move a few miles out of town, have abundant land and privacy, and still depend on fossil fuels to get into work. This is a choice that many of us face. How close we can live to our workplaces, farmers' markets, doctor's offices, and the like determine our means of transportation. This appears to be an either-or choice, but there is a middle ground. Australian permaculture designer David Holmgren reminds us of the importance of the "edge spaces"; he was able to find a delightful property on the edge of his town within biking distance and build a wonderful homestead there. The proximity, then, between living spaces and workspaces (or other spaces requiring frequent access) does need to be considered when we are in the position to make such choices.

The Biking Lifestyle

More and more people are willingly embracing car-free or low-car living. You are more likely to find these kinds of people in places where things are closer together (usually, in cities or towns) and where there are cycling or public-transportation initiatives, but biking and walking lifestyles are not necessarily limited only to these places. Two of my closest friends live in an old mill town and walk everywhere—they do not have driver's licenses or a vehicle. This is a lifestyle choice for them, a defining feature of how they enact their own druid beliefs in the world. Another friend of mine lives about 11 miles from his work and bikes each way, every day of the year. Yet another friend of mine in a larger city invested in an electric cargo bike and uses that not only to get herself up and down Pittsburgh's hilly terrain but to offer a delivery service for groceries. This biking lifestyle has led her to career opportunities.

Of particular interest are a growing number of efficient bicycles designed to embrace the biking lifestyle. With this new car-free lifestyle, we have seen tremendous advances in design of human-powered transportation options in the last ten years. In fact, a growing number of bicycles that are advanced, environmentally friendly, and efficient are now on the market—and there are free plans online for many. Cargo bikes are longer bikes that are designed to increase a bicycle's carrying capacity and often have saddle bags, a cart, or the ability to tow materials. Recumbent bicycles and tricycles have a different weight distribution than a standard bike and are much more comfortable to ride and pedal for long distances. For an "everyday" bike over long distances, especially for someone who may have back or muscular problems, these are a great option. Velomobiles are another new style of human-powered transportation. They are usually a recumbent bicycle that have a body and therefore extremely good aerodynamics; think about it like a little race car that you sit in that protects you from the weather and also happens to be very efficient in terms of your pedal power. Pedaling in a velomobile offers you three to four times more impact than a typical bicycle. They also can get up to 30 mph due to their design. Electric-assist bikes pair a small electric motor with the bicycle and may be incorporated into any of the above designs. The motor is particularly helpful for hills or heavy loads, or at the end of a long and tiring day.

Many of the above bicycles are much more of an investment than your standard bike, but DIY options are much cheaper, and you can use recycled and repurposed materials. I saw an amazing DIY bike that a high school student made—it was like a little car that you pedaled and had electric assist, complete with a full plastic cover to keep out the weather. He and his father built it one summer when he decided he wasn't interested in pursuing a car-based lifestyle, and he is now working to build a company and sell them more broadly.

The Walking Lifestyle

Sometimes there is just no better alternative than our own two feet! At various points in my life, I've enjoyed embracing the walking lifestyle and have delighted watching my car sit parked for weeks on end as I walk to work, to the bank, to the grocery store, to the coffee shop, to the library, and more. One of my favorite things about the "walking" lifestyle is how close it has brought me to nature. When I was driving my car back and forth to work for five years or carpooling with others, I had little chance to witness the beauty and majesty of the Earth while stuck in traffic. But after moving, I get to walk in all weather, and I can witness the beauty of the raindrops being directed by the tree's branches down its trunk and into its roots, the delight of the first snow or the frozen branches of the February morning, the flight of birds, the cool breeze against my cheek. Even though I'm in a small-town setting where the houses are closely spaced, nature still is present, and different pathways lead to different small discoveries—the chickweed and speedwell growing in the cracks along the sidewalks, the spaces where the brambles burst on the edge of a meandering stream. It has also allowed me to slow down, both physically and mentally, which is important to my spiritual practice.

Other Transportation Considerations

Alternative fuels and vehicles: For those with longer commutes, alternative fuels and alternative vehicles may also be an option. One possibility is running your vehicle on biodiesel or grease. This is a tricky area to enter and requires mechanical knowledge as well as commitment, but it can be highly rewarding. Most successful systems in place for biofuels are community driven and involve a number of individuals working toward a common goal. For example, Sirius Ecovillage in Massachusetts offers a "grease CSA [community-supported agriculture]" where the ecovillage members do the legwork of collecting grease from local restaurants and filtering it, and then people who have "greasecars" (those running on "straight vegetable oil" or SVO) could come, pay a small fee, and pick it up. Another group I was involved with in Michigan was seeking funding to create a small biodiesel operation that would be essentially another CSA. That project didn't get off the ground in the time I was there, but I was excited to see that it was happening. Although some of these kinds of practices take time, they are real options and great possibilities for shifting away from fossil fuel and using existing resources in the community (such as old vegetable oil from restaurants with fryers, for example). If these aren't options, even hybrid and other fuel-efficient vehicles are possibilities, but I would suggest carefully researching your option and looking at the true environmental impact of any choice.

Car sharing: Given that a car may sit very frequently for long periods of time, another alternative model is car sharing. The idea is simple—rather than being the sole owner of a car, you might share it, or you might have a car share where you buy into the membership and have so many days/hours when you can use the car each month. It saves a lot of funds and allows us to more efficiently make use of limited fossil fuel resources.

Public transit: Public transit in many areas of the US is very poor or nonexistent; even some larger cities have challenged public-transportation systems. And yet, in many other places, public transportation is excellent and affordable. Here in the US, I learned about poor transportation systems the hard way while living in the "Motor City"; the public-transit system had been systematically dismantled in the 1940s and 1950s with the rise of the big-three auto companies, and a car was necessary to get anywhere in the city. Other places offer a variety of public-transportation options. When I can, I always opt for public transportation, since I want to support those services. What I have found, even in my small town, is that public pressure to improve public-transit systems (buses and trains, but also such things as bike lanes and bike trails) is highly effective—usually citizen groups are forming or existing for such work, and they are worth supporting with your energy and enthusiasm.

Distance travel: Airline travel remains an extremely fossil-fuel-intensive way to travel; many of us have, as time and resources permit, shifted to other kinds of transportation systems: buses, trains, carpooling, staycations, and so on. The train remains the least fossil-fuel-intensive way to travel and can be an incredible way to see the countryside!

Carbon offsets: Regardless of your transportation choices, a final option is available to you: supporting carbon offsets. When I do need to travel by air, I always do something to offset my carbon: planting more trees, buying carbon credits (such as through terrapass.com), supporting good organizations who are reforesting and protecting habitat, and more. That way, even if you are "stuck" using a particular transportation mode, you can offset some of the impact of that mode of travel.

Intentional and Community Living

We might also think about the role of community in our daily living. As one response to the challenges of our current age, people are moving from "conventional" ways of living and into more-community-based structures that are organized in an intentional manner. An international movement of intentional community living—of many varieties—has been gaining momentum and offers an alternative to conventional living for those interested in this path. Here are some of the most common kinds of structures.

Cohousing: Cohousing is a collaborative neighborhood where individuals each own their private home within the neighborhood but share common areas such as gardens, childcare facilities, and other facilities. Cohousing neighborhoods are typically focused on sustainable living, where resources are shared, projects are done as a community, and long-term relationships are formed.

Housing cooperatives: A housing co-op is where a legal entity owns a piece of real estate—typically one or more residences—and people live within the residences. This might be in an urban, suburban, or rural setting.

Intentional communities: Intentional communities vary widely; commonly a community organization owns all permanent structures, and residents pay "rent" or offer services to a land trust where multiple individuals are "founders" for the community and hold the property in trust.

Income-sharing communes: Income-sharing communes are places where everything in a community is shared among members. The community usually has several streams of income, and all individuals within that community work for the benefit of the community.

Intentional camps: Another spin-off of the community idea is the intentional camp, where those with small campers / RVs / tiny houses come for a season, stay, learn, and work together. These may be short term or longer term.

Intentional communities exist and are forming all over the world—if this is something you are potentially interested in as a way to develop a long-term response and engage in sacred action, I suggest you visit the Fellowship for Intentional Community (www.ic.org) and read *Creating a Life Together: Practical Tools to Grow Ecovillages and Intentional Communities* by Diana Leafe Christian.[81]

Conclusion

Cultivating Care and Creating Places We Want to Live

To conclude, most of what is covered in this chapter is really about bettering our local communities and our broader world, in making spaces that people care about, that they want to invest in, and that they feel proud about. These kinds of investments of time and energy can help us reconnect with each other, and the living Earth, and transition to more-sustaining and life-honoring lives.

Exercises and Rituals

Bardic Arts and Potlucks

Begin practicing a bardic art that you can share with others. Bardic arts include any creative arts: music, stories, singing, dancing, and more. The art of storytelling, for example, is one that people without other musical talents can still enjoy! Host a bardic circle at your home, partnered with other activities (a full-moon potluck, a permaculture meeting), and start building community. You can do this as part of a larger celebration or as something on its own.

Workplace Sacred Actions

Find allies at your workplace and meet to brainstorm ways to make your workplace more sustainable. Set one to three key goals that you can achieve over the period of a year and work to make it happen. You might opt to do something small as an individual first—office vermicomposting, keeping reusable silverware for lunch, using a camping towel in place of paper towels, and so on. And if you are ready—get a small group of people together and help work on a larger vision. A small group of people can make tremendous change in a few short months or years!

Earth Ambassadorship

Find a small way that you can engage in Earth ambassadorship every so often. For me, this involves giving local plant walks and teaching people about the healing plants local to our ecosystem, as well as running a local permaculture meet-up. Look for opportunities to share your knowledge, even informally, and teach people more about the living Earth.

CHAPTER 8

Samhain

Sustainable Ritual Tools, Items, and Objects

At Samhain, we turn to the sacred work we do: with the tools of our craft and our tradition, with the plants and spirits that work with us on our journey, and with the ancestors that guide us. Samhain is a time to reflect back as well as look forward and, for many pagans, is our most sacred holiday. This chapter explores how to create a "sustainable paganism" by exploring the ethics of fair share and Earth care in our pagan practices and the tools we regularly use as part of them. Thus, in this chapter, we consider ways to make our spiritual uses of plants, tools, and offerings sustainable. The triad that guides this chapter is the following:

Three considerations for sacred tools:

Sacred plants for guidance
Tools for manifestation
Offerings of and for the land

Sacred Plants and Sustainable Plant Relationships

From before humanity had recorded history, the plant spirits were there, growing with us, guiding us, healing us, and supporting us on our journey. Our ancestors—of our lands, of our blood, and of our tradition—worked with plants in a multitude of ways, and when we cultivate relationships with those same plants, it is a way to honor them and their knowledge. Today's modern pagan practice continues this sacred plant work: we burn plants for smudging, clearing, and helping to energize spaces. We use trees and plant-based incenses as part of divination and sacred rites. We use plants as healers, for magical healing and physical healing, and to connect with spirit on deep levels. Plants have long been friends of humans—and have long walked beside us, hand in hand, as we do our sacred work.

And yet, in the twenty-first century, we are seeing the demand for certain "sacred" plants used commonly in pagan practices so high that it is threatening these species worldwide. In fact, many plants that are favorites of the pagan community that are easy to purchase at local pagan shops (such as white sage, frankincense, palo santo, and sandalwood)[82] are critically endangered or threatened according to the International Union for the Conservation of Nature's Red List.[83] These plants are critically endangered *because* of their overuse, particularly by people who are far disconnected from their growth, harvest, and ecosystems and who don't realize the impact of purchasing these plants. As this book explores in a multitude of ways, we can consider our use of plants in ritual and sacred purposes from several angles: from the ethics of people care, fair share, and Earth care as well as from perspectives of physical (outer/material) and spiritual (inner/sacred) perspectives.

The Physical: Land, Livelihood, Indigenous Practice, and Ecosystems

I already grow and use a lot of my own herbs for spiritual and medicinal purposes but occasionally still enjoy the choice rare ingredient that I purchase or that is given to me as a gift. Recently, I was burning a piece of palo santo a friend had given me, and received this distinct question: "Do you even know me?" The answer was, shamefully, no, I did not. So I started to research it, and I found a host of material that suggests that the ethics of palo santo are all about the sourcing: it can be harvested sustainably by local peoples or it can be stripped bare. In holding my own piece of palo santo wood, I realized I couldn't answer the important questions: Where did this come from? How was it harvested? Who harvested it? Who profited from it? A few days later, after doing some research, I saw a post shared by a friend on social media. This post came from a woman native to Colombia who said that palo santo was being stripped from her forests, and she was begging people to stop using it.

Palo santo is hardly unique in this respect—there are so many plants that are now in global demand due to their uses for medicine or spiritual purposes. Kelly Ablard's research[84] on essential-oil plants is useful to this discussion. As she describes, as global demand for certain plants rise, the plants become so lucrative that they are overharvested and can be poached, reducing biodiversity and threatening local people's traditions and livelihoods. Thus, in purchasing plants for spiritual supplies, we can make choices that encourage people care (enhancing local and indigenous people's livelihoods), Earth care (supporting biodiversity and the continuance of endangered species), and fair share (supporting ethical and sustainable harvesting). Or, we can make unknown choices that may be threatening the very plants we hold sacred. Thus, knowledge of sourcing is critically important.

In fact, I have witnessed the vicious cycle of overharvesting driven by global demand firsthand here in the Appalachian Mountains. When I was a child, my grandfather used to harvest with beautiful wild ginseng roots, and we would brew ginseng tea and enjoy it, quietly sipping it as we observed the land around us. I remember those roots—the look of them, the feel of them, the energy of them. This was ancestral medicine, and he had cultivated a patch that had been shown to him by his own grandfather. Grandpa would only ever bring back a small amount, as he told me once, "My grandkids will be able to harvest this as I did." However, the patch was stripped bare by ginseng wild harvesters ages ago—every last root was taken. A good-quality dried American ginseng root, wild harvested, currently goes for between $500 and $800 a dried pound, and the demand globally for ginseng is growing each year. What happens is that people literally scour our mountains, and when they find the roots, they harvest all they can. Over the years, I have covered thousands of miles of forests in this region, and yet, since I was a child, I've never seen a single wild ginseng plant. The demand for ginseng is primarily from China—a far-off place wanting to pay top dollar for high-quality ginseng. Chinese people buying American ginseng have no idea of the impact their purchasing has on wild ginseng populations here. Locals here don't even get to see the plant, much less build a relationship with it—it is no longer part of our forest ecology. That same story can be told about many, many of these in-demand sacred plants—and I think it's useful to see that this overharvesting problem can happen anywhere.

Thus, knowing which plants are of particular concern and how they are harvested is also an important part of engaging in sacred action. A lot of plants that are endangered are "whole plant" harvests, with ginseng being a good example—if harvesting wood or roots, or all the aerial parts of a plant, what is left of that plant afterward? One good source of information on certain plants in North America is the United Plant Savers.[85] In 2018, white sage was added to their list due to wild harvesting and overharvesting.

The other challenging piece of this that ties to our ethic of "people care" is cultural appropriation. While smudging (smoke cleansing) is used widely globally, the use of particular plants for smoke cleansing is tied to certain indigenous practices. White sage has been in the spotlight recently as one such plant. Increased demand for white sage use is driving up the prices and reducing native access to wild white sage (due to commercial wild harvesting), and putting plants at risk. The questions that I am left with are these: Is it right or ethical that we use these plants to the point of their extinction? Is it right to create such demand for plants that native peoples who depend on them for spiritual practices cannot find them to use? Can we find a better way?

The Spiritual: Energy, Honoring, and Connections

Even if we put every physical consideration of people care, Earth care, and fair share aside, there are still spiritual matters to consider. In working with physical plants, we also work to honor, connect with, and work with the spirit of the plant. Attending to our connection and relationship with the spirit of a specific plant we are using matters if we want our spiritual practices to have effect. Yes, I could wave some rosemary and sage around to "clear" my room before doing a ritual, but if my relationship with sage is one rooted in blind consumption, and not connection or sustainable practice, is the spirit of that sage really going to want to support my efforts? As we explored in chapter 3, what energy tied to the plant's harvest and sale is being brought into my ritual at the same time? The way in which the plant was obtained has a direct relationship with the connection—and depth of connection—that one is able to have with the plant. If I purchase a plant from an unknown source, I am bringing all the energy of that source into my spiritual practice. Who harvested it, how it was harvested, how it was handled, how it was sold, how it was transported—and in the case of poaching and overharvesting to the threat of the species, that may be energy I do not want to have as part of my ceremony. What was that plant's life—and harvest—like? Was it harvested respectfully? If not, do I even have any hope of connecting with the plant spiritually? These questions are critical in developing spiritual practices surrounding plant use.

Any time we use a plant as part of our sacred practices, we are building relationships with that plant. Plants work physically and spiritually, but for many of the deeper spiritual uses, they really do require a deep connection. For example, many herbalists understand and quietly share about visionary properties of calamus (sweet flag). In order to connect with calamus on that level, you have to connect with the spirit of the calamus, building a relationship with it over a long period of time. As part of this, you have to work with the plant, tend it, plant it, spend time with it, meditate with it, and ethically and respectfully harvest it. At some point, sometimes years or decades later, calamus open you up for visions and experiences. This isn't something you can buy or purchase or force to happen. Calamus offers you a process of initiation—and it must be done with the utmost respect and patience. Most sacred plants work just like this.

Thus, the need to cultivate deep relationships to really "know" a plant and use it for good spiritual effect is necessary for every plant we might work with spiritually. Each plant offers us an initiation into its own mysteries, teachings, and magic, and having those initiations will allow you to use the plant to its full magical or spiritual effect. However, we have to build that relationship. It's hard to build a relationship with a plant that has had suffering, death, and pain as part of its sourcing. In the case of some plants, sure, you can use them spiritually, but you aren't ever going to breach that barrier into deeper work if these other concerns are present. I can burn my piece of palo santo, and it smells nice and produces a calming energy. But that experience is a very surface one. Under no circumstances could I ever build a deep relationship with that particular wood, given the conditions under which it was harvested and the energy that it now carries with it.

Ethical and Sustainable Plant Use

Given the above, I'd like to advocate for the key practice of ethical plant use in neopagan paths through the three ethics present in this book. People care encourages us to think about the sourcing of the plant (if you are not growing it yourself) and how the harvest of this plant is tied to local communities and local labor. Earth care asks us to consider how the harvest of this plant may have affected the plant and plant species itself, as well as the broader ecosystem where the plant grows. Fair share asks us to take only what we need of the plant, and, certainly, to make sure this plant is available to indigenous peoples who might depend on it—fair share can take place both on an individual level and a cultural level. Now let's consider a range of alternative practices to simply "consuming" plants in general, and then, I share a very specific example for handcrafting your own smoke cleansing / smudge sticks.

Substitutions: Palo santo, frankincense, sandalwood, and other exotic plants smell amazing—but many local substitutes can also be used. For example, the resin of many pine trees is a wonderful substitution for frankincense (currently threatened with overharvesting). You can often find this resin locally, collect it, and use it. White pine is one of my favorite resins for this purpose. It comes out of the tree sticky and, over a period of about a year or two, dries. You can burn it sticky or dried. Here are a few of the most endangered "spiritual" plants and some suggested alternatives.

- Frankincense can be replaced with any pine resin; each pine has its own distinct scent. See what pines are growing in your region and experiment. Pine resins can be harvested sustainably; when harvesting them, make sure you do not cut into the tree but take only what is dried or dripped on the trunk.

- Sandalwood can be replaced with cedar wood or juniper wood; again, see what is local and accessible. Nontreated cedar or juniper sawdust makes a great alternative to powdered sandalwood.
- White sage can be grown in pots or in a garden or can be replaced with any other sage; garden sage is a great substitution and is readily available. Each sage has its own unique smell.
- Palo santo is unique and is hard to replace. Sometimes combinations of herbs can get you to a similar scent. I like to combine herbs including lavender, mugwort, cinnamon, and rosemary.
- Rosewood is also unique; it can be replaced with a rose essential oil or rose petals.
- Atlas cedarwood can be replaced with other more-local cedars.

Ethical purchasing: Purchasing has power: you can leverage your dollars in ways that support sustainability and that help honor the plant and build livelihoods and ecosystems for local peoples. If you are buying locally or online, before you buy, ask some good questions to ensure an ethical and sustainable harvest. Here are some questions you can ask:

- Where does this plant come from? Look for places engaged in sustainable harvesting and that specify who harvests it, how the plants are sustained over time, and ecological considerations. If this information is not present, sustainability and ethics are likely not being considered.
- How is this plant harvested? Learn about your plant. Root, bark, or wood harvests are most damaging and can often kill the plant, but other harvests, such as leaf or resin, may also be extremely damaging, particularly if they harm the plant or prevent it from going to seed. Find out where your plant is grown and what its conservation status is.
- Who harvested this plant? Under what conditions? How are individuals, cultures, and communities affected by this harvest? Be skeptical of a "wild harvest" label without any clarification, recognizing the lack of oversight for many wild-harvesting operations.
- Who is profiting from this plant? Are local people gaining the bulk of the profit?

- If purchasing locally, if the shop owner can't tell you the answers (especially to the first three questions), perhaps encourage that person to consider a different source. If buying online, you can ask the same information if it is not available. As an example, Mountain Rose Herbs describes their ethical sourcing of palo santo and their conservation efforts, specifically, how purchasing palo santo from them supports Ecuadorian people and the replanting of palo santo trees. To me, this is critical—a good purchase can do a lot of good and support people care, Earth care, and fair share.

Ethical growing: The easiest way to manage a population and cultivate deep relationships is to grow it yourself, if you can. For example, I never buy white sage, but I love the smell and I do like to use it as part of certain incense blends that I make and use regularly. Because I know it is so endangered, I have learned to grow it myself and save seeds of it each year. Even if you don't have land to grow large amounts of plants on, you can still grow a number of your own magical herbs in pots in your home or patio. In fact, many garden herbs are potential magical allies and readily available for purchase in the spring. A pot of rosemary, garden sage, white sage, bay laurel, thyme, or lavender would each be very useful culinary, magical, and medicinal allies—and you build your relationship considerably with each time and each plant. See the list that follows for some ideas if you are in the East Coast or Midwest regions.

Ethical wild harvesting: Some plants, and trees, are harder to grow in pots in your windowsill or garden but certainly can be wild-harvested ethically, taking only what you need, helping populations grow by spreading seeds. I like to wild-harvest plants on private lands (asking landowners, developing relationships with them) so that I know exactly how many people are harvesting there and how much is being taken. Harvesting on public lands presents a much-larger problem because even if you take only a little, you are never sure how much is being taken by others. Regardless, you can do this ethically by learning about the plant, the ecosystem, and seeing how much of the plant is available locally.

Creating Your Own Incenses and Smudge Sticks

To show how cultivating more-sacred and more-sustainable plant relationships can be done on a very specific level, I'll share information about creating your own smudge/smoke cleansing sticks with local, homegrown, or foraged ingredients. Creating homemade smudge sticks with local ingredients is a wonderful activity to do at Samhain. As the plants die back, you can harvest whatever you aren't using for other purposes to create a number of beautiful smudges. These can be used for clearing, honoring spirits, protection, setting intentions, letting go, bringing in, and preparing for ritual or mediation. You can craft smudges that can be used for different purposes and craft them with intent.

Here is a list of potential plants for the East Coast and Midwest regions of the US that can be used in your own smudges and incense blends. When harvesting any ingredients, take into consideration how much of the plant there is, so that you can ensure an ethical harvest. Part of why I strongly suggest making smudge sticks near Samhain is that most plants you would grow or wild-craft have gone to seed and have already reproduced and are in the process of dying off for the season; that way, you aren't taking something that may inadvertently harm the ecosystem.

Aromatic cultivated and wild-harvested herbs: This list represents plants that you can easily find in the wild or grow in a garden. (C) refers to the need to cultivate this herb, while (W) indicates that you can likely find it in the wild.

- **Bay leaf (C) (*Laurus nobilis*):** Bay has a wide range of magical uses: to banish or expel, to protect, to support, to prepare folks for deeper magical work. If you aren't sure what to use as smudge, bay is a great choice due to its flexibility! You can cultivate bay plants; alternatively, pick up some bay leaves in the spice section of the grocery store.
- **Coltsfoot (C) (*Tussilago farfara*):** Coltsfoot is used primarily for divination, and due to its very early bloom time in the spring and beautiful yellow flower, it is also associated with sun work and the coming of spring. Leaves can be harvested in the spring or fall; you can find it along roadways in full sun or partly shaded areas. The leaf is large and can be used as a wrap for other smudge ingredients. The flower, looking similar to a dandelion but smaller, and blooming in early spring, can also be used in smudges.

- **Eucalyptus (C) (*Eucalyptus* spp.):** Another herb for clearing work; its smolders nicely and produces a powerful scent. It combines beautifully with sage and lavender. While you can find it in craft stores in the US, it is often treated, so it is better to grow it yourself or wild-harvest it.

- **Hyssop (C) (*Hyssopus officinalis*):** Hyssop is an herb with ancient connections to purification work; you can also use this to keep away negativity. Hyssop smells wonderful when burned. Anise hyssop can be used in a similar way; it is more aromatic and smells like black licorice.

- **Lavender (C) (*Lavandula* spp.):** Lavender helps with clear thinking, relaxation, and focus. You can use both leaf stalks and flower heads in smudges—lavender flowers give smudges beautiful colors and appeal. Lavender combines beautifully with sage or sweetgrass.

- **Lemongrass (C) (*Cymbopogon* spp.):** Lemongrass can be used for cleansing, removing obstacles, and purification. You can grow this or even pick up organic stalks in the local grocery store. It burns with a lemony scent and produces good smoke.

- **Mugwort (W, C) (*Artemisia vulgaris*):** Mugwort is specifically tied to dreams and can produce very vivid dreaming. It is also wonderful for any other kind of trance or journeying work. Mugwort also grows beautifully straight and tall and really does do well in smudges.

- **Mullein (W) (*Verbascum thapsus*):** Soft, fuzzy mullein leaves have a nice "smoldering" quality—they smolder in the same way that sage smolders. They don't smell nearly as nice, but the smoke itself does have a beneficial impact on the lungs and can, medicinally, be used for "clearing out" the lungs of toxins. In Buddhist practice, the lungs are said to house grief. Thus, it can be used to clear out deep emotions and aid with emotional recovery.

- **Rosemary (C) (*Rosmarinus officinalis*):** Rosemary is another clearing and protective herb. Interestingly enough, you can use both the root and the plant of rosemary—and they have different qualities and burn differently. The rosemary stalks burn wonderfully in a smudge. Don't let them get too dried out before wrapping your smudge, or the needles fall off easily.

- **Sage (W, C) (*Salvia* spp.):** Sage is a clearing herb that helps purify and cleanse spaces of negative energy. All sages energetically work similarly, but they do have some fairly distinct smells. Here are some different sage options: **white sage** can be grown in gardens and has a potent, distinctive smell. **Desert sage** also has a lighter, sweeter smell than white sage; again, it can be cultivated or wild-harvested depending on where you live. **Garden sage** is a wonderful choice for multiple purposes—culinary arts as well as smudge sticks. I harvest back the garden sage plants in the fall for use in smudges and for cooking! Garden sage burns with a deeper sage smell. **Clary sage** has larger leaves and a muskier smell.

- **Scented geranium (C) (*Pelargonium* spp.):** Geranium is associated with prosperity, happiness, and love. The leaves and stalks of scented geraniums make wonderful smudge stick ingredients.
- **Sweet clover (W) (*Melilotus officinalis*):** Sweet clover is a great locally available plant that smells fairly similar to sweetgrass (and attracts spirits and honors them, like sweetgrass). Sweet clover is dotted over roadsides and fields around midsummer, where you can gather it and dry it in preparation for making smudges at Samhain.
- **Sweetgrass (C) (*Hierochloe odorata*):** Sweetgrass gets spirits' attention and can be used in any visionary or spirit-honoring work. I cultivate a patch of sweetgrass (moved with me several times and originally given as a gift), and it works great for smudges.
- **Thyme (C) (*Thymus vulgaris*):** This gentle garden and culinary herb is an incredibly powerful magical plant. Thyme helps with the removal of negative emotions, healing, and emotional healing.
- **Tobacco (C) (*Nicotinana rustica*):** Homegrown tobacco is my go-to offertory plant, for making offerings in particular to the spirits of the land, particularly of the plant kingdom. Tobacco also amplifies the power of other plants.
- **Valerian (C) (*Valeriana officinalis*):** Valerian is one of the most powerful and potent cleansing and clearing herbs. A little valerian root goes a long way. The flowers, stalks, and root all can be used. Be warned: valerian has a very potent "sweet wet dog" smell as it dries, but it clears out negativity better than anything else. Burn with the windows open!
- **Wormwood (C, W) (*Artemisia absinthium*):** Wormwood burns beautifully and functions like valerian, but with less intensity; thus, it can be used for protection and clearing.
- **Yarrow (C, W) (*Achillea millefolium*):** Yarrow is another herb I like to use a lot in my smudges for its energetic qualities. Yarrow is used for workings where you don't want to be seen or you need to hide or conceal something. It is also useful for strength and divination.

Trees and shrubs: Trees and shrubs offer many possibilities for smudges.

- **Eastern red cedar / juniper (*Juniperus virginiana*):** Juniper is a strongly protective herb and is useful for male strength and for banishing. Juniper burns beautifully in smudges but does have little prickly bits, particularly as it dries.
- **Eastern white cedar (*Thuja occidantalis*):** Eastern white cedar is a great smudge to help cleanse and open up a sacred space. It also helps with cleansing negative emotions, grief, or other pain. It is also tied to longevity and illumination. If you use the cedar branches when they are first dried, they smell wonderful but literally crackle and pop when you burn them due to all the volatile oils they contain. However, if you hang the cedar in your house for a few months and let it dry out, the oils slowly dry out of the cedar, and then you can make your smudge sticks.
- **White pine (*Pinus strobus*):** White pine is associated with peace (both outer and inner), drawing things out (including pain), cleansing and purification, and wayfinding. White pine needles burn beautifully and smell a bit like a pine vanilla when they burn. Wonderful in any smudge stick!
- **Blue spruce (*Picea pungens; Picea glauca*):** Spruce offers healing, resilience, strength, and getting past the darkness. The Latin name says a lot about the scent of the spruce tree: *pungens*—it is pungent! The blue spruce has a very musky smell, which goes well for working with animal magic and other nature-focused approaches. The white spruce is less musky and very strengthening and potent. Beware—most spruce needles are sharp and may need to be handled carefully when harvesting and making smudges.
- **Staghorn sumac (*Rhus typhina*):** Staghorn sumac is a wonderful addition to any smudge stick. If you are using the leaves, you need to get them into the center of the smudge stick or they crumble as they dry. You can make smudges with small clusters of berries or collect and use the leaves after they have gone red in the fall for the best smoke. Staghorn sumac has a very calming effect and smolders nicely—plus, it is a beautiful red color that provides visual beauty in your smudge. Staghorn sumac is a plant that offers creative approaches to thinking and encourages cunning and intelligence.

Visual components: You can craft smudge sticks not just energetically but also visually; this is where various wild flowers can lend a hand. Most of the flowers don't have a particularly strong smell when burned, but a bit of purple or yellow or white in your smudge can look absolutely beautiful (and add energetically to your smudge). A visit to any flower field at the height of the summer or in late fall will certainly give you much to work with: asters, goldenrods, and daisies are good choices. You can also cultivate flowers such as baby's breath to include in your smudges; dried yarrow flowers are particularly delightful! Again, I would not buy these commercially since they are almost always sprayed with chemicals, which you don't want to make airborne. Before including flowers in your smudges, I suggest burning a bit of the flower to make sure it has the smell you are looking for!

Step-by-Step Instructions for Making Your Smudge

Now that we have some sense of what ingredients can be used in a smudge, the next step is gathering them and actually making the smudge.

Step 1—gather materials: Go out and gather your materials. I have found that plants can be gathered and used fresh or dried. I typically make smudges at the following holidays: summer equinox and Lughnasadh for fresh herbs, and fall equinox or Samhain after the frost has wilted the plants a bit and they are starting to dry out naturally. You can gather your plant material from a variety of places, such a cultivated garden, an abandoned lot, an edge space, a field, or a forest. Before you gather your material, ask for permission from the plant and use inner listening skills to see if you can gather—I do not advocate taking any plant material without permission and an offering. If you are given permission, make an offering (*see below*) and then harvest a small bit of the plant. In addition to the herbs/plants you gather, you'll also need some cotton string (don't use anything synthetic, since you will be burning it) and some scissors.

Step 2—set intentions: Create a sacred space (see chapter 1, "Exercises and Rituals"). Different traditions would do this in different ways, of course, and you might just do something simple to set up your space. Light candles, call in the elements, and invite the energy of Samhain into your space.

Step 3—create your bundle: Start by laying out the herbs that you want to use in your smudge. Select whatever herbs speak to you, or use the lists I've offered earlier.

Step 4—wrap your bundle: Gather your ingredients up in one hand and loosely bunch them. Cut a long piece of the string and begin wrapping your ingredients. Start at the bottom of the bundle, tying off the string. Then wrap it up the bundle and back down, making sure the string wraps every inch or so around the bundle. If you wrap them too tight, the smudge may not burn (depending on what's in it), so experiment with your herbs/plants and tightness. I like to take my cotton string up and down the smudge twice, which helps hold it together a bit better than only one trip up and down.

Step 5—tie off: Tie your smudge off so that it's secure.

Step 6—trim: Once you've wrapped your smudge, you can trim it up a bit. I trim both the ends and the little bits that stick out (they will have trouble burning).

Step 7: Allow your smudge to dry out four to eight weeks (depending on what's inside and how wet it was when you put it in there).

SMUDGE STICKS

Recipes for Smudge Sticks

The following are some recipes you can use as you are creating smudges. You can use the same combination of ingredients for an incense blend as well—just chop finely and burn on a charcoal block. You may not have all the ingredients on these lists—you can eliminate ingredients you don't have or make substitutions. In the end, your intuition should be the best gauge for what plants to put together for what purposes. You can also use any of this list for incense blends rather than smudge sticks.

Recipes for the Wheel of the Year

- **Winter solstice smudge: for bringing the light back into the world.** Cedar, juniper, and white pine.
- **Imbolc smudge: for renewal.** Hyssop, rosemary, cedar, and sage.
- **Spring equinox smudge: purification.** Lavender, sage, and cedar.
- **Beltane smudge: fertility and creativity.** Wormwood, motherwort, lavender.
- **Summer solstice smudge: drawing strength and power.** Scented geranium, wormwood, juniper.
- **Lughnasadh smudge: land blessing/offering.** Tobacco, white pine, sage.
- **Fall equinox smudge: seeking balance.** Bay, rosemary, mullein, thyme, and white pine.
- **Samhain smudge: honoring the ancestors.** Bay, sweetgrass, sweet clover, cedar.

Recipes for Other Purposes

- **Visioning and journeying smudge:** Any of the following, individually or in combination: mugwort, bay, lavender, sweetgrass, sweet clover, yarrow, white pine, staghorn sumac
- **Letting go of grief/pain:** mullein, juniper, thyme, white pine
- **Really super cleansing:** valerian, rosemary, wormwood
- **Divination:** coltsfoot, mugwort, white pine
- **Establishing sacred/ritual space:** bay, yarrow, sage, cedar, staghorn sumac

Incense

The same recipes and materials above can be used not only for smudge stick making but for incenses of all kinds. All the recipes above can be made into a loose incense (noncombustible incense) that you can burn on a charcoal block. For all incense, you want your materials fully dried out. Thus, if you are growing them and harvesting them yourself, let them sit on a counter out of direct sunlight for a week or use a dehydrator on a low setting for twelve to twenty-four hours.

In creating your incense, you will want to attend to the balance of materials and try different combinations of ingredients. For example, for an ancestor incense, I would start with the base recipe above: bay, sweetgrass, sweet clover, and cedar. I'd use a powdered cedar as my base (4 parts) and then add 2 parts sweetgrass / sweet clover and 1 part bay. This recipe is one that I worked out on the basis of smell to my liking; how much bay to cedar to sweetgrass is somewhat a matter of taste.

For making any incense, start by making sure your materials are fully dry. Then, using a mortar and pestle (dedicated to this purpose), grind up your materials as finely as possible. You might find that you need to cut some of them with scissors, since leafy or stem material is harder to grind when it is large. Another tool that is useful for this process is a small dedicated coffee grinder. You can place a small amount of your incense ingredients into the coffee grinder and then grind them up. The smaller the materials are, the more consistently they burn.

Sustainable Ritual Tools, Clothing, and Objects

While plants have special consideration as part of nature, many other kinds of tools that we use as pagans all have natural sources, and thus we should consider them from a sustainability perspective as well. If we return to the discussion in chapter 4 about materialism, excess stuff, and waste, we can specifically apply many of the suggestions with regard to spiritual tools and objects. The basic principles here are, again, bringing in items into our spiritual lives that do not carry excess negative energy from their production, buying or using materials that are sustainable or offer "low impact," and considering what we need and how much we need for our spiritual practices.

Natural objects: Natural objects (sticks, stones, etc.) collected locally are wonderful because they have very little impact and can be used as tools and altar pieces. They can be harvested from nature locally, used for a period of time, and returned to nature. These produce no waste and are inherently sustainable. Natural objects from your local ecosystem are the most sustainable; however, when you are harvesting them, consider the impact. Taking a branch that has dropped in a storm is better than cutting one from a tree, for example.

Stones, gems, and crystals: Environmental and social impacts of mining for gems and stones are often hidden but can take the form of acid mine drainage (which pollutes thousands of miles of streams) or child labor practices. Unfortunately, it is frequently difficult to trace the origins of stones and crystals. For example, tourmaline, blue and smoky quartz, citrine, and amethyst coming from the Congo region employ children as young as seven to work in the mines, and the mines have almost no environmental regulation. Most gems aren't purchased from mines, however, but rather at large gem and mineral trade shows, where a seller of stones may not know where the stones they are buying are from—and thus, when you buy them, the origins are unknown. Gathering your own stones or finding stones that are ethically mined can help you engage in sacred action. Most states in the US have at least one "dig your own" mine, and these mines are often more sustainably run than large-scale industrial mines that extract crystals and stones. Consider asking the same kinds of questions you would for plants: Where does it come from? What is the environmental impact? Who mined this and under what conditions?

Repurposed and created materials for tools, altars, and more: Thrift stores, yard sales, or even someone's "spring cleaning" pile can be excellent places to find basic ritual tools such as bowls, candlesticks, offering plates, and so forth. For these kinds of finds, if you are concerned about the energy that they have, on the basis of previous ownership, place them in the sunlight for a few days to "clear" them. Additionally, you might consider working to make your own tools and supplies, and then you can control what materials go into the tools and also source materials in an ethical manner.

Handcrafted supplies: Supporting regional or local artists is another great way to support good people doing good work. For example, for statuary, jewelry, or clothing, consider finding a small-scale artist who hand-produces their work. Online marketplaces or local art festivals can often connect you to these artisans; additionally, working with the artist allows you to ask questions about the materials and their origins.

Clothing: The clothing industry is one of the most environmentally destructive in the world, polluting waterways, employing child labor, and generating massive amounts of waste and carbon each year. You can look for robes and other ritual-wear clothing options that are made from sustainable fabrics and materials, such as organic cotton or hemp, and that are made by small-scale producers at a living wage. Wool is another very sustainable resource that can make a great ritual robe for colder climates. You can also sometimes find very good ritual wear at thrift stores (such as simple robes and dresses) or learn to make your own.

Offerings and Sustainability

Another critical pagan practice is making offerings. Offerings may be made in honor of deities, ancestors, spirit guides, spirits of the land, or the Earth mother herself, or to other spirit beings. In most traditional pagan books, you may see suggestions for offerings on the basis of their appropriateness or historical significance, such as offering wine, a coin, a pinch of salt, whiskey, and so on. While many of these suggestions are rooted in history, in the twenty-first century, purchasing them is often now wrapped up in the same consumerist system that is damaging the planet. Take, for example, the humble bottle of wine you pick up at the supermarket for your next ritual. The supermarket bottle of ritual wine has at least three potential issues associated with it. First, the physical production and transport of the simple bottle of ritual wine has a network of various energies, resources, and potential pollution tied up in it. Where does the wine come from? Who produced it? How were the grapes grown and processed? How many pesticides were used to grow them? How far did it have to travel, and how many fossil fuels were burned on that trip? If this wine was not produced sustainably and harmed the Earth in its creation and transport, is this the offering you want to make? Additionally, we should consider the spiritual energies associated with the same bottle of wine. How many other people handled it before you? What other energies might be present? How do those energies interfere with your intentions? The final issue is internal to you—your intentions and energy expended in getting the offering. By doing something so effortless as grabbing a wine off the shelf, paying for it, and uncorking it for your offering, is this really an "offering" in the traditional sense? For those of us who have lived our whole lives in consumerist society, going to the store and purchasing a bottle of wine doesn't really seem like an issue. It's something we don't even think about—we need an offering, so we go buy one. And yet, as this book has demonstrated over and over again, the easy choices are often not the most-sustainable ones, and for something as sacred as an offering, it may be useful to take a different approach.

I'd like to suggest three general principles for sacred action with regard to offerings. If we look at the traditional role of offerings (as described beautifully in Catherine Bell's *Ritual* book),[86] we can see that offerings were often inherently tied to people's land, livelihoods, and harvests. Wine was a traditional offering because it took work: growing the grapes, harvesting them, pressing them, and fermenting them took months of labor, and thus, offering wine was offering some of that labor in thanks. This is also why we see first-harvest offerings of bread or meat—again, it is a real gesture to honor spirit. If we think about offerings in these terms, they are inherently tied not only to the bounty of the local land, but to the labor of those making the offering. These were the offerings of our ancestors: things grown where they lived, and produced by their own hands.

To honor our ancestors, we might consider three basic principles for more-sustainable and more-meaningful offerings: first, an offering should hold some value and meaning to you. Second, an offering should, at minimum, not cause the Earth any harm (in its production) and, ideally, shoud support and nurture the Earth in some way. Third, an offering cannot only be physical (wine, herbs) but also energetic (investing your time). Let's now consider some alternatives for offerings.

Handmade or grown offerings: Consider how investing your time in something handmade or hand grown holds power. You might do some baking, make a woodburning or a fallen stick and then offer it to the fire, or offer a handcrafted bundle of herbs. Using suggestions from chapter 6 and the above list of herbs in this chapter, you might consider growing a small patch of offering herbs. Grow lavender, mugwort, and rosemary; harvest it at a fortuitous time (such as the fall equinox or Samhain); dry the herbs; and carry them with you in an offering bag. Home brewing is another popular method of creating sustainable offerings. The important thing here is that offerings come from the heart.

Offerings of energy and time: Another way you might make an offering is by investing your time in conservation or cleanup efforts. Three hours of planting trees with a local conservation group, for example, sends a strong message to spirits. Picking up garbage along a trail, helping replant damaged ecosystems, doing a river cleanup, and many other options all are ways that you can make an offering that supports and nurtures the land.

Nonphysical offerings: Nonphysical things make wonderful offerings as well, and they do not have an environmental cost. Musical practices such as drumming,

Offering Herbs

dancing, and singing can be a great offering of your time, energy, and spirit. Prayers, sayings, or poems are also great offerings. I will also note here that music in particular is a great offering if you want to honor the spirits while others are around—I like to take my flute to majestic places (which often have other people visiting them) and play a song or two. The intention of the song is an offering to the spirits of the land, but it doesn't hurt to have others hear it too. Think about what gifts that you have that you might offer in this way—or what gifts you might cultivate.

Gifts of the body: As discussed in chapter 3, you can also offer "liquid gold" to plants as a direct offering of nitrogen. Give of your body to nature, just as nature has given to you. You might also do this with simple breath: breathe directly on leaves, knowing that they are taking in your carbon dioxide and releasing oxygen for you.

Conclusion

What I hope this chapter has shown is that there are many possibilities to engage in sacred action though the creation of meaningful ritual objects, ritual gear, and offerings. Our spiritual practices can be a blessing not only to ourselves, but to our broader lands. In cultivating this blessing, we connect more deeply to the land, her spirits, and the divine.

Exercises and Rituals

Researching a Local Substitute

Choose one of your favorite herbs or materials that you regularly purchase as part of your spiritual practice. Research that item, seeing if you can find a sustainable source for it. If you can, consider switching to that sustainable source. If you cannot, consider exploring your local ecosystem to see if you can find a substitute that will work for you both physically and energetically.

Herbal Wild-Crafted Blessing Oil

An herbal blessing oil is a simple magical tool that you can make that directly comes from the living Earth. The herbal blessing oil can be used to bless ritual tools, trees, yourself, other people, or anything else you like. Your own unique blend of herbs and wild-crafted ingredients allow you to create something unique to you. For this, you want to gather fresh or dried plant material. Fresh material can obviously be gathered in season; you can purchase or dry your own plant material otherwise. The list under "smudge sticks" can give you some good ideas about what plant matter to try.

Gathering aromatic plant material: Use the instructions above for how to make an offering and gather aromatic plants. Aromatic plant material is that which has a high concentration of volatile oils (which is what essential oil is made from). When you crush the leaves of a plant or needles of a conifer and you can smell that wonderful smell, this is an aromatic plant. Even if it's winter, you can gather conifers to make a potent oil.

Purchased material: If you purchase your material, make sure it is organic and ethically sourced. You don't want any chemicals in your blend, and you want to make sure that materials are ethically sourced. Even though you purchased it, I suggest still making an offering to the land in thanks for the herbs before proceeding.

Fresh plant material: Once you've gathered your plant material or have obtained dried material, chop up the plant material into small pieces (1 inch or so in length). Spread the plant material out on a baking tray or similar surface. Allow the plant material to wilt on the counter indoors for a day, so that some of the water is removed from it (wilting it in the sun will strip it of the aromatic oils). Wait till it dries out at least partially to reduce or eliminate the water in your sacred oil—water makes the oil go rancid. Water will shows up like small bubbles at the bottom of the oil.

Making Your Oil

Open a sacred space: Open up a sacred space (as described in chapter 1).

Making your oil: Start with a pint mason jar or other glass jar. Using a pair of scissors or a mortar and pestle, break up the large plant material / grind up the plant material. As you do this, chant, sing, or set your intentions, then loosely pack the plant material into the jar. Now, take a good-quality organic olive oil or other shelf-stable oil (ethically sourced fractionated coconut oil or almond oil are other good choices) and pour the oil over the plant matter until it is completely covered.

Infusing your oil: Let the plant matter infuse in view of the sun and moon (such as in a windowsill) for at least seven days, during the period of Samhain. If the plant matter is wet, you want to infuse it for no longer than seven days. For dried matter, you can infuse it longer, up to a single lunar cycle.

Straining your oil: On the seventh day (or end of the lunar cycle), get a fine strainer and strain the plant matter out. If you don't have a strainer, one ply of a paper towel can work, but it takes a while to drip through. Sometimes, a cheesecloth or thin paper towel (one layer) can be used to get final bits of plant matter out. Getting out as much plant matter is critical because plant matter will make the oil go rancid much more quickly.

Finishing your oil: At this point, if you want, you can add a few drops of your favorite essential oil. You can get a small portable bottle and take the oil with you. Store your oil in a cool, dark place. It will stay good for one to two years if all the plant matter is carefully removed. Make sure you label it carefully and write your recipe down, so if you want to make more, you will remember how to do so!

Using Your Oil
Here are just some of many uses for this kind of oil:

- Put it in a magical bag or in a bottle necklace and take it with you to bless trees, rocks, or anything else on your journey
- Consider using it to support meditations and dreams; you can dab a bit on your temples before meditation, dreaming, ritual work, journey work, and more.
- Dress candles with it, using traditional folk methods. Dressing a candle means putting oil on your finger and holding the candle in front of you. If you bring your finger from the bottom of the candle and up, toward you, you are "bringing in." If you do the opposite and move your finger away from you and down the candle, you are "removing." You can do this and then burn the candle (I like the little 4-inch chime candles for this purpose). Use this for healing, meditation, and more.

Samhain Natural Offerings
One of my favorite things to do at Samhain is to create small natural offerings. As the last of the leaves are falling and the Earth is growing quiet at this time of year, go collect sticks, acorn caps, pieces of bark, and stones. Bring these indoors and create a walnut-based ink (very easy; get fallen walnuts and boil them for a while, adding some vinegar to preserve the ink). Or, you can use a simple India ink or marker. Place a protective symbol (of your choosing, such as a rune or ogham) on each of the items. Bless them as part of your Samhain ceremony. Find or create a bag to keep them in, and take them with you on your journeys. Doing this each year ensures that you will always have something to offer that is sustainable.

CONCLUSION

Growing Where
We Are Planted

I leave you, dear reader, with the understanding that the journey into sacred action is very much like the spiral—with each step, we wind ourselves deeper and deeper into sacred connection with the land. With each change, we move ourselves further away from materialist culture and begin to embrace Earth-based living. The important thing is starting the journey and making the decision to walk it each day. And as you continue to walk this spiral, ever deepening, you will return to those different areas of your life. Just as the Wheel of the Year, the wheel of the seasons, spirals around you, so can you ever return and deepen this sacred work.

A final important lesson about the work of sacred action can be found from nature. This is the idea of "growing where you are planted." Remember that when an acorn falls from a tree or is planted by a person or squirrel, the seed has little choice in the matter. It grows where it is planted. But regardless, the seed is going to do all that it can to grow into that mighty oak. In the same way, we, too, can be proud to grow where we are planted. That is, we can need to do the work we are meant to do where we are, in whatever circumstances we are. Part of the work of living in a sacred manner is about living better in the circumstances that make up our current reality, not dreaming of a lifestyle that may not be tenable for our reality. Dreaming of a new way of living in some far-off place is a good goal to work toward if our life circumstances allow, but we can also get lost in the "what-ifs" rather than focusing on here and now. We need people to do what they can, using the best aspects of their own contexts to make it happen: abandoned lots in Detroit becoming gardens, apartment dwellers learning vermicomposting, a local school planting a garden, urban beekeeping, converting an old bus into a home.

The journey of sacred action is a journey into our future, not only as individuals but as the collected human race. This journey can be taken not only as a spiritual practice but, literally, as a life-honoring and life-saving practice for the whole world. We close with a ritual that helps you continue your journey into sacred action in the coming years.

Final Ritual: Honoring the Journey

Timing: This ritual is best completed at night, close to or on the winter solstice, one year after you have completed the journey of this book; see footnote in chapter 1: ritual for other appropriate times.

Preparation and Materials

Candles: Nine candles; place one at a central altar location, and place the other eight at stations around the room in a circle. These should be unlit at the start of the ceremony, except for the central candle. In line with sacred action, consider candles purchased secondhand (thrift store, yard sale, etc.) or beeswax candles produced locally (see chapter 4).

Journal: Your journal that you have kept along the journey into sacred action

Representations of the four elements: Place representations of Earth, air, fire, and water on your central altar in positions appropriate for each element. The central candle represents fire (placed in the south). You'll need a representation of air (incense, a bell, or a feather; placed in the east), water (bowl of water, shells; placed in the west), and Earth (bowl of Earth, stone; placed in the north).

Decorations: You may also include altar decorations appropriate to the season, gathered locally.

The Rite

Open up a sacred space in your tradition. Alternatively, use the sacred-space opening from the first ritual in chapter 1. Instructions are in plain text; spoken words are in *italics*. Say:

> *Today, I once again stand at the darkest point of year. But this year's journey has been filled with light. And even though the darkness surrounds me on this night, the darkness is not a stranger.*

> *I have returned, once again, to the place where many things are obscured, but this time the darkness takes on a new form. It is a representation of slowing down, of attuning, of paying attention, of engaging in the sacred.*

Spend a few moments quietly reflecting in the darkness on the journey you have taken in the last year. When you are ready, light the candle or remove the hooded lantern, and say.

> *A light shines in the darkness, and I am that light!*

Pick up the central candle and move to the first of the eight candles, in the eastern part of the circle. Light the candle.

> *The path of Oak knowledge brings light and hope to our Earth.*

At this point, review your journal and discuss the kinds of Oak knowledge and reskilling, the work that you have done and of which you are proud. Move to the next candle, in the southeast, and light it.

> *The path of fair share brings respite and relief to our Earth.*

Now, speak aloud about your journey toward sacred action through reducing consumption and waste, the work that you have done and of which you are proud. Move to the next candle, in the south, and light it.

> *The path of sacred action in the home brings peace and health to our Earth.*

Speak about your journey toward sacred action in your home and daily living, the work that you have done and of which you are proud. Move to the next candle, in the southwest, and light it.

The path of sacred action through nourishment brings abundance and regeneration to our Earth.

Speak about your journey toward sacred action through eating a more Earth-friendly diet, the work that you have done and of which you are proud. Move to the next candle, in the west, and light it.

The path of sacred action in my landscape brings blessings and joy to our Earth.

Speak about your journey toward sacred action through growing plants or gardens, the work that you have done and of which you are proud. Move to the next candle, in the northwest, and light it.

The path of sacred action in my community brings vision and reconnection.

If you wish, speak about your journey toward sacred action through community or workplace actions, the work that you have done and of which you are proud. Move to the next candle, in the north, and light it.

The path of sacred action in my life brings nourishment and wisdom.

Return to the central altar and pause for a moment.

*Caring for the Earth **<pause>***

*Caring for those of my human tribe **<pause>***

*Taking only my fair share in the world, that others may live **<pause>***

I continue this path of sacred action in the world!

At this time, reread that story you wrote of yourself, in your journal, a year ago during the first ceremony. Now that you have had a chance to reflect upon your work in this last year, set new goals for yourself in the coming year.

Close the space by using the closing in chapter 1 or any other appropriate closing.

Appendix: A Good Library

Gardening and Homesteading

Ashworth, Suzanne. *Seed to Seed: Seed Saving and Growing Techniques for Vegetable Gardeners.* White River Junction, VT: Chelsea Green, 2002.

Campbell, Stu. *Let It Rot! The Gardener's Guide to Composting.* Vol. 3. North Adams, MA: Storey, 1998.

Coleman, Eliot. *The New Organic Grower.* White River Junction, VT: Chelsea Green, 1989.

Coleman, Eliot. *The Winter Harvest Handbook: Year-Round Vegetable Production Using Deep-Organic Techniques and Unheated Greenhouses.* White River Junction, VT: Chelsea Green, 2009.

Deppe, Carol. *The Resilient Gardener: Food Production and Self-Reliance in Uncertain Times.* White River Junction, VT: Chelsea Green, 2010.

Fell, Derek. *Vertical Gardening: Grow Up, Not Out, for More Vegetables and Flowers in Much Less Space.* Emmaus, PA: Rodale, 2011.

Jeavons, John. *How to Grow More Vegetables (and Fruits, Nuts, Berries, Grains, and Other Crops) Than You Ever Thought Possible on Less Land Than You Can Imagine.* Berkeley, CA: Ten Speed, 2012.

Riotte, Louise. *Carrots Love Tomatoes: Secrets of Companion Planting for Successful Gardening.* North Adams, MA: Storey, 1998.

Permaculture / Whole-Systems Living

Bane, Peter. *The Permaculture Handbook: Garden Farming for Town and Country.* Gabriola, BC: New Society, 2012.

Hemenway, Toby. *Gaia's Garden: A Guide to Home-Scale Permaculture.* White River Junction, VT: Chelsea Green, 2009.

Hemenway, Toby. *The Permaculture City: Regenerative Design for Urban, Suburban, and Town Resilience.* White River Junction, VT: Chelsea Green, 2015.

Morrow, Rosemary. *Earth User's Guide to Permaculture.* Hampshire, UK: Permanent Publications, 2006.

Beekeeping

Conrad, Ross. *Natural Beekeeping: Organic Approaches to Modern Apiculture.* White River Junction, VT: Chelsea Green, 2013.

Hemenway, Christy. *The Thinking Beekeeper: A Guide to Natural Beekeeping in Top Bar Hives.* Gabriola, BC: New Society, 2013.

Cooking and Fermentation

Katz, Sandor Ellix. *Wild Fermentation: The Flavor, Nutrition, and Craft of Live-Culture Foods.* White River Junction, VT: Chelsea Green, 2016.

Morell, Sally Fallon, and Kaayla T. Daniel. *Nourishing Broth: An Old-Fashioned Remedy for the Modern World.* London: Hachette UK, 2014.

Prentice, Jessica. *Full Moon Feast: Food and the Hunger for Connection.* White River Junction, VT: Chelsea Green, 2012.

Wild Foods, Foraging, Bushcraft, Plant Identification, Herbalism

Buhner, Stephen Harrod. *The Lost Language of Plants: The Ecological Importance of Plant Medicines to Life on Earth.* White River Junction, VT: Chelsea Green, 2002.

Dawson, Adele Godchaux. *Herbs, Partners in Life: A Guide to Cooking, Gardening, and Healing with Wild and Cultivated Plants.* Rochester, VT: Healing Arts Press, 1991.

Elpel, Thomas J. *Botany in a Day.* Pony, MT: Hops, 2004.

Gatty, Harold. *Finding Your Way without Map or Compass.* North Chelmsford, MA: Courier, 1998.

Greer, John Michael. *Mystery Teachings from the Living Earth: An Introduction to Spiritual Ecology.* Newburyport, MA: Weiser Books, 2012.

Jaeger, Ellsworth. *Wildwood Wisdom.* Bolinas, CA: Shelter, 1999.

Oslund, Clayton, and Michele Oslund. *What's Doin' the Bloomin'?* San Diego, CA: Thunder Bay, 2011.

Thayer, Samuel. *Forager's Harvest.* Bruce, WI: Forager's Harvest, 2006.

Thayer, Samuel. *Nature's Garden: A Guide to Identifying, Harvesting, and Preparing Edible Wild Plants.* Bruce, WI: Forager's Harvest, 2010.

Tierra, Michael. *The Way of Herbs.* New York: Simon and Schuster, 1998.

Wood, Matthew. *The Earthwise Herbal, Volume I: A Complete Guide to Old World Medicinal Plants*. Berkeley, CA: North Atlantic Books, 2011.

Wood, Matthew. *The Earthwise Herbal, Volume II: A Complete Guide to New World Medicinal Plants*. Berkeley, CA: North Atlantic Books, 2011.

General Sustainable Living

Briggs, Raleigh. *Make Your Place: Affordable, Sustainable Nesting Skills*. Portland, OR: Microcosm, 2014.

Endnotes

1. Ancient Order of Druids in America, http://aoda.org/.
2. Order of Bards, Ovates, and Druids, www.druidry.org/.
3. Permaculture design system, rooted in patterns of nature, helps humans restore and regenerate ecosystems while providing for their own needs. We'll be drawing on permaculture in various ways in this book. For a detailed introduction, see David Holmgren, *Principles & Pathways beyond Sustainability* (Hepburn, Australia: Holmgren Design Services, 2002).
4. Dana O'Driscoll, *The Druid's Garden* (blog), https://druidgarden.wordpress.com/.
5. Stephen Harrod Buhner, *Sacred Plant Medicine: The Wisdom in Native American Herbalism* (New York: Simon and Schuster, 2006).
6. Joanna Macy and Molly Young Brown, *Coming Back to Life: The Guide to the Work That Reconnects* (Gabriola, BC: New Society, 2014).
7. Wendell Berry, *The Unsettling of America: Culture & Agriculture* (Berkeley, CA: Counterpoint, 2015).
8. Mark Shepard, *Restoration Agriculture: Permaculture for Farmers* (Greeley, CO: Acres U.S.A., 2013).
9. United Nations Environment Programme, *Mainstreaming Environment and Climate for Poverty Reduction and Sustainable Development: A Handbook to Strengthen Planning and Budgeting Processes* (New York: United Nations, 2016).

Emery, Carla. *The Encyclopedia of Country Living: The Original Manual for Living off the Land & Doing It Yourself*. Seattle, WA: Sasquatch Books, 2012.

Seymour, John. *The Guide to Self-Sufficiency*. Popular Mechanics Books. New York: Hearst Books, 1976.

Wigginton, Eliot, ed. *Foxfire 2: Ghost Stories, Spring Wild Plant Foods, Spinning and Weaving, Midwifing, Burial Customs, Corn Shuckin's, Wagon Making and More Affairs of Plain Living*. New York: Anchor, 1973. (This and any other Foxfire book!)

10. Holmgren, *Principles & Pathways beyond Sustainability*.
11. In the Druid tradition, the bardic arts include the many forms of human creative expression: poetry, music, writing, song, dance, visual arts, and the crafts. See also Dana Driscoll, "Channeling the Awen Within: An Exploration of Learning the Bardic Arts in the Modern Druid Tradition," Order of Bards, Ovates, and Druids, nineteenth Mount Haemus Lecture, www.druidry.org/events-projects/mount-haemus-award/nineteenth-mount-haemus-lecture.
12. For a more detailed discussion of these limits, I recommend Dennis Meadows and Jorgan Randers, *The Limits to Growth: The 30-Year Update* (Abingdon-on-Thames, UK: Routledge, 2012).
13. Holmgren, *Principles & Pathways beyond Sustainability*.
14. Indigenous Corporate Training, "What Is the Seventh Generation Principle?," www.ictinc.ca/blog/seventh-generation-principle.
15. There are a number of options for this, but I suggest the Center for Sustainable Economy's Ecological Footprint calculator at www.myfootprint.org/, or the Earth Day Footprint Calculator, www.earthday.org/footprint-calculator.
16. Joanna Macy in *Coming Back to Life* (Gabriola Island, BC: New Society, 2008) argues that part of healing work we must do is to be able to feel and experience our full emotions surrounding what is happening to the Earth. The first part of this ritual gives us safe space for our grief and then works to help us move beyond it.

17. Ancient Order of Druids in America, www.aoda.org.
18. For more on the "threefold breath" and other discursive meditation techniques, see John Michael Greer, *The Druidry Handbook: Spiritual Practice Rooted in the Living Earth* (Newburyport, MA: Weiser Books, 2006).
19. David G. H. Parsons, "The History of 'the Frog's Courtship': A Study of Canadian Variants." *MUSICultures* 18 (1990).
20. Barry Cunliffe, *The Ancient Celts* (Oxford: Oxford University Press, 2018).
21. Laura Ingalls Wilder, Cherry Jones, and Paul Woodiel, *Little House in the Big Woods* (New York: Harper & Row, 1953).
22. Alicia Bay Laurel, *Living on the Earth: Celebrations, Storm Warnings, Formulas, Recipes, Rumors & Country Dances Harvested by Alicia Bay Laurel* (New York: Random House, 1971).
23. Eliot Wigginton, ed., *Foxfire 2: Ghost Stories, Spring Wild Plant Foods, Spinning and Weaving, Midwifing, Burial Customs, Corn Shuckin's, Wagon Making and More Affairs of Plain Living* (New York: Anchor, 1973).
24. For a great example of connecting sacred awareness with a practical skill, see Mark Angelini, "Carving Away: An Initiation of the Trees through Spoon Carving," *Trilithon: The Journal of the Ancient Order of Druids in America* 2 (2015): 60–68. In this article, Mark describes his spiritual relationship with spoon carving and offers insights on how spoon carving connects him deeply with the spirit of the trees and his own path of druidry.
25. Paul Hawken, Amory B. Lovins, and L. Hunter Lovins, *Natural Capitalism: The Next Industrial Revolution* (Abingdon-on-Thames, UK: Routledge, 2013).
26. Victor Lebow, "Price Competition in 1955," *Journal of Retailing* 31, no. 1 (1955): 5–10.
27. Monique Grooten and R. E. A. Almond, *Living Planet Report 2018: Aiming Higher* (Gland, Switzerland: WWF, 2018), 22–100.
28. Hermes Trismegistus, "The Emerald Tablet," in *The Alchemy Reader: From Hermes Trismegistus to Isaac Newton*, ed. Stanton J. Linden (New York: Cambridge University Press, 2011), 27–28.
29. Annie Leonard, *The Story of Stuff: How Our Obsession with Stuff Is Trashing the Planet, Our Communities, and Our Health—and a Vision for Change* (New York: Simon and Schuster, 2010).
30. Kathy Marks and Daniel Howden, "The World's Rubbish Dump: A Garbage Tip That Stretches from Hawaii to Japan," *The Independent* 5, no. 1 (2008): 3.
31. Dana Gunders and Jonathan Bloom, *Wasted: How America Is Losing up to 40 Percent of Its Food from Farm to Fork to Landfill* (New York: Natural Resources Defense Council, 2017).
32. Peter Wardrop, Jeff Shimeta, Dayanthi Nugegoda, Paul D. Morrison, Ana Miranda, Min Tang, and Bradley O. Clarke, "Chemical Pollutants Sorbed to Ingested Microbeads from Personal Care Products Accumulate in Fish," *Environmental Science & Technology* 50, no. 7 (2016): 4037–44.
33. Glenn Albrecht, Gina-Maree Sartore, Linda Connor, Nick Higginbotham, Sonia Freeman, Brian Kelly, Helen Stain, Anne Tonna, and Georgia Pollard, "Solastalgia: The Distress Caused by Environmental Change," *Australasian Psychiatry* 15, no. S1 (2007): S95–S98.
34. Caitlin Johnson, "Cutting through Advertising Clutter," CBS News, 2006, www.cbsnews.com/news/cutting-through-advertising-clutter/.
35. Learn more at www.ecobricks.org/.
36. See http://thesecomefromtrees.blogspot.com/ for more information.
37. Arnold Schecter, Linda Birnbaum, John J. Ryan, and John D. Constable, "Dioxins: An Overview," *Environmental Research* 101, no. 3 (2006): 419–28.
38. For philosophy and detailed instructions, see Kathleen Meyer, *How to Shit in the Woods: An Environmentally Sound Approach to a Lost Art* (Berkeley, CA: Ten Speed, 2011).
39. Monika A. Bauer, James E. B. Wilkie, Jung K. Kim, and Galen V. Bodenhausen, "Cuing Consumerism: Situational Materialism Undermines Personal and Social Well-Being," *Psychological Science* 23, no. 5 (2012): 517–23.
40. See more at the Global Footprint Network at www.footprintnetwork.org/.

41. Abraham Harold Maslow, "A Theory of Human Motivation," *Psychological Review* 50, no. 4 (1943): 370–96.

42. For those more interested in rocket stoves, I would highly recommend Ianto Evans and Leslie Jackson, *Rocket Mass Heaters*, 3rd ed. (Coquille, OR: Cob Cottage, 2014).

43. Of course, furry companions and sleeping partners offer many of the same benefits!

44. Yoshihide Wada and Marc F. P. Bierkens, "Sustainability of Global Water Use: Past Reconstruction and Future Projections," *Environmental Research Letters* 9, no. 10 (2014): 104003.

45. See, for example, Janet Wilson, "Nestle Is Still Taking National Forest Water for Its Arrowhead Label, with Fed Help," *Desert Sun*, June 13, 2019, www.desertsun.com/story/news/environment/2019/06/13/nestle-still-taking-public-forest-water-its-arrowhead-label-feds-help/1362211001/.

46. A good resource for understanding this issue more thoroughly is a documentary called *The Bottled Life*.

47. Visit www.findaspring.com to see a mapping of springs all over the globe.

48. The kind of soap you use will substantially affect the consistency, but not cleaning ability, of the detergent. Plain Ivory soap works for a good consistency; I usually use a local goat milk soap. Some handmade soaps don't allow the finished detergent to "gel" as fully. I would not recommend glycerin soaps, since the end result stays very watery (but still usable).

49. Usually, you can find Arm and Hammer brand Super Washing Soda in the laundry aisle in the US. Not all stores carry it, and you may have to hunt around a bit. It is very much worth finding.

50. The best resource for learning more about people power is Tamara Dean, *The Human-Powered Home: Choosing Muscles over Motors* (Gabriola, BC: New Society, 2008).

51. Becky Bee, *The Cob Builders Handbook: You Can Hand-Sculpt Your Own Home* (Azalea, OR: Groundworks, 1997).

52. Ianto Evans, Linda Smiley, and Michael G. Smith, *The Hand-Sculpted House: A Philosophical and Practical Guide to Building a Cob Cottage* (White River Junction, VT: Chelsea Green, 2002).

53. Amanda D. Cuéllar and Michael E. Webber, "Wasted Food, Wasted Energy: The Embedded Energy in Food Waste in the United States," *Environmental Science & Technology* 44, no. 16 (2010): 6464–69.

54. Robert J. Diaz and Rutger Rosenberg, "Spreading Dead Zones and Consequences for Marine Ecosystems," *Science* 321, no. 5891 (2008): 926–29.

55. Donald R. Davis, "Declining Fruit and Vegetable Nutrient Composition: What Is the Evidence?," *HortScience* 44, no. 1 (2009): 15–19.

56. Wendell Berry, *The Unsettling of America: Culture & Agriculture* (Berkeley, CA: Counterpoint, 1996).

57. Tanya Basok, *Tortillas and Tomatoes: Transmigrant Mexican Harvesters in Canada* (Montreal: McGill-Queen's University Press, 2002).

58. David S. Wilcove and Lian Pin Koh, "Addressing the Threats to Biodiversity from Oil-Palm Agriculture," *Biodiversity and Conservation* 19, no. 4 (2010): 999–1007.

59. Marne Coit and Kim Bousquet, "GMO Labeling: An Emerging Food Labeling Issue," *Drake Journal of Agricultural Law* 23, no. 1 (2018): 21–28.

60. Irene Shaver, Adina Chain-Guadarrama, Katherine A. Cleary, Andre Sanfiorenzo, Ricardo J. Santiago-García, Bryan Finegan, Leontina Hormel, et al., "Coupled Social and Ecological Outcomes of Agricultural Intensification in Costa Rica and the Future of Biodiversity Conservation in Tropical Agricultural Regions," *Global Environmental Change* 32 (May 2015): 74–86.

61. United Nations, *Wake Up before It Is Too Late: Make Agriculture Truly Sustainable Now for Food Security in a Changing Climate* (New York: United Nations, 2013), https://unctad.org/en/pages/PublicationWebflyer.aspx?publicationid=666.

62. Shepard, *Restoration Agriculture*.

63. Mark Bubel and Nancy Bubel, *Root Cellaring: Natural Cold Storage of Fruits and Vegetables*, 2nd ed. (Adams, MA: Storey, 1991).

64. Jessica Prentice, *Full Moon Feast: Food and the Hunger Connection* (Hartford, VT: Chelsea Green, 2006).

65. Meaning the dominance and intentional cultivation of only a single crop; in this case, grass.

66. Lois B. Robbins, *Lawn Wars: The Struggle for a New Lawn Ethic* (New York: iUniverse, 2009).

67. Lakis Polycarpou, "The Problem of Lawns," Colombia University, State of the Planet: Earth Institute (2010), https://blogs.ei.columbia.edu/2010/06/04/the-problem-of-lawns/.

68. Jamie L. Banks and Robert McConnell, "National Emissions from Lawn and Garden Equipment," paper presented at the International Emissions Inventory Conference, San Diego, CA, 2015.

69. NASA did a study of lawns, including a map of where lawns are concentrated. You can see it here: http://earthobservatory.nasa.gov/Features/Lawn/.

70. For those interested in this kind of lawn activism, I refer you to two sources: the national Grow Food Not Lawns movement, spearheaded by Heather Jo Flores (www.foodnotlawns.com/), and Lois Robbins's Lawn Wars (www.lawnwars.org/).

71. For more on these resources, see Monarch Watch (www.monarchwatch.org/) and the World Wildlife Federation (www.nwf.org/certify).

72. See David Jacke and Eric Toensmeier's *Edible Forest Gardens* for more details about how these guilds function: David Jacke and Eric Toensmeier, *Edible Forest Gardens, Vol. 1, Ecological Vision and Theory for Temperate Climate Permaculture* (White River Junction, VT: Chelsea Green, 2005), 128.

73. You can check out *Carrots Love Tomatoes* by Louise Riotte for basic annual interplanting ideas for annual crops: Louise Riotte, *Carrots Love Tomatoes: Secrets of Companion Planting for Successful Gardening* (North Adams, MA: Storey, 1998).

74. A really good resource for this: Jon Young, Ellen Haas, and Evan McGown, *Coyote's Guide to Connecting with Nature: For Kids of All Ages and Their Mentors* (Duvall, WA: Wilderness Awareness School, 2008).

75. Thomas L. Friedman, *Hot, Flat, and Crowded: Why the World Needs a Green Revolution— and How We Can Renew Our Global Future* (Westminster, UK: Penguin Books, 2008).

76. Al Gore, *An Inconvenient Truth: The Planetary Emergency of Global Warming and What We Can Do about It* (Emmaus, PA: Rodale, 2006).

77. Masoom Gupte, "Why Thomas Friedman Chooses Hypocrisy over Being a Denier," *Economic Times*, May 31, 2018.

78. Drew Johnson, "Al Gore's Inconvenient Reality: The Former Vice President's Energy Use Surges up to 34 Times the National Average despite Costly Green Renovations," National Center for Public Policy Research, National Policy Analysis #679, August 1, 2017.

79. Neil E. Klepeis, William C. Nelson, Wayne R. Ott, John P. Robinson, Andy M. Tsang, Paul Switzer, Joseph V. Behar, Stephen C. Hern, and William H. Engelmann, "The National Human Activity Pattern Survey (NHAPS): A Resource for Assessing Exposure to Environmental Pollutants," *Journal of Exposure Science and Environmental Epidemiology* 11, no. 3 (2001): 231–52.

80. Doug Vine, "Transportation Emissions Roll Over Power Sector Emissions," Center for Climate Energy and Solutions, June 20, 2016, www.c2es.org/2016/06/transportation-emissions-roll-over-power-sector-emissions/.

81. Diana Leafe Christian, *Creating a Life Together: Practical Tools to Grow Ecovillages and Intentional Communities* (Gabriola, BC: New Society, 2003).

82. Please note that I have capitalized names of specific plants as a sign of respect for the living beings and spirit of the plants.

83. International Union for the Conservation of Nature, "ICUN Red List," www.iucnredlist.org/.

84. Kelly Ablard, "Conservation of Essential Oil and Carrier Oil-Bearing Plants," www.kellyablard.com/blog/conservation-sustainability-of-essential-carrier-oil-bearing-plants/.

85. United Plant Savers, "Species at-Risk List," https://unitedplantsavers.org/species-at-risk-list/.

86. Catherine M. Bell, *Ritual: Perspectives and Dimensions* (New York: Oxford University Press, 1997).

About the Author

DANA O'DRISCOLL has been a practicing animist druid for more than 15 years and currently serves as the Grand Archdruid in the Ancient Order of Druids in America. She is also a druid-grade member of the Order of Bards, Ovates, and Druids and is the OBOD's 2018 Mount Haemus Scholar. She writes at *The Druid's Garden* blog and is the creator of *Tarot of Trees*. Dana is a certified permaculture designer and teacher; she has taught sustainable-living courses and wild-food foraging in her local community and in university settings. Dana lives at a 5-acre homestead in rural western Pennsylvania with her partner and a host of feathered and furred friends.